Reading in Christian Communities

Christianity and Judaism in Antiquity Series

Gregory E. Sterling, *Series Editor*

VOLUME 14

The University of Notre Dame Press gratefully acknowledges the generous support of Jack and Joan Conroy of Naples, Florida, in the publication of titles in this series.

Reading
in *Christian*
Communities

Essays on Interpretation
in the Early Church

edited by

Charles A. Bobertz
David Brakke

University of Notre Dame Press

Notre Dame, Indiana

Library of Congress Cataloging-in-Publication Data
Reading in Christian communitites : essays on interpretation in the early
church / edited by Charles A. Bobertz and David Brakke.
p. cm.—(Christianity and Judaism in antiquity ; v. 14)
Includes bibliographical references and index.
ISBN 0-268-03165-7 (cloth : alk. paper)
ISBN 0-268-04017-6 (pbk. : alk. paper)
1. Bible—Criticism, interpretation, etc.—History—Early church, ca. 30–600.
I. Bobertz, Charles A., 1957–   II. Brakke, David.   III. Greer, Rowan A.
IV. Series
BS500 .R387   2002
270.1—dc21
2002010182

∞ *This book is printed on acid-free paper*

Christianity and Judaism in Antiquity Series (CJAS)

The Christianity and Judaism in Antiquity Program at the University of Notre Dame came into existence during the afterglow of the Second Vatican Council. The doctoral program combines the distinct academic disciplines of the Hebrew Bible, Judaism, the New Testament, and the Early Church in an effort to explore the religion of the ancient Hebrews, the diverse forms of Second Temple Judaism, and its offspring into religions of Rabbinic Judaism and the multiple incarnations of early Christianity. While the scope of the program thus extends from the late Bronze and Early Iron Ages to the late antique world, the fulcrum lies in the Second Temple and Early Christian periods. Each religion is explored in its own right, although the program cultivates a History-of-Religions approach that examines their reciprocally illuminating interrelationships and their place in the larger context of the ancient world.

During the 1970s a monograph series was launched to reflect and promote the orientation of the program. Initially known as Studies in Judaism and Christianity in Antiquity, the series was published under the auspices of the Center of the Study of Judaism and Christianity in Antiquity. Six volumes appeared from 1975 to 1986. In 1988 the series name became Christianity and Judaism in Antiquity as the editorship passed to Charles Kannengiesser, who oversaw the release of nine volumes. Professor Kannengiesser's departure from Notre Dame necessitated the appointment of a new editor. At the same time, the historic connection between the series and the CJA doctoral program was strengthened by the appointment of all CJA faculty to the editorial board. Throughout these institutional permutations, the purpose of the series has continued to be the promotion of research into the origins of Judaism and Christianity with the hope that a better grasp of the common ancestry and relationship of the two world's religions will illuminate not only the ancient world but the modern world as well.

Gregory Sterling, *Series Editor*

To

ROWAN A. GREER
Colleague, Teacher, Friend

Contents

x   Contents

PART TWO   LOCATING INTERPRETERS

Acknowledgments

The editors of this volume especially thank the scholars, all colleagues, students, or friends of Rowan A. Greer, who contributed their effort and time in writing these essays to honor Professor Greer. All of us are bound together by our association with this marvelous man, who has taught us so much so clearly, and with such great *humanitas*. We have all enjoyed the smell of his pipe and the friendly grin of a large Irish setter.

David Brakke also thanks his graduate assistant, Aaron Hughes, for his valuable editorial assistance and, for general moral support, J. Albert Harrill and Mary Jo Weaver.

Charles Bobertz is especially grateful to the Committee on Faculty Development at St. John's University (Minnesota) for its financial assistance and to graduate assistants Mark and Danielle Nussberger, who, along with Tracy Schar, were so willing to help out in so many ways. Charles' family—wife Mary, daughter Sarah, and son Thomas—has been, as usual, greatly encouraging and supportive.

Thanks also to Professor Gregory Sterling, Rebecca DeBoer, and the folks at the University of Notre Dame Press for making this tribute to Professor Greer possible.

Finally, we thank Professor Greer. As our teacher and now friend, he continues to inspire us both. We wish him many more years of productive scholarship and are happy to offer to him this small token of our gratitude and esteem.

Introduction

DAVID BRAKKE

The study of Christian biblical interpretation, like the humanities in general, underwent a dramatic transformation in the last decades of the twentieth century. Forty years ago scholars were confident that their modern critical methods had enabled them to discover the true, objective, historical meaning of biblical texts, against which they could assess the interpretive efforts of their ancient and medieval predecessors. They applauded early Christian fathers who belonged to "the school of Antioch," which championed a historical approach to scriptural exegesis against the "fanciful" allegorical method practiced by "the school of Alexandria." Antiochene exegetes, the moderns believed, adhered more closely to the "literal" meaning of texts, which they tied to the original historical contexts in which the works of scripture were produced. The Antiochenes provided a rare moment of attention to history within the centuries of theologically driven allegory that preceded the birth of critical scholarship in the Enlightenment. For the guild of Christian scholarship, this narrative served a politics of academic labor: historians and biblical scholars were eager to defend their roles as arbiters of the original "literal" meaning of the Bible against any encroachment on their turf by theologians and ethicists.

But decades of literary theory, ranging from structuralism to reader-response theory to deconstruction, have called into question the stability, even existence, of such a "literal" meaning and have emphasized instead the active role of the reader in creating meanings. Modern historical criticism began to lose its status as "objective" and "scientific," as critics pointed out that it was a particular practice developed in a particular culture. The distinction between historian and theologian became increasingly obscure. An early

1

and outstanding example of this changing perspective was the agenda for studying the history of early Christian biblical interpretation that Rowan Greer sketched in 1973 in his *The Captain of Our Salvation: A Study in the Patristic Exegesis of Hebrews*.[1] By pursuing in a more intentionally theological manner the descriptive method of Maurice Wiles,[2] Greer sought to avoid the pitfalls of the predominant mode of such studies, which often criticized patristic exegesis as determined by theological concerns and unfaithful to the original meaning of the biblical text. Such criticism is, Greer argued, "anachronistic," for "it judges by a later standard, whether that standard be the historical method evolved in the last two or three centuries or the exegetical consensus that is its present result."[3] The main point of this statement is to encourage an approach to ancient biblical interpreters that places them in their own contexts, in which "exegesis and theology were largely indistinguishable."[4] Thus, the use of scripture by, say, Cyril of Alexandria cannot be studied apart from the theological controversies over the person and nature of Christ for which his interpretations served. In *Captain of Our Salvation*, Greer was interested very specifically in the role of discursive theology in biblical exegesis, but his later works broaden the focus to see scripture as a part of the entire way of life of early Christian communities or, we might say, of their cultures.[5] It is now generally accepted that studies of early Christian interpretation are flawed if they do not see past interpretations as embedded in the communities in which they were formed.

Recent studies of early biblical exegesis have sought to place ancient readers and their readings within cultural worlds in which interpretation informs and is informed by communal life and its diverse practices. The material and social conditions of the ancient production, transmission, and collection of books, as well as social conflicts over authority and communal formation, shaped the rise of early Christian writings to the status of scripture and their subsequent canonization.[6] Allegorical reading could support social postures of cultural revision, not merely of cultural accommodation, and even the most aggressively sectarian modes of Christian identity exhibited flexibility in biblical reading under changed social circumstances.[7] Not only internal conflict but also debates with contemporary Jews over the significance of biblical promises shaped Christian notions of the text's "literal" and "spiritual" meanings.[8] In addition to the use of the Bible in theological and philosophical debates, the monastic movement produced new reading strategies as ascetic Christians sought to transform themselves spiritually through the Bible and to legitimate a form of life that appeared at odds with some biblical, especially Old Testament, passages.[9] In general, early scriptural interpretation must be viewed as part of the process by which Christians formed a new culture or "totalizing discourse" for the emerging Christian empire.[10]

But Greer's argument not only required that scholars historicize their accounts of past exegesis but also challenged them to recognize the contingent, culturally specific character of the historical-critical method itself. We modern scholars should not be so quick to "assume" that, thanks to our superior method, "we know what the text means" since historical criticism itself has produced readings suspiciously in tune with modern theological positions.[11] The distinction between what the text "meant" and what it "means" that biblical scholars cherished so highly is perhaps not so clear after all.[12] In this point, Greer, without the benefit of French post-structuralist thought, anticipated objections to the dominance of the supposedly "objective" historical criticism lodged from both the "post-liberal" right and the "postmodern" left. At Greer's Yale, Hans Frei, George Lindbeck, and their students decried the loss of the "narrative" dimension of scripture that came with the new attention solely to historical reference and called for a form of theology that allowed the Bible's "story" to shape Christian thought and practice.[13] Meanwhile, liberation theologians and biblical scholars indebted to literary and cultural theory challenged the objectivity of historical criticism by pointing to its embeddedness in an academic culture of economically privileged males of European descent.[14] Even before these developments Greer invited historians of exegesis to reflect not only on specific interpretations of the past but also on the act of interpretation in the present.

The essays in this volume take up this agenda by studying the connections between the act of interpretation and the formation of religious identity. The essays in Part 1, "Interpretive Locations," study specific examples of early Christian biblical interpretation as a means of creating Christian identity in the pluralistic ancient world. In keeping with an interest in scripture's place in the wider culture of a community of faith, the authors examine interpretation as it takes place in a variety of genres and media: not only commentaries, but also martyrdom accounts, Gnostic apocalypses, catechetical homilies, art, and even a bestiary. By examining genres of interpretation beyond the strictly exegetical, the contributors explore several of the functions that scripture played—and plays—in the creation and maintenance of faith communities, in the locating of Christian groups with respect to other Christians as well as Jews and pagans.

For example, Frederick Weidmann and David Brakke study how early Christians used the scriptural narrative as a tool of self-definition, both to create their own identity as the people of God and to label their own opponents as estranged from the biblical tradition. In his article on the *Martyrdom of Polycarp*, Weidmann shows how the author of this martyrdom account juxtaposes the biblical images of "sojourning" and "dwelling" in its depictions of the Christian and Jewish communities in second-century Asia Minor. By describing the Christians as "sojourning," the author identifies the Christian community as alien to the Roman imperial society in which it lived, but as conformed to Abraham and the ancient Israelites, who sojourned in lands not their own. In contrast, the Jews "dwell" in Roman Asia Minor and thus are now "in league with the pagan establishment," alienated from their biblical past. Christians' use of the biblical story to define themselves often carried with it the negative task of delegitimating contemporary Jews. The *Martyrdom of Polycarp* joined other second- and third-century Christian writings in depicting Christians as a "third race," neither Gentile nor Jewish.

Racial symbolism even more strongly pervades the Gnostic writings studied by Brakke in his essay. Taking issue with scholars who dismiss Gnostic reworkings of the Bible as "arbitrary," Brakke argues that Gnostics used the Genesis story of Noah and the flood much as their "proto-orthodox" contemporaries did, as an opportunity to reflect on who is in and out of the saved community and why. The flood account provided Gnostic writers with a set of characters on which to map their own social world and so to identify themselves as the elect of the true God and to characterize Jews, other Christians, and pagans as misguided or ignorant. The result is a picture of Gnostic theology and exegesis that highlights diversity and subtlety rather than determinism and caprice. Like the case of the *Martyrdom of Polycarp*, the Gnostics' efforts to find themselves in the biblical narrative entailed a delegitimation of opponents, in this case, the emerging Great Church, which in one Gnostic work is simply erased from history through the erasure of its symbol, the ark.

As Richard Norris's essay shows, the proto-orthodox heresiologist Irenaeus would reject the idea that the Gnostics were placing themselves in the biblical narrative, although it is Irenaeus' polemic against the Valentinian school that Norris considers here. Scholars have long debated whether there is a coherent plan that organizes Irenaeus' five-volume *Against the Heresies* (and if so, what it is). Norris studies the place of Book 2 in Irenaeus' anti-Valentinian polemic and argues that the book aims to defend Irenaeus' mode of reading the biblical narrative, but does so by attacking the Valentinians' mode on nonscriptural grounds. Irenaeus adopts this strategy because, although he recognizes that the Valentinians interpret the Bible in narrative fashion as he does, he believes that their *hypothesis*, their narrative of cosmic emanation and return, is not found in the scriptures, indeed is foreign to them. When they find their myth in biblical passages, the Valentinians are not uncovering the narrative within the Bible, but conforming the Bible to a narrative that is not its own. Thus, Irenaeus, at least in a preliminary way, eschews engaging the Valentinians over interpretations of specific biblical texts in favor of exposing the absurdity of their *hypothesis* apart from scripture. As an exegete and theologian, Irenaeus is committed to a narrative framework for biblical interpretation and theological argument, but he discovers that the scriptures themselves are insufficient for the defense of that position.

Alan Scott's essay on Origen and the *Physiologus* uncovers different strategies by which early Christian interpreters related the biblical story to the natural—not merely the social—world. In the case of Origen, the natural world "is the background, not the foreground": he turns to zoological knowledge for essentially two purposes, to answer pagan critics or to solve exegetical problems in the biblical text (compounded by the appearance of exotic animals in the Septuagint). It is the spiritual world of scripture that the Platonizing Origen seeks to understand through allegorical interpretation: nature itself is scarcely of interest. Not so for the author of the *Physiologus:* for him nature itself is a revelatory text and thus a proper subject for allegorical reading. Even the owl can serve as a medium for the theological significance of the conversion of Gentiles to the one God. Scott points out that the readings that the *Physiologus* produces are not nearly as profound or satisfying as those of Origen, but this theological attitude toward nature has an appeal that perhaps would escape even the great Alexandrian, Platonist that he was. It would appear that biblical texts are not the only "scripture" to which early Christians turned for theological insight. Moreover, the juxtaposition of these two works raises in a refreshing way the problematic relationship between the church's work of interpretation and the methods and results of "secular" forms of knowledge.

The criticism of Christian scripture by Porphyry of Tyre, studied here by Michael B. Simmons, has often been seen as another ancient example of this problem: the pagan Porphyry's perceptive historical debunking of such texts as Daniel may be depicted as a precursor of the modern use of historical criticism. Simmons's essay challenges such a facile comparison. Considered apart from the context of his overall theology, Porphyry's criticisms of the Bible may appear superficially similar to those of modern historical critics, but Simmons demonstrates that they are dependent on Porphyry's own theological convictions. Committed to the superiority of "reason" over religious faith and to the soul's need to escape the material conditions of this world,

Porphyry sought to elaborate a "universal way" to human salvation found in Neoplatonic philosophy and revelatory pagan oracles. So committed was Porphyry to his own religious agenda, Simmons argues, that he probably participated in an early imperial conference that led to the persecution under Diocletian. Porphyry hardly emerges as an ancient model of "disinterested" biblical criticism. Still, Simmons's essay forms an intriguing companion to those of Weidmann and Brakke: if Christians base their identity on their place within the "biblical story," how vulnerable are they to attacks on the historical accuracy of that story? This problem appears to have arisen far earlier than the Enlightenment.

Likewise, the program of shaping the culture of a faith community through the biblical narrative does not guarantee that the same culture will result, as Arthur Shippee's essay shows. Following Greer, we have seen in the work of Irenaeus the emergence of the notion of a Christian Bible with a narrative framework: the Bible is now seen to tell a story with a beginning (creation), a middle (redemption), and an end (eschatology), summarized in the rule of faith.[15] But this story did not dictate either the method or the results of interpretation carried out from within this framework, which fostered, rather than suppressed, pluralism in Christian readings.[16] Shippee explores this pluralism on a large scale by outlining the different ways in which Western and Eastern theologians, exemplified by Augustine and John Chrysostom, resolved the tension already present in the New Testament between the present availability of salvation and the kingdom of God and the future realizations of these gifts at the resurrection. While Chrysostom and his colleagues in the East tended to emphasize the extent to which Christians now participate in the heavenly life through the Church and its sacraments, Augustine initiated a contrasting Western emphasis on the distinction between the present earthly life and the future heavenly life. While heaven may be said to meet earth in the Eastern church, Augustine's Western church is most definitely a pilgrim community, on its way to a place it has not yet reached. Shippee traces this divergence not only to a tension between these two views in the New Testament itself, but also to the differing philosophical and political climates of the two halves of the Roman empire. The difference Shippee outlines here cannot be called one of "mere emphasis," for surely these contrasting interpretations of the biblical story produced in their respective faith communities quite dissimilar "moods and motivations," to use the language of Clifford Geertz.[17]

Shippee points to the Eastern church's more thorough appropriation of the Platonizing ideal of contemplation of God as one factor in the development of its more "realized" eschatology: Wayne Meeks and Martha Meeks's essay provides a rich analysis of how scripture informs the vision of God portrayed in a fifth-century mosaic from the Latomou monastery, formerly the Church of Hosios David, in Thessaloniki. The Meekses criticize one (mainly Protestant) approach to Christian art that would treat it primarily as illustration of the Bible, and indeed in the case of the Latomou mosaic such a perspective has led to fruitless efforts to conform the image to a single biblical text. Instead, they explore the mosaic's roots in a long Jewish and Christian tradition, originating in the Bible, of imagining how one could see the unseeable. The exegetical puzzles posed by passages in which such figures as Moses and Ezekiel see the God who said, "No human person shall see my face and live" (Exod 33:20), proved fertile ground for early Christian christologies, for Jewish mysticism, and for the iconic spirituality found in the Latomou mosaic. Here is a vision of God that arises out of the full spiritual life of a community faith that is deeply informed by scripture and further shaped by liturgical and interpretive tradition. The scholar may separate the strands of scripture, liturgy, and theology in his or her work of interpretation, but they are inseparable in how those who saw the image also saw the divine. The Meekses remind us of a function of scripture not often recognized by modern historians. Scripture is not only used for theological discourse and historical research by learned authors, but also for spiritual growth or for a relationship with God, whether by a community gathered in worship or by an ascetic in his or her solitude.

Together the essays in Part 1 present a complicated picture of how interpretations of scripture were created in early communities of faith, and they raise difficult questions about the possibilities and problems that religious communities face when they base their theology and practice on a single canonical collection, which is not a universal phenomenon among religions. Does finding one's communal identity in a normative story necessarily involve the delegitimation of other religious communities who lay claim to the same story? How should the community of faith respond when its scriptures become the subject of alternative readings developed by outsiders, whether professedly "neutral" scholars or outright enemies? How should the community adjudicate between contrasting appropriations of the same biblical narrative, if at all? How do alternative media of divine revelation, such as ritual, mysticism, and the natural world, affect the interpretation and normative status of the Bible? In what ways does the generic location of interpretation affect the outcome of readings?[18] It is possible that a more rigorous and self-conscious appropriation of social-scientific and cultural theory may clarify the terms in which such questions can be fruitfully addressed.[19] The contributions to Part 1, following Greer's lead, suggest also that any convincing answers will be found only when theoretical proposals are grounded in the "thick description" of specific communities.[20]

The four essays in Part 2, "Locating Interpreters," consider specific cases of interpretation as well, but they move from these to examine the general problem of interpretation within communities of faith, whether ancient or modern, which face the task of maintaining a coherent identity in a multicultural environment. As we have seen, Greer's emphasis on the integrity of patristic exegesis in the face of modern historical criticism represented not only a methodological proposal for studying early Christian exegesis, but also a problematization of historical criticism's claims to have discovered "the" meaning of the text. The recent attacks on historical criticism and the postmodern emphasis on the contextual nature of all reading have renewed calls for the development of a specifically Christian (and Jewish) reading of the Bible as a canonical whole.[21] The contributors to Part 2 all identify themselves as speaking from within the Christian tradition (in one case, Christian feminism) and as seeking to explicate a mode of interpretation appropriate to that location. Still, just as the essays in Part 1 show that diversity characterizes even readings that share a commitment to the biblical narrative, these proposals in Part 2 offer differing readings of the interpretive position of the Christian scholar.

Writing in the relatively recent tradition of feminist interpretation, Mary Rose D'Angelo addresses the multiple readings that even interpreters who share the same Christian feminist commitments have given for Gal 3:28, arguably the most conflicted site for the contemporary discussion of the roles of women in the Church. Sifting through the varied proposals for what Paul or the Christian baptismal ritual that he quotes meant in claiming that there is "no male and female . . . in Christ," D'Angelo suggests that the phrase may not have had a single meaning for Paul or for the early Christians who read Galatians or heard the phrase in baptism. The inclusion of all humanity, the abolition of disadvantage based on gender, and the abrogation of patriarchal marriage are all possible implications of the phrase within its ancient context. Its meaning in any particular instance may have depended on how differently located Christians performed it in creating their new identity "in Christ." The Christians addressed by Paul, D'Angelo points out, were not simply and uniformly Christian, but performed their Christian identities in locations ranging from traditional married life, to female missionary partners, and possibly to a community of male celibates. Locating the interpreter, whether in the first century or the twenty-first, may be the key to identifying which meaning or meanings an interpretive activity produces.

D'Angelo's depiction of first-century diversity provides a fitting introduction to Charles Bobertz's reflections on a ritual/liturgical reading of the Gospel of Mark and his complicated picture of the present-day Christian interpreter as located at the intersection of several overlapping communities. Taking up the postmodern emphasis on the embeddedness of the reader in a specific location, Bobertz proposes "the liturgical gathering, historical and modern," as "a location from which meaning (those gathered might say 'the meaning') emerges." Bobertz works with a chastened version of the classic distinction between "what it meant" and "what it means" by proposing a reading of Mark that seeks the Gospel's origins in the early Christian community's ritual life and that forthrightly comes from a modern reader who identifies with the modern Roman Catholic liturgical community. Bobertz exposes the anti-ritual bias that pervades modern historical criticism, developed as it was primarily by Protestants interested in the bare "kerygma," and shows how that bias has produced distorted readings of Markan scenes having to do with Jesus and ritual purity. Still, Bobertz does not offer his own location within the Roman Catholic community as a simple contrast to the historical-critical perspective; rather, Bobertz describes what is the case for most professional interpreters of the Bible at work today: a location in several different overlapping communities (the academy in general, one's own college or university, one's faith community, etc.) that renders any attempt at a monovocal articulation of one's social position impossible. The result is a play among "strong readings" originating from several traditions that creates a conversation that may be open-ended, but does not lack (especially in the academic environment) standards of adjudication.

Does, however, the "strong reading" that emerges from a specific community simply reflect that community's preexisting values and commitments, thus depriving scripture of its potential to challenge or critique the community? Frederick Norris thinks not: he believes that the close, theologically informed reading strategies practiced by such early Christians as Origen and John Chrysostom can "transform" the Church rather than simply confirming it in its own predilections. Norris portrays Origen and Chrysostom as "savvy and humble deconstructionists" who attend closely to textual details, expect "resistance" from the text, and do not separate interpretation from ethics. Still, unlike contemporary deconstructionists, Origen and Chrysostom do indeed believe in a Logos whose speech lies behind the scriptural text, which they expect to "light the soul." One recalls perhaps Stanley Fish's famous characterization of Christianity as "structuralism *with* a transcendental subject."[22] Although he does not elaborate on this point, Norris's vision does not appear to countenance a nostalgic return to the centuries before the rise of the historical-critical method, for he eschews a "wooden sense of inerrancy." What Norris proposes for communities of faith is a mode of reading that aims at transformation of one's self and community, which he identifies as both "ancient" and "postmodern."[23]

Stanley Hauerwas makes the most vigorous case for a practice of interpretation specific to the Christian community. Drawing on Greer's discussion of Paulinus of Pella in *Broken Lights, Mended Lives*,[24] Hauerwas argues for a Christian posture of "endurance" in a world that appears to have lost its moorings. He thinks of this posture in terms not so much of withdrawal as of friendship: the creation of an alternative community, enabled by God, with God and with one another. Accordingly, his essay presents a warm and engaging portrait of himself, Rowan, and their productive friendship, from which Hauerwas learned "how to read." Since history is always "written to and for a specific community," Christian history will be written to and for the Christian community and its circle of friendship, differing from secular history perhaps even in its methods. Christian historians may learn a great deal from their non-Christian colleagues, but their aim will be not an elusive "objectivity" but (as Frederick Norris suggests) transformed lives. With Hauerwas we perhaps return full circle to Weidmann and the *Martyrdom of Polycarp*, for here we find in modern dress the second-century identification of Christians as a community in exile, living "the paradox of alien citizenship."

"The paradox of alien citizenship" may provide the appropriate metaphor to understand the overall theme of this collection, for the interpretive perspective that Rowan Greer's work opens up does not belong to any one community, not even the religious community. Consider the diverse locations of the contributors to this volume, all of whom have been inspired by Greer, who spent his career in a university divinity school (which may itself be an example of "the paradox of alien citizenship"): most are professors in free-standing Prostestant seminaries, university divinity schools, Roman Catholic colleges and universities, private and state universities; some are also working clergy. Such differences in location are bound to produce different modes of appropriating the contextual method that Greer advocated. For example, the professor who teaches New Testament in a state university is bound to quarrel with Hauerwas's assertion that "the study of Scripture only makes sense as a theological task of the church." In postmodern fashion, he or she is likely to ask, "only makes sense" for *whom?* And what kind of "sense" is imagined here? To be sure, the theological interpretation of scripture by and for communities of faith indeed has its own integrity that the chastened historical critic must respect. But in a pluralistic age in which communities of faith make specific demands for public policy based on "biblical values," the interpretation of scripture is far too urgent to be left to communities of faith alone: the Bible has entered the public domain and so is now, as it was in Porphyry's day, open to readings from persons of a variety of locations, especially from those whose lives may be adversely affected by particular readings of the Bible. Moreover, as the essays in this volume make clear, even readings from within communities of faith that share fundamental principles can differ markedly. In this sense, it is scripture itself that is the "alien citizen": created and interpreted by diverse human communities, it belongs to all of them, and thus to none of them.

That "alien" character of Christian scripture may be most evident in the two historical moments between which this volume works: "late antiquity" and "late modernity." The early Christians started out with a set of scriptures that belonged primarily to another religious community, the Jews: they faced the tasks of making that Bible their own (the "Old Testament") and of creating, limiting, and interpreting a new canon of their own writings. What "Christian scripture" is and how it should be read were, for much of the early period, up for grabs. Late modern or postmodern Christians face the equally daunting task of reclaiming as their own a Bible that, thanks to three centuries of historical criticism, has been rendered "alien" to them in unprecedented ways: the Bible's historical accuracy, theological unity, and moral relevance are now up for grabs. The example of the early church suggests that the strategies by which contemporary Christians accomplish this task will be diverse and that they will have to be theological proposals. Historical criticism, especially as practiced by theologically engaged scholars, can contribute to this project, if only by continuing to show how "alien" scripture is, how it challenges faith communities as it nourishes them. But Rowan Greer's question may be even more apt now than it was twenty-five years ago: "May it not be the case that we, like the Fathers, are obliged to take our theologies and, while revering the text and respecting its autonomy, use them boldly in our exegesis?"[25]

NOTES

1. Rowan A. Greer, *The Captain of Our Salvation: A Study in the Patristic Exegesis of Hebrews* (BGBE 15; Tübingen: J.C.B. Mohr, 1973).

2. Maurice Wiles, *The Spiritual Gospel* (Cambridge: Cambridge University Press, 1960); *The Divine Apostle* (Cambridge: Cambridge University Press, 1967).

3. Greer, *Captain of Our Salvation*, 3.

4. Greer, *Captain of Our Salvation*, 2.

5. Rowan A. Greer, *Broken Lights and Mended Lives: Theology and Common Life in the Early Church* (University Park: Pennsylvania State University Press, 1986); *The Fear of Freedom: A Study of Miracles in the Roman Imperial Church* (University Park: Pennsylvania State University Press, 1989).

6. Harry Gamble, *Books and Readers in the Early Church* (New Haven: Yale University Press, 1995); Helmut Koester, "Writings and the Spirit: Authority and Politics in Ancient Christianity," *HTR* 84 (1991): 353–72; David Brakke, "Canon Formation and Social Conflict in Fourth-Century Egypt: Athanasius of Alexandria's Thirty-Ninth *Festal Letter*," *HTR* 87 (1994): 395–419.

7. David Dawson, *Allegorical Readers and Cultural Revision in Ancient Alexandria* (Berkeley: University of California Press, 1992); Maureen Tilley, *The Bible in Christian North Africa: The Donatist World* (Minneapolis: Fortress, 1997).

8. Robert L. Wilken, *Judaism and the Early Christian Mind: A Study of Cyril of Alexandria's Exegesis and Theology* (New Haven: Yale University Press, 1971); idem, "*In novissimis diebus:* Biblical Promises, Jewish Hopes, and Early Christian Exegesis," *JECS* 1 (1993): 1–19.

9. Douglas Burton-Christie, *The Word in the Desert: Scripture and the Quest for Holiness in Early Christian Monasticism* (New York: Oxford University Press, 1993); Elizabeth A. Clark, *Reading Renunciation: Asceticism and Scripture in Early Christianity* (Princeton, N.J.: Princeton University Press, 1999).

10. Averil Cameron, *Christianity and the Rhetoric of Empire: The Development of Christian Discourse* (Berkeley: University of California Press, 1991); Frances M. Young, *Biblical Exegesis and the Formation of Christian Culture* (Cambridge: Cambridge University Press, 1997).

11. Greer, *Captain of Our Salvation*, 2–3.

12. The classic formulation of this distinction is Krister Stendahl, "Biblical Theology," *IDB* 1.418–32, alluded to by Greer, *Captain of Our Salvation*, 2.

13. Hans Frei, *The Eclipse of Biblical Narrative: A Study in Eighteenth and Nineteenth Century Hermeneutics* (New Haven: Yale University Press, 1974); George Lindbeck, *The Nature of Doctrine* (Philadelphia: Westminster, 1984); idem, "The Story-Shaped Church," in *Scriptural Authority and Narrative Interpretation* (ed. Garrett Green; Philadelphia: Fortress, 1987), 161–79; Ronald Thiemann, *Revelation and Theology: The Gospel as Narrated Promise* (Notre Dame, Ind.: University of Notre Dame Press, 1985).

14. See Elisabeth Schüssler Fiorenza, *In Memory of Her: A Feminist Theological Reconstruction of Christian Origins* (New York: Crossroad, 1983); Stephen D. Moore, *Literary Criticism and the Gospels: The Theoretical Challenge* (New Haven: Yale University Press, 1989); The Bible and Culture Collective, *The Postmodern Bible* (New Haven: Yale University Press, 1995); Vincent L. Wimbush, "*Contemptus Mundi* Means '... Bound for the Promised Land ...': Religion from the Site of Cultural Marronage," in *The Papers of the Henry Luce III Fellows in Theology* (ed. Jonathan Strom; 2 vols. thus far; Atlanta: Scholars Press, 1996–), 2.131–61.

15. James L. Kugel and Rowan A. Greer, *Early Biblical Interpretation* (Philadelphia: Westminster Press, 1986), 155–76; cf. Wayne A. Meeks, *The Moral World of the First Christians* (LEC; Philadelphia: Westminster, 1986), 154–60.

16. Kugel and Greer, *Early Biblical Interpretation*, 177–99.

17. Clifford Geertz, "Religion as a Cultural System," in his *The Interpretation of Cultures* (New York: Basic Books, 1973).

18. Not much or even at all in the early Church, claims Young (*Biblical Exegesis*, 216).

19. See Kathryn Tanner, *Theories of Culture: A New Agenda for Theology* (Guides to Theological Inquiry; Minneapolis: Fortress, 1997), and David Brakke, "Cultural Studies: Ein neues Paradigma us-amerikanischer Exegese," *Zeitschrift für Neues Testament* 2 (1998): 69–77.

20. For an example based on study of modern communities, see Mary McClintock Fulkerson, *Changing the Subject: Women's Discourses and Feminist Theology* (Minneapolis: Fortress, 1994).

21. See Brevard S. Childs, *Old Testament Theology in a Canonical Context* (Philadelphia: Fortress, 1985); Jon D. Levenson, *The Hebrew Bible, the Old Testament, and Historical Criticism: Jews and Christians in Biblical Studies* (Louisville: Westminster/John Knox, 1993).

22. Stanley Fish, "Structuralist Homiletics," in his *Is There a Text in This Class? The Authority of Interpretive Communities* (Cambridge, Mass.: Harvard University Press, 1980), 181–96, at 182.

23. The invocations of the term "postmodern" in religious thought are diverse and suggest different things for different authors, even within this collection. A useful start to sorting out these gestures is Paul Lakeland, *Postmodernity: Christian Identity in a Fragmented Age* (Guides to Theological Inquiry; Minneapolis: Fortress, 1997).

24. Greer, *Broken Lights and Mended Lives*, 193–95.

25. Greer, *Captain of Our Salvation*, 359.

The Work of Rowan A. Greer

An Appreciation

CHARLES A. BOBERTZ

Rowan A. Greer, Walter H. Gray Professor of Anglican Studies at Yale University *emeritus*, began his now forty years of productive theological and patristic scholarship with a remarkable first book: *Theodore of Mopsuestia: Exegete and Theologian.*[1] In the foreword to the book, Reverend Frederic Hood, then Canon and Chancellor of St. Paul's Cathedral, London, was remarkably prescient in describing "the young American priest" as possessing "exceptional promise." Written four years *before* his actual Yale doctoral dissertation, "The Antiochene Exegesis of Hebrews,"[2] *Theodore of Mopsuestia* clearly developed several themes which would become characteristic interests of Greer's later work.

The first and most important of these themes is the role played by the late antique quest for virtue in early Christian theology.[3] Greer identified this theme at the center of Theodore's theological thought, and as one that logically followed from the more general Antiochene[4] insistence on an "assumed man" Christology. This Christology—which Greer clearly contrasts with the "word/flesh" Christology of Alexandria—took as bedrock the doctrine that the Word of God united with a *fully human person* in Christ. What has happened in the incarnation of Christ does not change or alter the humanity of Christ. An essential aspect of that nature is that humanity is morally free, free to choose between good and evil and thus free to conduct an *authentic* quest for virtue. Greer clearly describes Theodore's understanding of Jesus Christ: if Jesus did not possess freedom of choice and act as a free moral agent, then the humanity of Christ disappears. At any time prior to the glorification of the resurrection Christ could have repudiated the indwelling of the Word (*Logos*); only at the words "it is finished" from the Cross is the incarnation complete.[5]

This theme—that Christ was fully human as well as divine and thus able to be the model and goal of the Christian quest for virtue—led Greer to recognize and describe two other themes which have had, and continue to have, profound impact on the study of patristics. First, Greer emphasized that Theodore and the other patristic authors read and interpreted scripture from prior theological, ecclesial, and cultural commitments. Such scriptural interpretation often appears to us to be "eisegesis" (reading meaning *into* the text). Yet as Greer shows us, those very commitments also paradoxically emerged from, and were transformed by, the continued reading of scripture.[6] Indeed, Greer's later work in exploring the nuances of this paradox, in page after page of insightful reading of primary patristic texts, is perhaps unparalleled in modern scholarship.[7]

Moreover, much of this work on ancient scriptural interpretation was published in the 1960s and 1970s, just as claims for the "objectivity" of the historical-critical method in biblical interpretation were most far-reaching. Greer helped many to see what should have been obvious: it is not only the ancients who read scripture from commitment, to text, and back to commitment, but ourselves as well. With characteristic understatement, Greer helped to explode the Enlightenment myth of objectivity in biblical interpretation and, judging from several of the essays in this volume, there will be no attempt soon to rebuild.

A second theme of Greer's exposition of Theodore's characteristically "Antiochene" theology emerged in his analysis and evaluation of the transformation of this theology toward the end of the Roman imperial period.[8] The late antique quest for virtue, which lay at the foundation of Christian theology and ethics and was a characteristic of Christian preaching and teaching in the fourth century, was transformed both by a new theology grounded in the *sovereignty* of God rather than the *freedom* of humanity and by a change in culture, as increasing numbers in the empire sought salvation through the patronage of holy ascetics and the cult of the saints and martyrs. In contrast to this understanding of God and church so characteristic of western medieval Christianity and hence foundational for the modern church (one thinks here of the cult of saints *and* the doctrine of justification by faith alone),[9] Greer constantly invites his readers to engage an earlier time, one marked by the free quest for virtue, in their dialogue with the ancient traditions of Christianity.

The Fully Human Nature of Christ

In several studies, beginning with *Theodore of Mopsuestia,* Greer carefully develops the nuances behind the insistence by the fourth- and fifth-century theologians of Antioch upon the fully human nature of Christ.[10] Their Christology begins with the then-conventional Platonic anthropology that "humanness," the essential quality of what it means to be a human being, is located exclusively in the human capacity for rationality; rationality inheres in an immortal soul which is also a "spark" of the divine fire, the very rationality that governs the universe. Rationality, however, requires the capacity, or freedom, to choose—in this case the capacity to choose between good and evil (Gen 3:1–6)—and so Theodore and the other Antiochenes established rationality and freedom at the heart of their understanding of human nature. But these theologians were also readers of the biblical story beginning with Genesis, and here they understood God as the creator of humanity and therefore understood humanity not as a "spark" of the divine fire (destined for reunification) but as essentially other than God: as *created.* Salvation was then understood to be the *communion* of created humanity with God rather than (re)*union* with the divine.[11] Mankind was destined for immortality and even immutability in the age to come, but was not destined to *become* divinity. And while Jesus Christ, free and rational in his human nature (for he was God and human both) has, with providence, already achieved this blessed condition, we remain part of *this* age, baptized to utilize our own moral freedom to choose obedience and so one day attain immortality in communion with Christ and with God. Christ is thus both model and goal of salvation.[12]

The fully human Christ is "assumed by" the fully divine Word of God, and the two natures are joined in the one "person" (*prosopon*) of Jesus Christ,[13] the "assumed man."[14] What follows, therefore, is a unique combination of Platonic assumption (humans are free and rational)[15] with biblical logic: God is that which is "uncreated" and humanity is "created" by God. Humanity is therefore created rational and free, the good creation of God. If Jesus Christ is not also rational and free, then his humanity disappears and we no longer have a model for the full realization of God's good creation. Moreover, the Antiochene theologians read biblical story in a way that takes seriously, even literally, the historical story of Israel as well as the gospel narrative (expressed, of course, in each of the four canonical Gospels). Humanity, in the story of Israel, has undergone an "education," training, as it were, to be able to exercise free rationality in obedience to God, while in Jesus Christ such free obedience, even in the face of Satanic temptation, has been achieved.[16] The perfect governance of rationality (Christ did not choose wrongly) mirrors—the Antiochenes use the biblical language of "image"—God's governance of the created universe: the immortal body of resurrection is the result.[17] Thus Antiochene theology and Christology —in the midst of rival understandings and biblical interpretations[18]—developed a simultaneous emphasis on the fully human nature of Christ and human freedom to pursue the quest for virtue.

The Quest for Virtue: Reading Scripture from Within

What Greer describes as the late antique quest for virtue is often presented more generally as a central tenet of the ancient Hellenistic worldview. This worldview was dominated by the philosophical tenets of Stoicism, emphasizing the rational governance of the universe and control of the passions, and its eclectic partner Middle Platonism, emphasizing the connection between knowledge and ethics: "to know the good is to do the good." A fundamental insight of Greer is that this worldview in its Christian manifestation was built upon the emerging church's conversation between a Hellenistic inheritance and its own reading of the scriptural text. Greer shows us clearly that the patristic writers he studies—among them Irenaeus, Origen, Athanasius, Cyril, Gregory of Nyssa, Apollinaris, Augustine, and especially the "Antiochenes," Diodore, Theodore, and Nestorius[19]—read the biblical text from *within* the dominant worldview of Hellenism and from *within* the different theological and liturgical traditions then emerging in the church. Perhaps more important, he shows us how these biblical interpreters were themselves transformed by what they encountered. Greer's descriptions reveal, in the exquisite detail of which only he is capable, that patristic exegesis and theology are marked by true dialogue between prior cultural and Christian commitments and the biblical narrative. The result is that church and culture are constantly being transformed by such committed interpretive acts. As a theologian who is himself in dialogue with the contemporary church, he then holds this out as one model for our own reading of scripture.[20]

Beginning with Irenaeus (second century), Greer traces the history of the church's dialogue between culture and scripture. He notes that one description of Irenaeus' reading of scripture emphasizes its Platonist assumptions, in that Irenaeus understands the biblical story of salvation as one of a "return" to the pristine origin of things (Genesis). Christ is the "new Adam," uncorrupted, prior to the "Fall." Christians are caught up in the myth of the return to paradise lost as they enter "into Christ."[21] Yet Greer, without denying the influence of Platonism, reads Irenaeus as most deeply affected by the biblical narrative he reads. Irenaeus integrates the story of Israel, creation, and history[22] into his understanding of salvation. Christ as the incarnation is active throughout the whole history of creation. The creation of humanity (Adam) is followed by humanity's maturation and education as it moves toward the perfect vision of God which renders humanity incorruptible (the resurrection of Christ).[23] While it is true that this "reading" of scripture took place in dialogue with Gnostic Christians (themselves greatly influenced by Platonism), whom Irenaeus accuses of either rejecting the Old Testament altogether (and thus any importance of the story of Israel) or perniciously misreading it, Greer shows us that Irenaeus was equally motivated by the desire to incorporate the story of Israel into the story of mankind's redemption because of his prior conviction that the God of Israel was the God of creation.[24] Thus creation, and humanity's role within it, is inherently "good." God's plan of redemption is not salvation *from* the world (a Platonic assumption) but salvation *of* the world, a plan that of necessity incorporates both the human story and the story of Israel.[25]

Origen, often regarded as the great Hellenizer of Christianity, was perhaps the most important expositor of scripture in the early church. Yet Greer shows how he too was profoundly influenced by his reading of the biblical narrative. While the vast majority of Origen's interpretation of scripture was allegorical (seeking the inner and more spiritual meaning of the literal text), he did also pay attention to the literal text. Moreover, and most important to the later development of Christian biblical interpretation in Antioch, Origen in his reading of the biblical story insisted on the *simultaneous* action of God's providence and human freedom. Origen therefore adopted the notion of *paideia*, the education of free and rational humanity, guided by providence, toward its eventual redemption. And while Origen understood this *paideia*, in both corporate and individual terms, as the ascent of the soul in stages from earth to heaven (and so *not* in the temporal sphere),[26] the later biblical interpreters of Antioch made the metaphor temporal: *paideia* in our age means building virtue, which guides us toward redemption in the age to come.[27]

Greer, after paying close attention to various theologies and interpretive strategies between the time of Origen (third century) and the latter half of the fourth century,[28] highlights two influences which were of central importance in the emerging theology of fourth- and fifth-century Antioch. First, Irenaeus' reading of the centrality of the historical story of Israel as part of the story of God's good creation, guided by providence, precedes the Antiochenes' conviction that humanity matures "historically" and finds its culmination in the Christ who, fully mature, freely chooses to obey God, even in the midst of temptation, and so is met by the fullness of divine providence in the resurrection. Second, with Origen, the theologians of Antioch insist that constitutive of Christ's humanity, and so of all humanity, is freedom, a freedom which is met but not overcome by providence. And following Origen's strong biblical reading which posits God as sole Creator ("eternally creating"), the relationship between the human, created soul of Christ and the uncreated God is described as communion rather than union. Yet while Origen, undoubtedly influenced by Plato, reads the scripture as explaining the communion of the Word of God (*Logos*) with the preexistent soul of Jesus, the Antiochenes read the scripture as presenting a fully human Christ, body and soul, establishing a relationship with the Word through steadfastness in the face of freedom.

Similarly, in tension with the reading of Irenaeus, with the reading of contemporary Alexandrian theologians, and with some Arian readings, the Antiochenes resisted the notion, common in philosophical parlance, of the outright divinisation of humanity, first of Christ (as the Alexandrians later came to understand it, Christ is one nature and that nature is divine) and then of the rest of those "in Christ" (so Athanasius, "Christ became human so that we might become divine").[29]

Rowan Greer's scholarship in the history of exegesis in the early church—most notably his study of the history of the interpretation of Hebrews[30]—is a *tour de force* just because it so clearly describes this pattern of reading from within constantly emerging theological and cultural positions, in this case paying particular attention to the exegetical tradition associated with Antioch in the fourth and fifth centuries. Thus while the Alexandrian theologians can seemingly ignore Heb 5:7–9, which refers to the *human* suffering of Christ, while treating other similar verses as part of the *communicatio idiomatum* (the awesome condensation of the Word in the incarnation, the one nature of Christ the Word acting in the "guise" of human), the exegetes of Antioch insist that just these verses point directly to the full humanity of Christ. They show that he is the "assumed man" who retains his freedom of will and who is, by the providence of God, joined in *moral* union with the Word in the person (*prosopon*) of Jesus Christ.[31]

The overall picture Greer paints thus becomes clear. The early church read scripture from within both cultural and theological commitments, while these same commitments were themselves profoundly shaped by the reading of scripture. There is no place, then or now, from which one can begin that exchange. Rather, one always begins in the middle and moves on from there. Greer's sense of ecclesiology, arising from his strong Anglican identity, also becomes apparent. He views the church not as a voluntary association of believers, but as an institution with commitments and tradition. To quote Newman, the church is "established by the divine will of Christ," a prior reality to which one comes to belong.[32]

The Quest for Virtue Transformed

In an article which should be required reading in all graduate patristics courses,[33] Greer carefully rehearses the history of the ideas of freedom and providence in the early church. Rooted in the Jewish interpretation of scripture during the Second Temple period as well as the philosophy of Middle Platonism, patristic theology prior to Augustine held both that humans were morally free (therefore allowing for virtue and vice, praise and blame) and that, on a higher level, providence guided humanity toward its ultimate salvation. Hence providence was understood to be general in character while "free" individual actions brought consequences.[34] Providence was understood to be persuasive rather than coercive; the beauty of the beloved naturally attracted the affection of the lover.[35]

Greer underscores the fact that the quest for virtue laid the foundation for the relationship between doctrinal theology and ethics in the church, both of the East and of the West, before Augustine. On this pre-Augustinian understanding, humanity with its rational soul (mind) and body stood as a microcosm of the universe, itself constituted by rationality governing a physical world. Moreover, as Genesis relates, in the beginning when mankind failed to exercise proper rational control there were universal consequences: physical corruption, including death, was introduced into the world. Hence the proper ordering of mind to body, including the control of the passions, was the prerequisite to the acquisition of virtue and incorruption. Jesus Christ exemplified this ordered self with the result that his body was rendered incorruptible in the resurrection. And so he becomes the paradigm, differently understood in Alexandria and Antioch,[36] of the pursuit of virtue.[37]

But there is more to this Christian version of the quest for virtue. It is the vision of God (the Beloved), mediated by Christ in creation, in scripture, in the Incarnation, and, importantly, in the sacraments of the church, which empowers the mind to its task. Thus "the moral dimension finds its place in the broader context of the Christian church."[38]

In the final pages of *Broken Lights and Mended Lives,* Greer begins to describe the transformation of the "quest" in the common life of the church in the fourth and fifth centuries and in the theology of Augustine. In *The Fear of Freedom* he elaborates on how and why this is a pivotal transition in the history of the church. Greer picks up Peter Brown's description of the emergence and function of the holy ascetic and the cult of the saints as powerful brokers (patrons) of divine power,[39] and sees in this development the beginning of a profound change. The pivotal role of the quest for virtue in doctrinal theology, preaching, and ethical practice was giving way to an emphasis on the sovereign *power* of God in salvation, mediated directly by holy patrons and the church itself.[40]

Thus Augustine, whose Platonic education and proclivities made him amenable to the quest for virtue at the beginning of his ecclesial career (not to mention the fact that he was greatly influenced by a champion of the quest, Ambrose),[41] soon finds himself, on the basis of personal and ecclesial experience, emphasizing the sovereignty of God more than human freedom. To be sure, Greer understates his own sense of disappointment over this development, but his description makes it quite clear that Augustine's theology— at least that of the later Augustine—represents the antithesis to the theology of Theodore and the other Antiochene theologians, rooted as it is in the free human nature of Christ.[42] We come away from this part of Greer's work with a strong sense of being invited as Christians to rediscover the wellspring of Christian theology, which bubbles in the vicinity of Antioch rather than Hippo.

Final Matters

By focusing on Greer's contributions to the history of theology and biblical interpretation, I have of course failed to give adequate account of the range and depth of interests with which all those who know him or who have had the privilege of hearing him lecture are familiar. Among the most important of these interests is his attention to, and concern over, the shape and identity of the worldwide Anglican communion, expressed most often in his extensive and provocative reviews of contemporary Anglican scholarship.[43] Greer has also been intrigued throughout his career by the question of the relationship of church to society, both ancient and modern,[44] describing what in one place he calls "the marvelous paradox": Christians live as citizens of the earth as well as aliens. With Augustine, Greer concludes that our experience here only takes on its true meaning when related to our destiny in God.[45] Utilizing a study of hospitality in the early church, Greer characteristically (i.e., through his reading of ancient texts) warns us in the modern church of the danger of Christian practice motivated soley by a bland moralism or institutionalization. In ancient monastic culture true fellowship with God came first; hospitality, important as it was, served the higher purpose of leading folks toward perfect fellowship with God.[46]

Finally, perhaps it is most important to say that Rowan A. Greer, my mentor and friend, always teaches and writes as a man who lives the "marvelous paradox." His scholarship, always impeccable by worldly standards,[47] is motivated by a profound concern for the spiritual destiny of the church. For he has understood, and continues to teach us, that it is our committed dialogue with scripture and tradition that transforms us toward that destiny.[48]

NOTES

1. Rowan A. Greer, *Theodore of Mopsuestia: Exegete and Theologian* (Westminster, U.K.: Faith Press, 1961).

2. Subsequently revised and published as *The Captain of Our Salvation: A Study in the Patristic Exegesis of Hebrews* (Tübingen: Mohr [Siebeck], 1973).

3. In his book *The Fear of Freedom: A Study of Miracles in the Roman Imperial Church* (University Park: Pennsylvania State University Press, 1989), 178, Greer provides the following description of the quest for virtue:

> The predominant theology of the fourth century is Christian Platonist in character, and it focuses attention upon human freedom and our natural capacity for virtue. God's gift to us is his image, and that gift enables us to discern good and evil. Moreover, we have the power to act upon that discernment. Choosing the good, in the first instance, means the difficult struggle involved in taming the passions and establishing the mind as the governing principle over the body and its passions. The moral virtue thus achieved enables us to move toward the full contemplation of God. Virtue then, is both moral and spiritual. It represents human destiny. At the same time, we cannot accomplish this destiny apart from God. He has made us for himself and implanted us with a nature yearning for our proper goal. In baptism the spirit awakens this free capacity, and the Christian life progresses as an education in which God always remains the beneficent teacher.

4. By use of the term "Antiochene" in this essay, I generally refer to the group of theologians connected to the church at Antioch and extensively studied by Greer throughout his career. In particular see Greer, *Theodore of Mopsuestia; The Captain of Our Salvation; The Fear of Freedom,* 23–28, 48–56; with James L. Kugel, *Early Biblical Interpretation* (Philadelphia: Westminster Press, 1986), 185–99; "The Analogy of Grace in Theodore of Mopsuestia's Christology," *JTS* 34 (1983): 82–98; "The Image of God and the Prosopic Union in Nestorius' *Bazaar of Heraclides,*" in *Lux in Lumine: Essays to Honor W. Norman Pittenger* (ed. Richard Norris; New York: Seabury Press, 1966), 46–61; "The Use of Scripture in the Nestorian Controversy," *SJT* 20 (1967): 413–22; "The Antiochene Christology of Diodore of Tarsus," *JTS* 16 (1966): 327–41.

5. Greer, *Theodore of Mopsuestia,* 45, 51–53.

6. Greer, "The Use of Scripture," 421: "Objectivity derives from its reference to the community and from the fact that it has always been corrected by scripture itself and by the ongoing tradition."

7. Good examples include Greer's *Broken Lights and Mended Lives: Theology and Common Life in the Early Church* (University Park: Pennsylvania State University Press, 1986), 76–90; *The Captain of Our Salvation,* passim; *The Fear of Freedom,* 8–87; *Early Biblical Interpretation,* passim; "The Use of Scripture"; "Diodore of Tarsus."

8. This is the subject of *The Fear of Freedom.*

9. Note Greer's insightful comments in "The Man from Heaven: Paul's Last Adam and Apollinaris' Christ," in *Paul and the Legacies of Paul* (ed. William S. Babcock; (Dallas: Southern Methodist University Press, 1990), 181.

10. Primarily, though not exclusively, *Theodore of Mopsuestia;* also Greer, *The Captain of Our Salvation,* 178–223; "The Analogy of Grace"; "Image of God"; "The Man from Heaven"; "The Use of Scripture"; "Diodore of Tarsus."

11. Greer, "Image of God," 51.

12. See especially Greer, *The Captain of Our Salvation,* 129–77. Greer elaborates on how Theodore, at least, viewed Christian salvation: while we are part of the "first age," Christ has already ushered in the final age. We live in the hope, strengthened and spurred on by the "vision of God" provided in the liturgy (sacraments belong to the final age but are available to us here), of attaining the final age "in Christ" (*Theodore of Mopsuestia,* 72–76).

13. Greer, "Image of God," 47.

14. Several metaphors are used to express this union, primary among them the "indwelling of the Word as in the Temple" and the grace of God acting through and within human nature (Greer, *Theodore of Mopsuestia,* 51–55; *The Captain of Our Salvation,* 210–35).

15. Greer, *The Captain of Our Salvation,* 16.

16. Ibid., 22; Greer, *The Fear of Freedom,* 81.

17. Greer, *Broken Lights,* 111, explains that the church fathers, following Greek philosophy, argued that salvation involved the perfection of the mind in governance over the body and its passions. Christian life, modeled on Christ, involves the stable

acquisition of virtue and also the perfect control of the body which renders it incorruptible in the resurrection of the dead.

18. One thinks here of Apollinarianism (the Word of God displaced the human soul of Christ), Arianism (denying the full divinity of Christ), and the "Word/Flesh" Christology of Alexandria, among others.

19. On Irenaeus: *Theodore of Mopsuestia*, 22, 153–57; *Early Biblical Interpretation*, 165–79; "The Dog and the Mushrooms: Irenaeus's View of the Valentinians Assessed," in *The Rediscovery of Gnosticism*, vol. 1 (ed. Bentley Layton; Leiden: Brill, 1980); on Origen: *Early Biblical Interpretation*, 180–82; *The Captain of Our Salvation*, 64; Foreword, in *Origen: Selected Works*, trans. Rowan A. Greer (Classics of Western Spirituality; New York: Paulist Press, 1979), xv-xvi; *Theodore of Mopsuestia*, 157–61; on Athanasius and Cyril: *Early Biblical Interpretation*, 187; *The Captain of Our Salvation*, 87–96; on Gregory of Nyssa: *Broken Lights*, 45–60; "The Analogy of Grace," 92; "The Leaven and the Lamb: Christ and Gregory of Nyssa's Vision of Human Destiny," in *Jesus in History and Myth* (ed. R. Joseph Hoffmann and Gerald A. Larue; Buffalo: Prometheus Books, 1986); "The Man from Heaven," 176–80; "Augustine's Transformation of the Free Will Defense," *Faith and Philosophy* 13 (1996): 475; on Augustine: *Broken Lights*, 90; *The Fear of Freedom*, 170–77; "The Analogy of Grace," 96–98; "Augustine's Transformation"; Apollinaris: "The Man from Heaven"; for the "Antiochenes" see n. 4 above.

20. Greer concluded his study of the history of patristic exegesis of Hebrews, *The Captain of Our Salvation*, with the following:

> Should we not in our own time take more seriously the role of theology in the exegesis of scripture? Much of the hermeneutical discussion now seems to assume that if one persists in historical or linguistic exegesis of scripture, theological norms will somehow emerge. This is like saying that by persistent beating one can turn milk into whipped cream. Either the exegesis follows its historical path without contributing a theological message for us; or the theology, despite claims to the contrary, is imposed on the text. In neither case does theology emerge full-grown from the Bible. Perhaps the fact that the hermeneutical debate is largely a Protestant one indicates that the various solutions proposed are nothing more than a sophisticated and at times obscurantist way of preserving a "scripture alone" principle. May it not be the case that we, like the fathers, are obliged to take our theologies and, while revering the text and respecting its autonomy, use them boldly in our exegesis? (p. 358)

21. Greer, *Theodore of Mopsuestia*, 22–23.

22. It should be noted that "history" here denotes less our sense of the subject than the obvious narrative meaning of the text.

23. Greer, *Early Biblical Interpretation*, 167–70.

24. Greer, *The Captain of Our Salvation*, 206; "The Dog and the Mushrooms"; *Early Biblical Interpretation*, 167–70.

25. Greer, *Broken Lights,* 37–43; Greer also points out that Irenaeus' Christology remained in some tension with his reading of scripture as the story of the education (*paideia*) of creation toward its redemption. Namely, he possessed a strong view of the *union* of human with the divine nature in Christ. Salvation was therefore akin to "becoming divine"—a view thoroughly compatible with the philosophical assumptions of the day.

26. The transformation does, however, involve change: in the beginning all rational beings are incorporeal and equal; in the end, when the full contemplation of God through his Word (*Logos*) is restored, the rational beings have bodies and are therefore unequal (Greer, *Early Biblical Interpretation,* 180).

27. Greer, *Theodore of Mopsuestia,* 153–54; *The Captain of Our Salvation,* 221.

28. Especially Greer, *The Captain of Our Salvation,* 65–128, and *Early Biblical Interpretation,* 177–99.

29. Greer, *Theodore of Mopsuestia,* 153–60.

30. Greer, *The Captain of Our Salvation.*

31. Greer, *Theodore of Mopsuestia,* 50; "Image of God," 47.

32. Rowan A. Greer, "The Good Shepherd: Canonical Interpretations in the Early Church?" in *Theological Exegesis: Essays in Honor of Brevard S. Childs* (ed. Christopher R. Seitz and Kathryn Greene-McCreight; Grand Rapids: W. B. Eerdmans, 1998), 329.

33. Greer, "The Analogy of Grace."

34. Greer uses the metaphor of the law of the land (general providence) bringing about specific, educative penalties or praise for particular (free) actions.

35. This is particularly true in the theology of Gregory of Nyssa, described by Greer in "The Leaven and the Lamb."

36. Alexandrian theology emphasized a Word/flesh Christology, namely, that the Word joined to Jesus Christ enabled him to act with complete rationality (virtue); our hope is to be caught up "into (the divine) Christ." Antioch emphasized the indwelling of the Word by grace so that it was the free rational obedience of the human Christ which rendered him incorruptible; our hope is, with the same grace of God, to emulate the rational obedience of Christ.

37. Greer, *The Fear of Freedom,* 86; Greer adds here that the defeat of death in Christ not only supplies Christian hope for the age to come but also makes that hope a force in this world; the fathers of the church attribute our tendency to sin to our mortality. Once death is robbed of its power, it becomes possible to live the life of virtue.

38. Greer, *Broken Lights,* 111.

39. Peter Brown, *The Making of Late Antiquity* (Cambridge: Harvard University Press, 1978); *The Cult of the Saints* (Chicago: University of Chicago Press, 1981); *Society and the Holy in Late Antiquity* (Berkeley: University of California Press, 1982).

40. Greer, *The Fear of Freedom,* 147, explains that this is at least partly why there was a concerted effort by the church in this period to bring holy ascetics (monks)

and the cults of the saints and martyrs under the aegis of the church hierarchy. Greer alludes to, but does not elaborate upon, the apparent irony here. The ideal of the holy ascetic, one who controls the passions, is itself rooted in the quest for virtue. Yet as it is "applied" to mediate divine power it is bereft of its original premise of human freedom.

41. Greer, *Fear of Freedom*, 36–42.

42. Rowan A. Greer, "The Transition From Death to Life," *Int* 46 (1992): 248; "Augustine's Transformation," 42.

43. See especially his reviews of Stephen W. Sykes, ed., *Authority in the Anglican Communion: Essays Presented to Bishop John Howe;* J. Robert Wright, ed., *Quadrilateral At One Hundred: Essays on the Centennial of the Chicago Lambeth Quadrilateral 1886/88–1986/88;* and Stephen W. Sykes and John Booty, eds., *The Study of Anglicanism, Anglican and Episcopal History* 58 (1989): 226–31; review of Donald Gray, *Earth and Altar: The Evolution of the Parish Communion in the Church of England to 1945, ATR* 70 (1988): 112–113; review of Robert D. Cornwall, *Visible and Apostolic: The Constitution of the Church in High Church Anglican and Non-Juror Thought, ATR* 76 (1994): 379–81; review of Peter B. Nockles, *The Oxford Movement in Context: Anglican High Churchmanship, ATR* 77 (1995): 247–48; "Anglicanism as an On-Going Argument," *Witness* 81 (1998): 23.

44. One is reminded here of his contributions to the discussion of contemporary priesthood: Rowan A. Greer, "Who Seeks for a Spring in the Mud? Reflections on the Ordained Ministry in the Fourth Century," in *Theological Education and Moral Formation* (ed. Richard John Neuhaus; Grand Rapids: W. B. Eerdmans, 1992); "Reflections on Priestly Authority," *Saint Luke's Journal of Theology* 34 (1991).

45. Rowan A. Greer, "Alien Citizens: A Marvelous Paradox," in *Civitas: Religious Interpretations of the City* (ed. Peter S. Hawkins; Atlanta: Scholars Press, 1986), 54–55.

46. Rowan A. Greer, "Hospitality in the First Five Centuries of the Church," *Monastic Studies* 10 (1974): 48.

47. See, e.g., Rowan A. Greer, "Reckonings in the Study of the Ancient Church," *ATR* 73 (1991).

48. Just as this volume was submitted for publication, Rowan Greer's latest book, *Christian Hope and Christian Life: Raids on the Inarticulate* (New York: Crossroad, 2001) came to my attention, regrettably too late to be included in this essay.

Interpretive Locations

"To Sojourn" or "To Dwell?"

Scripture and Identity in the *Martyrdom of Polycarp*

FREDERICK W. WEIDMANN

In his essay "Références patristiques au 'chrétien-étranger' dans les trois premiers siècles," Johannes Roldanus considered early Christian usage of several related terms, including "foreigner" (ξένος), "sojourner" (πάροικος), "alien" (παρεπίδεμος), and their cognates, asserting, "In all these cases, the condition of the stranger appears in a context of exhortation: it means to inspire an attitude of detachment."[1] In his essay "The Christian Bible and Its Interpretation," Fr. Greer used the related notion of pilgrimage as a kind of metaphor to make a broader point about patristic exegesis: "Built into the patristic understanding of exegesis is the conviction that the Christian's theological vision continues to grow and change, just as the Christian life is a pilgrimage and progress toward a destiny only dimly perceived. The framework of interpretation, then, does not so much solve the problem of what Scripture means as supply the context in which the quest for that meaning may take place."[2]

Greer began his study with a passing reference to Polycarp, bishop of Smyrna and teacher of Irenaeus, but did not analyze the writings associated with Polycarp. For his part, Roldanus began a word study of "to sojourn" (παροικέω) with references to several writings, including Polycarp's *Letter to the Philippians* and the *Martyrdom of Polycarp*, but with no follow-up discussion of either of these documents.[3]

In what follows, I will examine the use of "to sojourn" (παροικέω) in *Mart. Pol.*, particularly in juxtaposition with the use of "to dwell" (κατοικέω) in the same document. Although the evidence provided by *Mart. Pol.* is very limited, it is highly suggestive, and concentration on it is enlightening for the student of *Mart. Pol.* and of early Christian literature generally. In the social-historical setting of Asia Minor in the middle to late second century of the common era, the juxtaposition of the terms "to sojourn" and "to dwell" found within *Mart. Pol.* serves as a signifier of community identity, definition, and purpose vis-à-vis both (non-Christian) Jews[4] and pagans (called "Gentiles"). Further, it illustrates an approach to, and method for, understanding Hebrew Scripture. Finally, it negatively defines contemporary Jews vis-à-vis scriptural descriptions and categories, which in turn suggests a Christian adoption or seizure both of the Jews' scripture and of their place within it.

Within *Mart. Pol.*, the "multitude" (τὸ πλῆθος, *Mart. Pol.* 3.2, 12.2) or "crowd" (ὁ ὄχλος, *Mart. Pol.* 9.2) appears several times. At one point, it is described specifically as "the whole multitude of Gentiles and Jews dwelling (κατοικέω) in Smyrna" (*Mart. Pol.* 12.2). Meanwhile, according to the address of *Mart. Pol.*, the Christians make up a third identity group. Unlike the "Gentiles" and "Jews," the Christians do not "dwell" in Smyrna; rather, they "sojourn": "The community of God which is sojourning (παροικέω) at Smyrna, to the community of God which is sojourning (παροικέω) in Philomelium, and to all the sojournings (παροικία) of the holy and catholic community throughout every place" (*Mart. Pol.* pref.). Such is the extent of the recorded evidence regarding these two verbs, "to sojourn" and "to dwell," within *Mart. Pol.* What might it mean? Both "sojourn" and "dwell" are terms and, more broadly, concepts familiar in the Septuagint (LXX), the Greek translation of the Hebrew Scripture. Consideration of these terms and concepts in the LXX along with their use in later early Christian writings will be the primary concern of this study. Moreover, these terms suggest contemporary technical usage within the Roman Empire.

In his study of 1 Peter, John Elliott reminds the modern reader that, "Politically and legally, persons did not become *paroikoi* because of their conversion to Christianity but as a result of a change in their geographical and legal status."[5] Given the imperial bureaucratic structure of the day, that is most certainly true. Elliott concludes that Christian use of "sojourn" may "have *both* literal *and* metaphorical connotations."[6] In any case, it "draws its rhetorical power from the actuality of lived experience."[7] Specifically, "from the perspective of 1 Peter the basic point is that conversion involved no alleviation of the predicament of social alienation but rather its intensification"; further, "this situation of social and cultural alienation" is "similar to that experienced by ancient Israel."[8]

What is of interest at the beginning of the present study is that the circle can be, and has been, completed by Elliott himself, through the reference to "ancient Israel." I am not concerned with the legal status of the author, addressees, or greater readership of *Mart. Pol.* To be sure, there may indeed be a literal connotation in *Mart. Pol.*'s use of "sojourn": regardless of the legal status of members of Christian community at Philomelium, Smyrna, or elsewhere, the ancient readers/hearers of the text would have been aware of the contemporary, legal meaning of the term, and that awareness could and quite likely would, whether consciously or subconsciously, inform their engagement with it. Still, my study will concern itself with the LXX usage of these terms and *Mart. Pol.*'s particular employment of the LXX usage.

As presented succinctly, though not exhaustively, in Elliott's consideration of the LXX usage, "the term ['sojourn'] refers to Israelites residing away from home as well as to resident aliens in Israel's midst or living elsewhere: e.g., Abraham and his seed in the land of Egypt (Gen 12:10, 15:13), among the Hittites (Gen 23:4), or in Canaan (Gen 17:8; Ps 104 [105]:12); Lot in Sodom (Gen 19:9) . . . [and] the patriarchs residing in Mesopotamia (Jdt 5:7, 8, 10); or generally of Israelites as resident aliens in a land left unnamed (1 Chr 29:15; Pss 38 [39]:12; 118[119]:19)."[9] There is no need here to discuss generally the use of "to sojourn" in these verses, several of which are treated by Elliot and/or Roldanus.[10] What is of immediate interest to this study is a text that presumes a posture similar to that exhibited by the voice of the narrator in *Mart. Pol.*, that is, a narrative hearkening back to earlier "sojourning" to define and describe a contemporary group.

Toward the end of 1 Chronicles, King David speaks before the whole "community" (ἐκκλησία, 1 Chr 29:10; cf. *Mart. Pol.* pref.) a prayer to God: ". . . we are sojourners before you, and are sojourning just as all our fathers" (1 Chr 29:10, 15). The direct connection between David's "community" and the forebears is made through the use of cognate forms of "sojourn" to refer to each. Just as the address of *Mart. Pol.* indicates three times that the "community," in both its wholeness and its particularities, "sojourns," so too 1 Chronicles depicts King David's "community" as "sojourning." However, what is indicated overtly in 1 Chronicles is merely implied in *Mart. Pol.*: such "sojourning" hearkens back to that of the patriarchs or, more generally, the Israelite nation.[11]

In virtually direct contrast to the verb "to sojourn," "to dwell" is used in reference to Israelites residing at home, that is, in the land of Israel-Palestine. For example, according to Deut 12:10, "you will pass over the Jordan, and you will dwell in the land" (cf. Deut 11:31). Likewise, Num 15:2 employs a cognate, κατοίκησις, in rendering God's command to Moses: "Speak to the children of Israel and say to them, 'when you come into the land of your dwelling. . . .'" Yet another cognate, κατοικία, is used throughout Leviticus and elsewhere to refer to individual dwellings within Israel; for example, "you will not do any work, it is a Sabbath to the Lord in every dwelling of yours" (Lev 23:3; cf. Lev 3:13; 7:26; 23:14, 21, 31).

Unfortunately for my purposes, the direct contrast in which I am interested does not always hold, at least not in a simple, clean manner. Hebrews 11, a passage familiar to Greer,[12] contains the following description of Abraham: "By faith he sojourned in a land of promise as though it were foreign, dwelling in tents with Isaac and Jacob, co-heirs of the same promise." In his commentary on Hebrews, Harold Attridge states what is, presumably, the obvious conclusion regarding "to sojourn" and "to dwell" in this verse: "the two verbs can, however, be used synonymously."[13] But is that so? Relative to the homeland from which he has been "called out" (Heb 11:8), Abraham is indeed as one who "sojourned" in Israel (cf. Ps 104[105]:10–12). Relative to the future history of the successors of Abraham in the land (that is, the people of Israel), Abraham and the following generations did/would "dwell" in the land. So, given the context of 11:9, Attridge's own previously stated rule of thumb would seem to hold: "The verb used to describe Abraham's 'sojourning' (παρῴκησεν) often has connotations of temporary dwelling and is frequently opposed to κατοικεῖν, used of a more permanent residence."[14]

Potentially more confusing is the use of "sojourn" and "dwell" in a document roughly contemporary with *Mart. Pol.*, the *Letter to Diognetus*.[15] In an extended discussion which means to "distinguish" Christians from "the rest of humankind" (*Diogn.* 5.1), the author begins by stating that "nowhere do they dwell in their own cities" (*Diogn.* 5.2). However, when considering where the Christians do live, the author employs the same verb, "to dwell": "while dwelling in both Greek and barbarian cities" (*Diogn.* 5.4). So, there is apparently no distinction sought between the theoretical "dwelling" in one's own city (*Diogn.* 5.2) and the actual "dwelling" in the city of another. Given our study of *Mart. Pol.*, one might have expected a change to "sojourn." In the next sentence, the author provides the expected change *and* employs it in a clearly metaphorical way: "They live (οἰκέω) in their own homelands, but as sojourners" (*Diogn.* 5.5). In contrast to the addressees of 1 Peter and possibly of *Mart. Pol.*, all or some of whom may literally be πάροικοι in the contemporary political sense, the Christians described in the *Letter to Diognetus* "dwell" and "live" in cities which they can literally claim as their own. Metaphorically, however, they are "sojourners."

In general, early Christians chose to identify themselves as "sojourners." Polycarp himself begins his letter to the Philippians with the term: "Polycarp and the elders with him to the community of God which is sojourning at Philippi" (Pol. *Phil.* pref.). The author of *Mart. Pol.* had to look no further than the great martyr himself for this particular usage of "sojourn." Prior to the writing of Polycarp's letter, the address of 1 Clement was written as follows: "The community of God which sojourns at Rome to the community of God which sojourns at Corinth." What is the significance of this self-understanding, especially as regards the Polycarp material?

Considering Irenaeus, *Haer.* 5.32.2, Roldanus notes: "Irenaeus refers to the speech of Abraham in Gen 23:4 in order to recall that the condition of the stranger is perpetuated throughout the life of the father of believers."[16] One wonders to what extent Irenaeus may have been influenced by his (ac)claimed teacher, Polycarp. Polycarp, after addressing his letter to "the community . . . which is sojourning," exhorts the addressees to "act as worthy citizens of [God]," "pleasing [God] in the present age" (Pol. *Phil.* 5.2). Indeed, those who are held up as models to be emulated have this in common: "they did not love the present age" (Pol. *Phil.* 9.2). For Polycarp, Christians are sojourners during their earthly lives, citizens of God working to please God, while detaching themselves—on some level, in some way—from the present age.

The author of *Mart. Pol.* develops a contrast between such "sojourning" Christians and the "dwelling" Jews. One recalls the description of "the multitude" in *Mart. Pol.* 12.2, which is the point within the narrative that "the Jews" are introduced: "the whole multitude of Gentiles and Jews dwelling (κατοικέω) in Smyrna." Immediately recognizable in this introduction is the contrast between the Jews and the Christians: while the preface states three times that Christians "sojourn," here one learns that the Jews "dwell." Further, the Jews are immediately and directly associated with pagans, while the Christians stand apart from both.

Greer himself has made the following observations about other second-century documents in discussing the matter(s) of "Christians and Jews" and "[Christianity's] Jewish heritage":

> The *Letter to Diognetus* (ca. 170? C.E.) distinguishes Christians so sharply from Jews that the inference of total discontinuity can be drawn. The *Preaching of Peter*, cited by Clement of Alexandria (ca. 200 C.E.), speaks of Christians as a "third race," neither Jewish nor Gentile. All ambiguity is removed by Marcion, who repudiates Judaism, the Hebrew Scriptures, and the God of Israel altogether.[17]

Greer's comment provides a narrative grid, defined by the *Letter to Diognetus* and the *Preaching of Peter*, on which to plot the characterization of Jews, Christians, and others in *Mart. Pol.* Like *Mart. Pol.*, the *Letter to Diognetus* includes a tripartite grouping of humanity in establishing the distinction of Jews and Christians. For example, the author writes that the Christians "do not consider those which are thought of as gods by the Greeks, neither do they keep the superstitions of the Jews" (*Diogn.* 1).[18] Later the groups are again all considered together, in the assertion that Christians are "battled by the Jews as foreigners, and persecuted by the Greeks" (*Diogn.* 5.17). So the division is consistent: Christians, Jews, pagans. What is different in *Mart. Pol.* is the direct pairing of the Jews with the pagans.

As noted above, in the *Preaching of Peter*, the Christians are identified with a "third race."[19] Clement of Alexandria quotes that document as follows: "But we Christians worship [god] in a new way, as a third race" (*Strom.* 6.5.41). As the culmination of a discussion of Greek and Jewish religious piety (*Strom.* 6.5.39−41), this statement highlights "worship" (σέβω) as that area in which Christians stand apart from the other two groups. *Mart. Pol.* employs a different word for "worship" (προσκυνέω). Nonetheless, there too worship (and worship practice) is of immediate concern. In *Mart. Pol.*, at the point at which the Jews are introduced, it is they who call out, together with the pagans, that famous charge against Polycarp: "This is the teacher of Asia, the father of the Christians, the destroyer of our Gods, who is teaching many neither to sacrifice nor to worship" (*Mart. Pol.* 12.2). As in the comparison to the *Letter to Diognetus*, *Mart. Pol.* differs from the *Preaching to Peter* in that it not only distinguishes Christians from Jews and pagans, but also directly pairs the Jews with the pagans. Together these two groups become offended and feel an "unrestrained anger" (*Mart. Pol.* 12.2), and together they charge Polycarp as one who teaches against their forms of "worship."

Indeed, this togetherness is confirmed and promoted even further in this section of *Mart. Pol.* After recording that the multitude failed in their attempt to urge that Polycarp be killed by a lion, the voice of the narrator continues: "Then it seemed good to them to cry out with one purpose (ὁμοθυμαδόν) that Polycarp might be burned alive" (*Mart. Pol.* 12.3). The depiction of Jews and Gentiles as crying out "with one purpose" is striking. The Greek term itself is quite pointed, being made up of the prefix meaning "same" and a stem suggesting "passion" or, as the term is defined in BAGD, "mind or purpose or impulse" (566). Further, the term appears only three times in the Pentateuch (Exod 19:8; Num 24:24; 27:21), most dramatically in the narrative of the theophany at Sinai: "So Moses came, summoned the elders of the people, and set before them all these words that the Lord had commanded him. The people all answered *as one:* 'Everything that the Lord has spoken we will do'" (Exod 19:8 NRSV). *Mart. Pol.* paints a far different picture: not only are the Jews oblivious to God's voice, which Christians hear and the narrator quotes (*Mart. Pol.* 9.1), but they also speak and act together—"with one purpose"—with the pagans.

The *Preaching of Peter* states outright that the Christians worship as "a third race." The same term, "race" (γένος), is used repeatedly in *Mart. Pol.* The narrator refers to "the . . . race of Christians" (3.2). During his final prayer, Polycarp himself refers to "the race of the righteous ones" (14.2), a phrase that the narrator uses later (17.1). Given the very clear and consistent separation of Christians from Jews and pagans maintained in *Mart. Pol.*, there is no question that this "race" of Christians is quite distinguishable from the other two groups and, as in the *Preaching of Peter,* that worship is a crucial arena of distinction (so *Mart. Pol.* 12.2).

So, returning to Greer's narrative grid, one might summarize as follows. The "inference of total discontinuity" of Christians vis-à-vis Jews which "can be drawn" from the *Letter to Diognetus* can be drawn also from *Mart. Pol.* The delineation of a third "race" such as is present in the *Preaching of Peter* appears also in *Mart. Pol.* As for Marcion, *Mart. Pol.*'s agenda is far from Marcionite, as its use of the LXX, among any other number of characteristics, would indicate. Greer says of Marcion's work that it "repudiates Judaism"; *Mart. Pol.* repudiates contemporary "Jews." However, in a manner qualitatively different than the *Letter to Diognetus* and *Preaching of Peter, Mart. Pol.* correlates the Jews with the pagans. These "Jews . . . dwell" in the Diaspora and act together "with one purpose" with the pagans. Clearly they have, at best, forgotten their heritage.

The description of the Jews' cooperation in preparing the fire for Polycarp's execution, coupled with the particular manner in which the event of the execution is dated, serves as a kind of caricature confirming much that is considered above. In Exod 35:3, Moses quotes the Lord as commanding: "You shall not burn a fire in any dwelling of yours on the Sabbath day."[20] *In Mart. Pol.* the Jews, who "dwell" in Smyrna (12.2), not only call for Polycarp to be burned but aid in the preparation of that fire (12.3, 13.1–2). What is more, all of this happens on a "a great Sabbath" (21.1).[21] Indeed, not only are these Jews presumably ignoring the Sabbath ordinance regarding fire, they revel in their questionable activity: "The Jews were assisting in these things enthusiastically, as was their custom" (13.1).

The Jews, as *Mart. Pol.* presents them, have forgotten their Scripture and their place (quite literally, since they "dwell" in Smyrna). Further, the Jews are fully in league with the pagans. The Christians, on the other hand, find their identity in one of the standard descriptions of the Israelites and their forebears in the LXX, "sojourners." And in much the same way that Polycarp asks his addressees to "act as worthy citizens of [God]," *Mart. Pol.* directs its audience to "[God's] heavenly kingdom" (20). The third-century theologian Origen sets up the following contrast: "The Christian doctrines are true, and are able to lift and raise up the soul and mind . . . [to] a certain citizenship, not like the earthly Jews, somewhere down here on earth, but in heaven."[22] Of such statements by Origen, Roldanus writes that "in this context, 'heaven' and 'earth' are not indications of place, but indicate a profound divergence of orientation and aspiration."[23] It is this early Christian construction of a "profound divergence" that the narrative descriptions of *Mart. Pol.* serve.

The questions are fundamental: how do Christians understand, appropriate, and use Scripture? What do Jews have to do with Scripture, and vice versa? How do Christians understand, describe, and define themselves vis-à-vis Jews and others? That these labels—"Christian," "Jew," "Scripture"—were and are themselves fuzzy is precisely the point. As Daniel Boyarin has recently put it, "There was as much shared religious life and development as partition, as much consensus as dissensus."[24] *Mart. Pol.* witnesses to both the consensus and dissensus, with the polemical, descriptive, and indeed prescriptive use of terminology and labeling that I have considered moving clearly in the direction of differentiation.

Mart. Pol. provides answers to our fundamental questions, answers that make sense within its author's and presumed audience's social-historical context. Through the juxtaposition of the terms "to sojourn" and "to dwell," as well as through other descriptions, the voice of the narrator presents a consistent and distinct picture of Christians as a community of integrity with a defined, unique place in the world. Neither pagan nor Jewish, the Christians, as "sojourners," form a separate "race." Further, Christians can and do, with integrity, use that Scripture which they have in common with Jews. They approach that Scripture as ones who identify with the Abrahamic promise. Indeed, they have now replaced the Jews as "sojourners," inheritors of that promise. The Jews have forgotten that promise and are in league with the pagan establishment trying to quash the faithful "sojourners."

The reader may detect in the categories and understandings established within *Mart. Pol.* the same logic evident, for example, in Ignatius' letter to Polycarp's community at Smyrna. There Ignatius remembers God's action in Jesus Christ as being "for [God's] holy and faithful ones, whether among the Jews or the Gentiles, in one body of [God's] community" (Ign. *Smyrn.* 1.2). On one level, these early Christians were concerned to delineate clear community boundaries precisely because those boundaries were fluid: from where would converts come, if not from among pagans or Jews? But it is another, more pervasive level from which these labels were constructed and on which they operated.

My summary statements above, especially that Christians have replaced the Jews as "inheritors," make *Mart. Pol.* sound harsher and more calculated than I had intended. Perhaps that is good—or at least fair and honest— since that document was formed in a place far different from my own. Boyarin writes suggestively regarding the interplay between Christian and Jewish (sub)groups evident in such literature as *Mart. Pol.* that "martyrdom was elaborated by rabbinic Jews and Christians together via a tangled process of innovation and learning, competition and sharing of themes, motifs, and practices."[25] I think so. Further and more particularly, I think that the on-going martyrdom tradition in Polycarp's city, Smyrna, indicates as much.[26]

The pointed usage of the verbs "to sojourn" and "to dwell" serves broad and central agendas within *Mart. Pol.*, those of community identity and use of Scripture. These agendas are not unique to *Mart. Pol.* among contemporary documents, but are carried out in a unique and perhaps under-recognized way. Returning to the scholarly quotations with which this study begins, one can observe that there is within *Mart. Pol.* both the concern to "inspire an attitude of detachment" from non-Christian ways (both Jewish and pagan) and to "supply the context in which the quest for . . . [the] meaning [of Scripture] may take place."[27] Toward the close of his essay "Alien Citizens: A Marvelous Paradox," Greer writes: "Martyrdom and alien Christianity made the Church a cause, exacting single-minded and exclusive loyalty."[28] That statement resonates well with the narrative of the *Martyrdom of Polycarp* and with the phenomenon of martyrdom more broadly.[29] In terms of the sweep of Christian literature, this "first of the martyr acts"[30] is also among the earliest, extended constructions of "alien Christianity."

Notes

1. Johannes Roldanus, "Références patristiques au 'chretien-étranger' dans les trois premiers siècles," in *Lectures anciennes de la Bible* (Cahiers de Biblia Patristica 1; Centre D'Analyse et de Documentation Patristiques, 1987), 27–52, at 32. Except when indicated otherwise, translations from ancient documents are my own.

2. James L. Kugel and Rowan A. Greer, *Early Biblical Interpretation* (LEC; Phila-delphia: Westminster, 1986), 107–208 at 198–99; cf. Rowan A. Greer, *Broken Lights and Mended Lives: Theology and Common Life in the Early Church* (University Park: Pennsylvania State University Press, 1986), esp. chaps. 3 and 6.

3. Roldanus, "Références patristiques," 29.

4. For purposes of this discussion I will regularly juxtapose "Christian" and "Jew." Of course, the use of such labels then and now is complex and problematic, and indeed some part of that complexity serves as the subject of this essay. For a recent discussion of the "fuzziness" of such labels, then and now, see Daniel Boyarin, *Dying for God: Martyrdom and the Making of Christianity and Judaism* (Stanford: Stanford University Press, 1999), 10 and passim.

5. John Elliott, *A Home for the Homeless: A Social-Scientific Criticism of 1 Peter, Its Situation and Strategy* (Minneapolis: Fortress, 1990), xxix.

6. Elliott, *Home for the Homeless*, xxix.

7. Elliott, *Home for the Homeless*, xxx.

8. Elliott, *Home for the Homeless*, xxx.

9. Elliott, *Home for the Homeless*, 27; regarding Ps 38[39], one could also add v. 54. References to "sojourners" within the land of Israel (that is, those whom Elliott refers to as "resident aliens in Israel's midst . . .") will not be considered here, though one might note that such usage confirms the notion that Israelites "sojourn" outside Israel, and "dwell" within it (contrast Deut 14:21 and 23:8 with 11:31 and 12:10).

10. Elliott, *Home for the Homeless*, 27–29; Roldanus, "Références patristiques," 28–32.

11. This same verse, 1 Chr 29:15, is cited in Karl Ludwig and Martin Anton Schmidt, "πάροικος", etc." *TDNT* 5:843, as an example of "why the LXX can some-times use κατοικεῖν when one would expect παροικεῖν," since in Codex B (Vati-cinus), the former does occur. In Rahlf's *Septuaginta* (Editio minor, 1979), the text as translated above is not questioned. Though the variant reading of B is noted, it is fur-ther marked with a dagger indicating "only the MSS. which we have cited and, at the most, not more than one minuscule which we have not mentioned have supported the reading in question" (explanation as stated by Rahlf, p. lxvii). Without any fur-ther evidence to the contrary, it would seem the safer assumption that this verse, with its repeated uses of "sojourn," confirms the expected LXX distinction of "to sojourn" and "to dwell."

12. Rowan A. Greer, *The Captain of Our Salvation: A Study in the Patristic Exegesis of Hebrews* (BGBE 15; Tübingen: J. C. B. Mohr [Paul Siebeck], 1973), esp. 34–36.

13. Harold W. Attridge, *The Epistle to the Hebrews: A Commentary on the Epistle to the Hebrews* (Hermeneia; Philadelphia: Fortress, 1989), 323.

14. Attridge, *Epistle to the Hebrews*, 323. The Abraham narrative, of course, pro-vides opportunities for further study of these terms and their nuanced usage, which is beyond the scope of this essay. For example, in the narrative description of Abram's first entry into the land promised him, the voice of the narrator notes, "the Canaan-

ites, then, were dwelling in the land" (Gen 12:6). After having departed "to sojourn" in Egypt (Gen 12:10), Abram returns to the promised land and now, according to the narrator, "Abram dwelt in the land of Canaan" (Gen 13:11). Study of word usage in Genesis supports the claim that the two terms "can . . . be used synonymously." For example, Gen 19:9 (as cited by Elliott above) records the words of the people of Sodom to Lot: "you came to sojourn." In contrast, Gen 13:12 states, "Lot dwelt . . . in Sodom." Of course, it is possible that the voice of the narrator and the people of Sodom have different perspectives on the matter, which are reflected in the verbs employed.

15. For a recent discussion of date, see Clayton N. Jefford, *Reading the Apostolic Fathers: An Introduction* (Peabody, Mass.: Hendrickson, 1996), 162; cf. Kugel and Greer, *Early Biblical Interpretation*, 122.

16. Roldanus, "Références patristiques," 36.

17. Kugel and Greer, *Early Biblical Interpretation*, 122.

18. For discussion of the charge of "superstition" posited in Jewish literature against Christians, see Boyarin, *Dying for God*, 103–4. On a related matter in Polycarp traditions particularly, see the recently published Harris Fragments on Polycarp and John which, distinct from *Mart. Pol.*, include the charge of "magic" among Polycarp's crimes and narrate that "the Jew[s]" alone charge Polycarp; *FrgPol* (d) 1–8 in Frederick W. Weidmann, *Polycarp and John: The Harris Fragments and Their Challenge to the Literary Traditions* (Christianity and Judaism in Antiquity 12; Notre Dame, Ind.: University of Notre Dame Press, 1999), 31, 45, 92–102.

19. For a similar (parallel?) development of the notion of "race" in Jewish literature, see Judith M. Lieu, *Image and Reality: The Jews in the World of the Christians in the Second Century* (Edinburgh: T & T Clark, 1996), 84–85.

20. The noun rendered "dwellings," κατοικία, as mentioned in the discussion of LXX usage of "to dwell" above, is a cognate of "to dwell"; cf. also the use of both "sojournings" and "to sojourn" in *Mart. Pol.* pref.

21. This reference to "great Sabbath" has engendered great (at least in terms of quantity produced) and often interesting scholarly debate; for discussion and bibliography, see recently Boudewijn Dehandschutter, "The Martyrium Polycarpi: A Century of Research," *ANRW* 27.1: 485–522, at 500–501, and William R. Schoedel, "Polycarp of Smyrna and Ignatius of Antioch," *ANRW* 27.1: 272–358, at 355.

22. *Cels.* 2.5 (trans. Henry Chadwick, *Origen: Contra Celsum* [Cambridge: Cambridge University Press, 1953], 70).

23. Roldanus, "Références patristiques," 43.

24. Boyarin, *Dying for God*, 17–18.

25. Boyarin, *Dying for God*, 126.

26. See, for example, the *Martyrdom of Pionius*, about a third-century leader within the Christian community at Smyrna who self-consciously stands in the tradition of Polycarp (*M. Pion.* 2.2). In a speech to the "Christian siblings" who visit him in jail (12.2), Pionius states: "I hear that the Jews are inviting even some of you into synagogues" (13.1).

27. Of course, on a different front, the sustained concern within *Mart. Pol.* to present Polycarp's as a "martyrdom according to the gospel" (or "Gospel") might also be considered an example of supplying "the context in which the quest for . . . [the] meaning [of Scripture] may take place"; see Leslie Barnard, "In Defense of Pseudo-Pionius' Account of Polycarp's Martyrdom," in *Kyriakon: Festschrift Johannes Quasten* (ed. Patrick Granfield and Josef A. Jungmann; 2 vols; Muenster: Aschendorff, 1970), 1:192–204.

28. Greer, *Broken Lights and Mended Lives*, 160.

29. See recently Lieu, *Image and Reality*, 82–86, on "Martyrdom and Self-Definition."

30. Schoedel, "Polycarp of Smyrna," 355.

The Seed of Seth at the Flood

Biblical Interpretation
and Gnostic Theological Reflection

DAVID BRAKKE

In the book that he co-wrote with James L. Kugel, *Early Biblical Inter-pretation*, Rowan Greer points to how "both Jews and Christians saw the task of interpretation as that of bringing Scripture to bear upon the present and upon the religious life of their respective communities."[1] Among such ancient biblical interpreters were the Gnostics, who engaged in the popular medium of "rewritten Scripture" to present their exegeses of the accounts of early humanity found in Genesis.[2] The driving question of Gnostic biblical inter-pretation was how it happened that fragments of the divine life, sparks of spiritual power present in the Gnostics themselves (and possibly, without their awareness, in others), had survived in a cosmos created and governed by demonic forces. The Gnostics corrected the stories of Adam and Eve and their progeny, originally written with little understanding by Moses, to answer this question and thus to account for their own remarkable presence in a hostile world.

The story of Noah and the flood, found in chapters 6 and 7 of Genesis, posed certain challenges to Gnostic mythmakers, who were united in their conviction that the God of Israel was not the ultimate God, but a vain, fool-ish, even evil lesser power named Ialdabaoth. How did the divine spark pres-ent in the Gnostics' spiritual ancestors, the descendants of Seth, survive a flood caused by the evil and false God of Israel when the only survivors of that catastrophe, Noah and his family, were human beings chosen for their particularly strong devotion ("righteousness") to that false deity? The Gnostics' own existence revealed that the true spiritual essence did survive, despite the best efforts of Ialdabaoth and his supernatural cronies. This theological crux reflected the Gnostics' own paradoxical social identity as persons who claimed to be the true heirs of a biblical tradition whose God they rejected. While many of the Gnostic mythmakers' interpretive moves in rewriting other biblical passages can be attributed to the need to solve certain "problems" in the biblical text recognized by other Jews and Christians,[3] their divergent readings of the flood narrative and of Noah's family history appear to have arisen less from troublesome details in the text than from tensions within the Gnostic sect over their own social identity with respect to Jews and Christians and over the problems of free will and salvation in their theological system. In their own way Gnostics participated in a project of forming a Christian identity through biblical interpretation similar to that pursued by such "proto-orthodox" interpreters as Irenaeus of Lyons.

Table 1 presents the six major witnesses to Gnostic retellings of the flood narrative and the interpretive cruxes that engaged and divided their authors.[4] Other ancient Jewish and Christian interpreters focused their energies on explaining who the "sons of God" were who mixed with human women (Gen 6:1–4), how God can be said to have "repented" (Gen 6:6) and to have become angry enough to destroy his creation, what virtues Noah displayed that made him worthy of rescue, and what is meant by his later drunkenness.[5] Likewise, several modern scholars have seen the "sons of God" incident as crucial to the Gnostics' use of the Bible, indeed as the origin of their myth.[6] In fact, however, none of these issues were the central concerns of the Gnostics, who seldom mentioned the "sons of God" incident in connection with the flood and saw in the capricious actions of the God of Israel only further confirmation of his lesser status. Instead, they focused intently on the people in the ark: who they were and by what supernatural aid they got into the ark, if indeed they even were in the ark at all. Just as third-century Christians such as Hippolytus and Callistus of Rome and Cyprian of Carthage used the little band of flood survivors as ciphers through which to debate the purity and discipline of the church,[7] so too the Gnostics saw in these primeval characters a microcosm of the human situation in their own day.[8]

Divine-Human Intercourse and the Cause of the Flood

The brief and enigmatic account of the "sons of God" who have intercourse with human women and so beget the "giants" has perplexed and fascinated

TABLE 1. GNOSTIC INTERPRETATIONS OF THE FLOOD STORY

Gnostic Witness	Who Causes Flood and Why?	Who Is Saved?	By Whom and How?	Gen. 6:1–4?
Irenaeus 1.30.10	Ialdabaoth, because humankind does not worship and honor him	*Noah and others*[1]	Wisdom, in the ark	Unlikely allusion, occurs before flood
Epiphanius 26.7–9	ruler (Ialdabaoth), in order to destroy Noria	(1) Noah (2) *Noria*	(1) ruler, in the ark ("coffer") (2) the higher powers and the Barbelo, ??	Absent
Epiphanius 39.3.1	"Mother" (Wisdom?), because humanity mixes with angels and may ally with them	(1) "*pure people*" = Noah + 6 (2) Ham	(1) Mother, in the ark (2) angels, secretly stowed in ark	Probable allusion, occurs before flood
Secret Book According to John II 28:32–30:11	Ialdabaoth, because of the superiority of human thought (?)	"*the immovable race*" = Noah and others	the light of forethought, in a place, in a luminous cloud	Certain allusion, occurs after flood, attempts to mix with human women fail and then succeed
Reality of the Rulers 92:3–93:2	rulers, because humanity multiplies and improves	(1) Noah and others (2) *Norea*	(1) Sabaoth, in the ark (2) Eleleth (?), ?	Unlikely allusion, rulers fail to rape Norea after flood
Revelation of Adam 69:2–71:8	Sakla, because of what humanity seeks after	(1) "*Those People*" (2) Noah and his family	(1) angels, moved to place where the spirit of life dwells (2) Sakla, in the ark	Absent

[1] The emphasized characters are ancestors or representatives of Gnostic humanity.

biblical interpreters of every era, including the ancient. In Gnostic myth, however, intercourse between human and supernatural beings is a continuous theme from the beginning: usually Cain, as well as Abel at times, is the product of such a liaison between Eve and some evil ruler, such as Ialdabaoth (e.g., *Ap. John* II 24:15–25). Thus, the specific incident in Gen 6:1–4 is, one might say, superfluous and thus not prominent in most Gnostic witnesses, as Table 2 below illustrates (information from Table 1 reorganized):

Gen 6:1–4 before Flood	*Gen 6:1–4 after Flood*	*Gen 6:1–4 Absent*
Epiphanius 39.3.1	Ap. John	Epiphanius 26.7–9
		Apoc. Adam
		Irenaeus 1.30.9 (?)
		Hyp. Arch. (?)

In the right most column, two accounts (Epiphanius' "Gnostics" and *The Revelation of Adam*) do not mention this incident at all, but the other two cases are ambiguous. Irenaeus reports that before the flood human beings "were introduced by the lower septet (of worldly demons) to all kinds of evil," possibly an allusion to the widespread notion that the sons of God corrupted the human women morally in multiple ways, thus provoking God to limit human lifetime to 120 years (Gen 6:3). But Irenaeus does not mention any sexual intercourse at this point and goes on to say that "the mother *always* secretly opposed them and preserved her own, that is, the secretion of light" (*Haer.* 1.30.9, emphasis added), suggesting that the reference is to an ongoing pattern of corrupting divine-human interaction, rather than to the discreet incident in Genesis 6. The attempted rape of Norea by the rulers in *The Reality of the Rulers* occurs after the flood and appears to be a better candidate as an allusion to Genesis 6 since sexual intercourse is explicitly in view, but in this witness as well, divine-human sexual intercourse does *not* occur, and only one woman appears (not multiple "daughters of humanity"): thus, even this episode fails to qualify.

That leaves only two witnesses that contain certain reworkings of the "sons of God" incident, and one of these diverges significantly from the biblical account. In *The Secret Book According to John,* the evil angels attempt to seduce human women *after* the flood. At first they do not succeed, but the angels then invent a "counterfeit spirit" in the image of the divine "spirit of life" that enables them to change their own images, to introduce humanity to wealth and its attendant anxieties and vices, and so at last to achieve their desired union with human women (II 29:17–30:11). The result is the ignorance of spiritual reality that plagues humankind even "down to the present time." Ialdabaoth had his crew make this effort because the flood had failed to destroy humanity, which was "superior" to him thanks to the work of "the afterthought of the luminous forethought" (II 27:33–29:1). In other words, Ialdabaoth causes the flood because of humanity's insight and superiority, rather than its moral depravity; hence, the "sons of God" incident makes no sense before the flood, but rather explains how ignorance arose even after the catastrophe left only "the immovable race" surviving (II 29:9–10).

This logic prevails in nearly all the other versions of the Gnostic myth. Ialdabaoth (or Sakla or the rulers in general) attempts to destroy humanity because of its adherence to higher divine reality: "humankind began to multiply and improve" (*Hyp. Arch.* 92:3–4); it would "seek after" higher things (*Apoc. Adam* 69:10–11); it would not "worship or honor" Ialdabaoth "as parent and god" (Ir. *Haer.* 1.30.10); or Norea, representative of enlightened humanity, "revealed the higher powers and the Barbelo from the powers" (Ep. *Pan.* 26.1.9). There is no room for a precipitating corruption of humanity by the angels in this scenario as long as the supernatural agents who cause the flood are the angels (rulers) or their chief, Ialdabaoth.

The only account of the myth in which Ialdabaoth or the rulers do not cause the flood, therefore, is also the only one that preserves the biblical sequence of intercourse between humanity and angelic forces, followed by the flood. Epiphanius reports that the "Sethians" believe that the "mother and female," most likely Wisdom, caused the flood because of "the frequent intercourse and confused impulse on the part of the angels and the human beings, so that the two tended toward mixture" (*Pan.* 39.3.1). This version of the myth foregrounds the struggle between the higher powers, led by the Mother, and the angels: factions of humanity form "alliances" with the two groups and thus participate on earth in a wider cosmic struggle. As Epiphanius tells it, this account is less interested in how people do or do not achieve acquaintance (*gnosis*) than in how the purity of the Sethian line and its "spark of righteousness" were preserved until the incarnation of Christ in Jesus, "a descendant of Seth by descent and by succession of peoples" (*Pan.* 39.3.5). This branch of the Gnostic sect appears to have emphasized more strongly than others the distinction between themselves and other people and to have tied this distinction most firmly to genealogy: a christology of messianic descent from Seth provided the model for this anthropology.

Ironically, then, this group comes closest within the Gnostic movement to displaying the stereotypical notion that the Gnostics taught salvation by fixed genetic origins, but does so by adhering most closely to the chronology of the biblical account: after corrupting interaction between humanity and angels, the "good" divinity causes the flood in order to destroy wicked people and to preserve the righteous. The extent of departure from the basic story line of the Bible in Gnostic myth, then, was not a function of the distance from "orthodoxy" in matters of soteriology and anthropology. Here a theology that adhered to the basic biblical narrative formed a communal identity of radical otherness based on "ancestry from Seth" (*Pan.* 39.1.3), whether such ancestry was believed to be literal or symbolic (see below). Given this highly sectarian anthropology, perhaps it is no surprise that, according to Epiphanius, the "Sethians" were "not found everywhere" and may already have disappeared completely (*Pan.* 39.1.1).

With the exception of a rare variety that emphasized its genetic ties to Seth, the Gnostics did not connect the flood to the incident described in Gen 6:1–4. For them the flood was caused by a lesser divinity hostile to people and to the higher divine life because of humanity's continued relationship with true spiritual reality: such a perspective obviated a provoking incident of corruption of humanity by angelic powers. A specific incident of sexual intercourse between the "sons of God" and human women faded from their imagination while the general principle that ignorance and vice resulted from corruption of humanity by evil lower supernatural beings loomed large. In some instances, most notably *The Reality of the Rulers,* the lesser rulers' erotic attraction to the spiritual power present in humankind becomes the primary motivation for action in the myth (see, e.g., 87:11–20). But this motif remains subordinated to and a function of the more basic Gnostic rejection of the ultimate divine status of the God of Israel, the cause of the flood. At the center of the Gnostic imagination was not the myth of the amorous "sons of God," fallen angels, but the conviction, based on first-hand knowledge (*gnosis*), that a truly spiritual, righteous, and good divine power resides above this troubled and demonic world and has miraculously remained present among the chosen human beings.[9]

Who's Who in the Ark: The Identity of the Saved

With only one exception, Gnostic sources are united in their belief that the flood was a bad thing, caused by the false God of Israel (Ialdabaoth) or a team of lesser powers. But they disagree markedly about who was saved from the deluge, by whom, and how. The Gnostics' fundamental disagreement with their "proto-orthodox" opponents was over the doctrines of God and creation, but their most significant disagreements among themselves apparently focused on anthropology and soteriology. Is every human being a potential Gnostic? How do people come to salvation? What about non-Gnostics? Are they lost forever? How are Gnostics related to the rest of humanity? Ancient and modern students of "Gnosticism" have tended to gloss over such differences within the sect by labeling its theology "deterministic." But the retellings of the flood narrative reveal considerable, but limited, diversity and subtlety among the Gnostics on these points.

Noah provided an excellent figure through which to think about such questions because the Gnostics' core beliefs about the biblical story made him problematic. If, as they nearly all thought, Ialdabaoth caused the flood to wipe out Gnostic or potentially Gnostic humanity, and if, as the Bible said, he also saved Noah and his family because of Noah's pronounced fidelity to him (and thus not to the higher powers), how is it that the Gnostic potential survived? Was Noah really one of the "pure" people? If so, how did he get on the ark without Ialdabaoth stopping him? Or were there other people stowed away on the ark? Maybe Moses was just confused about the ark entirely. These questions were not of merely antiquarian interest to the Gnostics, for whom the paradox of Noah was surprisingly close. The Gnostics themselves claimed to know the true content of the revelation of Jesus, the anointed one of Israel: that the god of Israel was not the true God.[10] Their rejection of that God made them saved, as opposed to the "proto-orthodox," whose devotion to that God left them in ignorance. And all this the Gnostics said could be found in the Scripture of that same God—if one knew how to correct its errors. The potential implications of these positions for the Gnostics' views of themselves with respect to Jews, Christians, and polytheists were bewildering. No wonder they could not get the passenger list of the ark quite straight.

Table 1 lays out the complexity of the Gnostic positions on this question, but it is possible to sort them into two general categories: a majority position (in terms of number of witnesses), in which two distinct groups of human beings are saved from the flood by two different divine agents; and a minority view, in which only one group of people is saved—Noah and his family—by the action of the higher powers. This "majority/minority" terminology cannot be pressed because one of the sources that contains the "minority" view, *The Secret Book According to John,* exists in at least four versions, a sign of its centrality and weight in Gnostic thought (or an accident of preservation), and because number of surviving sources is not a reliable indicator of number of adherents in any case. Still, the prevalence of the "two groups" model in the witnesses does suggest that it was the "easier" solution to the problem:

one could assert that somehow both "good" and "bad" people were saved, and thus there are Gnostics and non-Gnostics in the world today. The "one group" solution forces the question of how diversity in human salvation originated after the flood, and indeed the *Secret Book* must devote a lengthy dialogue to this very problem.

Although the "two group" model may imply that there are different "kinds" of people, distinguished by biological descent, even the sources that operate with this notion cannot easily be called "deterministic." This is the case even with the two witnesses that seem to most directly tie salvation to physical processes, the "Sethians" and "Gnostics" described by Epiphanius. We have already seen that Epiphanius' "Sethians" alone among the varieties of Gnostics identified one of the higher spiritual powers, the Mother, as the agent of the flood and retained the biblical sequence of human-angelic intercourse followed by flood. In their view, there were eight people in the ark: seven of the "pure people," Noah and six others, saved in the ark by the Mother; and one of the "evil people," Ham, secretly placed on board the ark by the angels. Thanks to Ham's survival, "forgetfulness, error, sinful undisciplined passions, and evil promiscuity" persisted among humanity despite the higher Mother's efforts (*Pan.* 39.3.2–4). As we have seen, this group directly connects salvation to ancestry: Gnostics are descended ultimately from Seth through Noah; non-Gnostics, from Cain and Abel, through Ham. The Gnostics are called "pure," "elect," and the like. It is likely, though, that this group did not simply divide all humanity into two such distinct groups since, although Epiphanius does not report on this point, Ham, the only "evil" person on the ark, must have had to mix with the "pure" in order to reproduce more evil people. There was, then, probably some room in this scheme of salvation by ancestry for some ambiguity among the human population, even if one does not demythologize this account into one of purely "symbolic ancestry."[11]

More dramatic is Epiphanius' controversial account of "the Gnostics": here the spiritual principle destined for salvation is identified as a "seed" within humanity and must be literally "collected" through sexual emissions and other physical activities. In this account, the ruler saves Noah from the flood in the ark ("the coffer") because Noah "put his trust in the ruler." Noah's wife Norea, however, is denied access to the ark because she "revealed the higher powers and the Barbelo from the powers"; in retaliation Norea burns the ark "many times," delaying construction "for many years." Somehow, however, by the agency of the higher powers, Norea appears to be preserved from the deluge, for she survives to reveal the sect's distinctive soteriology: "She made clear the necessity of collecting, from out of the power within bodies, the parts plundered from the superior mother by the ruler who made the world and by the others in its company—gods, angels, demons—by means of the emissions of males and females" (*Pan.* 26.1.7–9). This principle provides the rationale for the "shocking" practices of seed collection that Epiphanius goes on to report: ritual intercourse (both hetero- and homo-erotic), abortion, cannibalism, and so forth. At death human souls face two possibilities: if they have achieved acquaintance and have engaged in these practices designed to "gather one's self out of the world," they escape this world and enter into rest; if not, they are reincarnated in "swine and other living things" (*Pan.* 26.10.7–10). Nevertheless, here such psychological factors as "acquaintance," conversion, and the will are subordinated to the disciplined acts of collection of the divine principle.

Not surprisingly, modern scholars differ widely on whether and to what extent this sensational report ought to be accepted,[12] but its basic idea—that the spiritual presence must be freed from this material world through deliberate ritualized acts—is familiar enough from Manichaeanism,[13] whose possible influence on this group cannot be discounted.[14] The spiritual seed that is "sown" in humanity is both the fragmented presence of the higher divinity, gendered feminine, and the essence of the human self. So claims the *Gospel of Eve*, now lost except for a quotation by Epiphanius:

It is I who am you: and it is you who are me.
And wherever you are, I am there.
And I am sown in all: and you collect me from wherever you wish.
But when you collect me, it is your own self that you collect. (*Pan.* 26.3.1)

The divine stuff, as it were, is present in everyone: what is needed is awareness of its presence and the ritualized work of collecting it. Presumably anyone can come to this awareness, especially if they read the sect's special literature or interpret properly such biblical works as the Gospel of John and the Psalms, in which this message is presented symbolically (*Pan.* 26.8.1, 4–7). Hence, the rescue of Norea from the flood, outside the ark by the higher powers, was required not because Noah and his ilk were defective or lacked the spiritual principle, but rather because Norea possessed the insight into the human situation that had to be revealed to humanity. Even this highly physical soteriology left room for all people to be saved: the flood story emphasizes the continued availability of revelation, symbolized by Norea.

A strikingly similar version of the flood story is found in *The Reality of the Rulers*, which highlights Norea's role as revealer and mother of the Gnostic community, but makes Noah a more ambiguous figure than he appears in the myth of Epiphanius' "Gnostics." This work emphasizes the providential care of the ultimate God—everything happens "by the parent's will"—and ame-liorates somewhat the anti-Judaism of Gnostic myth by identifying the God of Israel, not as the satanic Ialdabaoth, but as Sabaoth, Ialdabaoth's repen-tant and rebellious son. When the rulers wish to destroy all life through a flood, it is Sabaoth ("the ruler of the powers") who saves Noah, his family, and the animals. Thus, in this version Noah is not portrayed as in league with the evil rulers, but he still denies Norea admission to the ark. This Noah is a more ambiguous figure, and thus the picture of the non-Gnostic humanity that he represents is not as dark as in Epiphanius' reports.[15]

Norea's role is likewise enhanced: she plays the role that Seth fills in other versions of the myth. When Norea, "the virgin whom the powers did not defile," is born, Eve announces: "He (most likely, the ultimate God) has begotten on [me a] virgin as an assistance [for] many generations of human-kind" (91:34–92:3), an allusion to the "voice" that "came forth from incor-ruptibility for the assistance of Adam" (88:17–19).[16] This declaration is fol-lowed by the author's statement that "then humankind began to multiply and improve," implying that Norea's "assistance" is responsible for this pro-gress, which provokes the rulers' plan to "obliterate all flesh" through the flood (92:3–8). The story follows the "two group" model in a manner similar to Epiphanius' "Gnostics": Noah and company are saved in the ark by a lower, albeit less evil, power (Sabaoth), while Norea, having burned up the ark once, is preserved mysteriously so that she can have her climactic encounter with the lustful rulers.[17]

The multidimensionality of the interaction surrounding the ark in this account presents a more complex view of the Gnostics' social world than do the two-dimensional narratives that we have seen in Epiphanius. The flood narrative reveals, rather, "three crucial oppositions: (1) between the Rulers and 'all flesh'; (2) between the Rulers and the Ruler of the Forces (probably to be identified not with Ialdabaoth but Sabaoth), who saves Noah and his chil-dren from obliteration; and (3) between Noah, the faithful servant of the Ruler of the Forces, and Norea."[18] To the extent that *The Reality of the Rulers* invited its Gnostic readers to re-imagine their own social world through the prism of this episode, they most likely saw in Noah and his children devotees of Sabaoth distinct among "all flesh," that is, their contemporaries who re-mained stubbornly, if mistakenly, devoted to the God of Israel. Issues of power within a religious community are played out in Noah's refusal of admis-sion to Norea to the ark, an act of authority that Norea resists.[19] Denying the

Gnostics a place in the "ark" of the wider church, the "proto-orthodox" doubt-less believed that these "heretics" were now vulnerable, like Norea, to hostile cosmic forces. But Norea's triumph assured the Gnostics of their own ulti-mate vindication.

But what made Gnostics "children" of Norea and others the mis-guided followers of Sabaoth? A pivotal passage suggests that the Gnostics have within them a spiritual presence, "the spirit of truth," that other people do not:

> But I (Norea) said, "Sir, am I too from their (the rulers') matter?" (Eleleth replies:) "You, together with your offspring, belong to the primeval par-ent; from above, out of the incorruptible light, their souls are come. Thus the authorities cannot approach them because of the spirit of truth pres-ent within them; and all who have become acquainted with this way exist immortal in the midst of dying humankind." (*Hyp. Arch.* 96:17–27)

While this passage can be read as implying that Gnostics, thanks to their descent from Norea, possess from birth "souls from above," absent in the rest of "dying humankind," other features of the work move against this reading. Norea, after all, is repeatedly identified as a "virgin," prompting the question, "how is it that the virginal Norea has children?"[20] Possibly she gives birth to them ritually, for Eleleth promises that, when "the true human being" comes, he "will anoint them with the ointment of eternal life, given unto that being from the undominated race. Then they will be freed of blind thought" (96:32–97:6). This promise could refer to the ritual of Gnostic baptism and its "five seals," which is familiar from other Gnostic writings, in which one might become an "offspring" of Norea and receive a soul from above.[21] In any case, a symbolism of spiritual descent need not imply literal inherited genetic superiority, nor need it preclude active efforts to recruit others.[22] But it may account for why some convert and others do not and so why, within the innu-merable mass of "all flesh," only a few ended up in the ark, and even fewer, only Norea, survived the flood based on the superiority of her "root" (93:13).

Among the Gnostic sources working with a "two group" model, *The Reve-lation of Adam* most elaborately uses the flood narrative and Noah's family to present a mythic account of its contemporary social world. Once again it is the ruler of the powers, here named Sakla, who causes the flood because of hu-manity's continual striving after higher spiritual reality, but his specific targets are "the people into whom had passed [the] life that belongs to acquaintance (*gnosis*)" (69:13–15). The two sets of survivors are "Those People," whom good angels spirit away to "the place in which the spirit [of] life dwells" (69:19–25), and Noah and his family, whom Sakla preserves in the ark.

The theme of power, played out suggestively in *The Reality of the Rulers*, is made explicit in the *Revelation of Adam*. Sakla "will cast his power upon the waters" and then "bestow power" on Noah and the other passengers on the ark (*Apoc. Adam* 70:8–12). As ruler of this world, Sakla is able to give controlling authority to Noah and his descendants: "Therefore, I shall give you and your offspring the land. With dominance you and your offspring will dominate it. And out of you will come no seed of humankind that will not stand in my presence in some other glory" (71:1–8). The story of the flood here accounts for the contemporary social fact that the world is governed by non-Gnostic humanity since the representatives of the Gnostics, "Those People," were simply absent during the deluge, enjoying the spirit of life in some removed "place." But in a world dominated by the ignorant majority, the Gnostics retain some freedom, for the higher powers "bring them in to their worthy land, and build for them a holy dwelling place" (72:2–5). The ensuing events reveal this "place" to be Sodom and Gomorrah: the Gnostics embrace the identity of the "Sodomites," the stigmatized "others" in the biblical tradition.[23]

While Norea actively resisted the dominant authority of Noah and the rulers, "Those People" merely retain some spiritual autonomy symbolized by geographical isolation. Their less aggressive resistance to non-Gnostic power appears again when their "land" is attacked with "fire, brimstone, and asphalt": once again "Those People" are rescued by angelic beings, who "take them above the aeons and the realms of the powers," where they "will come to resemble those angels" (74:26–76:7). *The Revelation of Adam* may make domination and power more explicit themes in its narrative than does *The Reality of the Rulers*, but it does so without the active subversion and resistance of the latter; instead, the primeval Gnostics are protected and saved through the three advents of "the luminary of acquaintance," that is, the great Seth.

Domination of the earth by non-Gnostics, particularly non-Gnostic Gentiles, is further explained through descent from Noah's sons. Shem's "posterity" remain faithful to Sakla, that is "God Almighty," the God of Israel, and so represent the Jews;[24] the descendants of Ham and Japhtheth form "twelve kingdoms," which are the Gentiles (72:31–73:29). The designation of the latter as "twelve kingdoms" highlights the social and political power of the Gentiles, particularly in contrast with the Jews, the Shemites, who "will serve in humility and fear [because] of their knowledge" (73:10–12). While "humility and fear" code the Jews as socially and politically inferior to the Gentiles, "their knowledge" makes them spiritually superior to the Gentiles but inferior to the Gnostics, who possess not merely "knowledge" (*eime*), but "acquaintance" (*gnosis*). Finally, from among the descendants of Ham and Japhtheth, "400,000 . . . shall go and enter some other land and sojourn with Those People who came into being out of great eternal acquaintance" (73:13–20). These renegades or apostates can only represent contemporary converts to the Gnostic sect: "The shadow of their (Those People's) power will guard those who have sojourned with them from all evil deeds and all foul desires" (73:20–24).[25] Indeed, it may be the 400,000, rather than Those People, who form the immediate model for the Gnostic readers of this work, for the "souls" of the primeval "great people" did not come into existence "by a defiled hand," but from a great commandment of an eternal angel" (75:1–8), and they seem to disappear from history into an angelic life after the attack by fire (76:3–5). By contrast, the 400,000 are made descendants of Seth by adoption, a common metaphor for conversion in antiquity.[26] Their sojourn with "the undominated race" disrupts the work's racial symbolism only from a perspective in which adoption is rare and viewed as lacking in comparison with biological descent. Such was not the case in Roman culture, where adoption was a common means of securing the strength of the family and legitimating heirs, whether financial or political.[27]

Once this map of the late ancient Gnostics' social and religious world has been charted through the primeval story of the flood and Noah's family, the ensuing action invites speculation into how far the myth can be read as a code for contemporary events. The descendants of Shem, the Jews, appear only once more in the narrative when they go to their God, "accusing the great men that dwell in their glory." These accusers tell their God that the "great" people "have overturned all the glory of your power and the dominion of your hand"; the speakers have "done all the will of yourself and of all the powers; while also Those People and the people who sojourn in their glory (the 400,000) have not done what is pleasing to you, [but rather] have upset your entire throng" (74:3–26). This accusation leads to the fiery attack on Those People and their removal from this world, leaving, it would seem, the 400,000. But the Shemites, representatives of the Jews, then disappear from the text, and the 400,000 renegades come only from the descendants of Ham and Japhtheth, representatives of the Gentiles. At the work's concluding poetic celebration of the incarnation, the Shemites do not show up to offer a possible explanation for the existence of That Human Being, as do the "twelve kingdoms" of the Gentiles, the 400,000 ("the thirteenth kingdom"), and "the undominated race" (77:27–83:4). Do we have here one Gnostic's mythological representation of the history of his or her sect as having originated in and broken with Judaism and then having gained converts only among Gentiles? If so, the story is a familiar one, remarkably similar to those of other forms of early Christianity, such as Pauline, Johannine, and Thomasine Christianities.

The sources that speak of two groups of people being saved from the deluge by different supernatural agents use the flood narrative to present a picture of different kinds of people. Characters such as Noah, Norea, and Noah's sons become archetypes for socioreligious groups in the Gnostics' present social world, but these types of people are not necessarily stable or predetermined. We have seen in each case some room for indeterminacy, for freedom among a wide range of people to come to acquaintance and thus to become children of Seth or Norea. But especially in *The Reality of the Rulers* and *The Revelation of Adam,* there is a polemical edge to the sociological picture, as it negatively highlights the power of Noah, human ally of either the evil Sakla or the ambiguous Sabaoth. The ark, symbol of the saved community in much early Christian interpretation, becomes a symbol of a misguided community that excludes the saved, who must be preserved from the deluge by some other means, outside the ark/church.

The two remaining Gnostic witnesses that envision a single group of saved people are, as one might expect, less sociologically focused in their retellings, interested less in delineating types of people with the flood narrative than in describing how all people can waver between ignorance and acquaintance. Thus, the unidentified "others," whose version of the myth Irenaeus reports immediately after that of the "Gnostics," believe that "the remaining multitude of humankind descended" from Seth and Norea. Still, despite the presence of "the secretion of light" in people, they could be led astray by the seven "worldly demons" into "all kinds of evil," while the Mother continued to work for humanity's spiritual improvement (*Haer.* 1.30.9). Humanity as a whole is in view at each point during the flood story. Discouraged by their failure to worship him properly, Ialdabaoth hopes by the flood "to destroy all people at once"; but "for the sake of the secretion of light which derived from her," Wisdom saves Noah and his family in the ark. Because of this light, "the world was again filled with human beings" (*Haer.* 1.30.10). The ark is not the site for encoding a "who's who" of human spiritual types; rather, all humanity oscillates between the corrupting influence of the demons of this world and the uplifting power of the light of Wisdom present within them.

This is not to say that these "others" did not reflect on their social identity with respect to Judaism in particular, but again this reflection is not marked by the kind of racial symbolism found in, for example, *The Revelation of Adam*. The Jews here are characterized as special servants of Ialdabaoth, who chose Abraham out of the mass of Noah's descendants and who brought the people out of Egypt through Moses; each prophet in the Septuagint was the spokesman of either Ialdabaoth or one of his six cronies. But the Jewish prophetic tradition was also the vehicle by which Wisdom continued "foretelling and reminding humanity of the incorruptible light" (*Haer.* 1.30.10–11). This paradoxical character of Judaism is reflected in this group's Christology, in which the human Jesus (like John the Baptist) had Ialdabaoth as his "parent," but served as the corporeal vehicle for the divine Christ (*Haer.* 1.30.12–13). The group is explicit about the analogy between Jesus Christ and the cosmos as a whole: "Jesus was united with the Christ" as "the incorruptible realm was united with the septet." But just as the divine Christ ultimately left behind the "worldly body" of Jesus, so too at "the end . . . the entire secretion of the spirit of light" would be "gathered together and caught up into the realm of incorruptibility" (*Haer.* 1.30.13–14). And so too these Gnostics, once necessarily united with the Jewish tradition, had now left it behind. The rescue of Noah had been completed.

Alone of our Gnostic sources, *The Secret Book According to John* places the flood story within a fully articulated theological context. It follows a lengthy dialogue concerned with the ultimate fates of human souls, which are seen as a function of how each person fares in the rivalry between two "spirits": "the spirit of life" that originates from above, and "the counterfeit spirit," its evil twin, created by the lower rulers. In this complex web of possible scenarios, which includes a series of multiple incarnate lives for the slow learners (akin to Origen's system), the only persons who seem to face an eternal loss of salvation are apostates from the Gnostic sect: "those who have gained acquaintance and then turned away" (II 27:22–23). The flood and, as we have seen, the *ensuing* intercourse between the rulers and human women, are invoked to explain the origin of this "counterfeit spirit" that works against the spirit of life in the human arena (II 27:32). This explanation draws heavily on biblical imagery.

Unlike most other Gnostic witnesses, the *Secret Book* makes use of Genesis 6:6: "And the Lord was sorry that he had made humankind on the earth, and it grieved him to his heart."[28] This "repentance" on God's part troubled most ancient interpreters, whose conception of God did not include the possibility of error, regret, or emotions of any kind, but posed no difficulties for the Gnostics, for whom this God was not authentic divinity anyway. Here, as in the biblical text, the flood is the result of such repentance: "And it (the ruler) repented of all things that had come to exist because of it. Again it made a plan: to bring down a flood upon the human creation" (II 28:32–29:1). This repentance occurs after the ruler had tried another scheme to enslave humanity: the creation of "fate" or "destiny." Although "destiny" had, by constraining human choices, fostered a variety of "sins" and especially "forgetfulness," a failure to recognize the ultimate deity, it was—it would appear—insufficient to "arrest" human "pondering" entirely (II 28:5–32).[29] Thus, a new plan, one of complete destruction, was required. Here the flood is not a limited attack on Gnostic humanity, but, as in the biblical account, a full-scale attempt to start everything anew, a result of the creator's regret.

Likewise, this version finds in the biblical story what other ancient Jews and Christians found: an opportunity for a great number of people to be saved, which was rejected by all except Noah's family. With little support in Genesis, many ancient interpreters (including Josephus, the Rabbis, 2 Peter, and Clement of Rome) concluded that Noah must have preached to other people, offering them a chance to repent of their wicked ways.[30] The *Secret Book* as well suggests that everyone had the chance to avoid destruction: "But the greatness of the light of forethought taught Noah, and he preached to all the posterity, that is, the children of humankind. And those who were alien to him did not pay heed to him" (II 29:1–5).[31] The long version emphasizes the expansive nature of this preaching by adding "all," which is absent in the short versions, and by specifying the group that did not respond ("those who were alien to him"), rather than implying, as the short versions do, that all the hearers "did not believe him" (cf. III 37:21–22; BG [Codex Papyrus Berolinensis 8502] 73:2–3). Similarly, the long version multiplies the number who did listen to Noah and thus were saved: in the short version, they are simply "also other people from the immovable race" (III 38:2–3); in the long, "*many* other people from the immovable race" (II 29:9–10). The emphasis here is on the effectiveness of forethought's response to the ruler's plan to destroy humanity completely: *all* people are offered a way out; a limited number do not listen, but "many" do and are rescued.[32]

The means of their rescue has been seen as a classic instance of Gnostic "reversal" or "rejection" of the Bible, but it may in fact be a bold attempt to salvage the basic historicity of the flood account or to reject the "Great Church" definitively:

They did not—as Moses said—hide in an ark; rather, it was in a certain place that they hid. Not only Noah, but many other people from the immovable race, went into a certain place and hid within a luminous cloud. And he recognized his absolute power.[33] And with him was that being which belonged to the light, who had illuminated them. For it (the ruler) had brought darkness down over all the earth. (II 29:6–15)

We have seen that in the "two group" sources where Noah does not belong to the primeval Gnostics, the ark is not the vehicle by which the higher powers save Gnostic humanity: indeed, in *The Revelation of Adam*, Those People are taken, as in the *Secret Book*, to "the place in which the spirit of life dwells" (69:20–21). But in these other witnesses, there still is an ark, and Noah is in it. In the *Secret Book* there is no ark at all: why could not the light have used that means? If, as has been suggested, the flood episode was a late addition in the *Secret Book*'s evolution,[34] this motif may simply have been borrowed from *The Revelation of Adam* because it appealed to this redactor. He or she may have considered the salvation of Noah and "many" others in an ark literally impossible, and thus meant to save Moses' basic story by correcting him on this point.[35] Or, even more dramatically, it is possible that by denying the salvific role of the ark the author was denying the salvific role of the emerging "Great Church," for which the ark was serving as a symbol in proto-orthodox exegesis. Erasing the ark from the flood narrative, the *Secret Book* erases the Great Church from biblical history.

Moreover, in the resulting version, the story of the flood becomes even more one about the renewal of creation in the face of the destructive force of the ruler. Salvation of the immovable race from the "darkness" covering the earth in a "luminous cloud" with illuminating "light" alludes to Gen 1:1–5, to the Johannine prologue, and to the struggle between "light" and "darkness" that drives the *Secret Book*'s own account of the origin of the material world (see esp. II 11:7–15) and pervades the final poem of deliverance (II 30:15–31:1). It ties the flood story, in a way familiar from other early Christian writings (e.g., 1 Pet 3:20–22), to Gnostic baptism: "the perfect forethought of the entirety" proclaims, "I raised and sealed that person, with the light of the water of the five seals" (II 30:12, 31:22–24). It may not have been "as Moses said," but the result is rich in biblical and ritualistic imagery that enhances the theological meaning of the narrative.

Biblically based too is the explanation of the present reality of mass ignorance despite the rescue of only the immovable race in the flood. As we have seen, it is at this point that the mythographer turns to Gen 6:1–4 and the "sons of God" incident, but the angels' attempt to copulate with human women fails until they "made a counterfeit spirit in the image of the spirit that had descended, by which they would befoul the souls" (II 29:23–25). This counterfeit spirit enables the angels to appear as human men and to introduce humanity to wealth and its attendant "anxieties" (II 29:26–30:1). The result is the present dire situation:

> Humankind grew old without having any leisure, and died without discovering any truth or becoming acquainted with the god of truth (cf. Heb 3:8–11; Ps 95[94]:7–11). And thus was the whole creation perpetually enslaved, from the foundation of the world down to the present time (cf. Dan 12:1; Matt 24:21; Rom 8:19–23). And they (the angels) married women and begot children out of the darkness, after the image of their spirit (cf. Gen 6:5). And their hearts became closed and hardened with the hardness of the counterfeit spirit (cf. Exod 8:15, 32; 9:7; etc.; Ps 95[94]:8; John 12:40; 2 Cor 4:4), down to the present time. (II 30:2–11)

The density of the biblical allusions in this passage firmly places this Gnostic work in the mainstream of Christian thinking about how human beings go astray and thus how divine aid is required for human salvation. It is the counterfeit spirit that blinds people, leads them into wickedness, and hardens their heart: there is no one immune to this process and no one for whom salvation by acquaintance is not possible, albeit perhaps over multiple lifetimes. And, in the apt words of a modern historian, this passage "also neatly links with the opening dialogue: it was not the Saviour who led people astray and hardened their hearts, as the Pharisee, Arimanius, had insinuated to John, but the demonic counterfeit spirit, the creation of the archons" (cf. II 1:13–17).[36] In the *Secret Book* the flood story illustrates the freedom of humanity to escape the bonds of fate and forgetfulness and vindicates the work of the Barbelo in fostering that liberation through the advent of the Christ.

After surveying the Gnostic versions of the flood narrative, one scholar has concluded: "We see that the story of the flood is accepted as far as the gnostics were able to use its contents. In an arbitrary way parts of it were accepted and rejected. The parts which were accepted were totally subjected to the intention of the authors of gnostic writings."[37] According to another, "Gnostic mythographers evaluated the biblical reports within a thought pattern that was radically different from the biblical point of view."[38] These statements imply that the Gnostics were unique in this respect and that most, if not all, other communities of Jews and Christians have accepted biblical stories apart from their need to "use their contents" or have not "subjected" the Bible to their own "intention." It is, however, unlikely, indeed impossible, that there have ever been such communities: after all, a book can function as scripture for a group only if its contents are "useful" to that group and coherent with the group's "intention."[39] Moreover, it can be said that, in comparison to their contemporaries, the Gnostics interpreted the flood narrative in "an arbitrary way" only if it was possible for any interpreters to ascertain "*the* biblical point of view" apart from the (inevitably not biblical) "thought pattern" by which they worked. Although such miraculous objectivity was once the dream of modern biblical scholars, it now appears that the "plain sense" of scripture, far from being stable and fixed in the text, is itself a product of social convention, of complex communal practices.[40] "Therefore, there always will be a literal reading, but (1) it will not always be the same one and (2) it can change."[41] If Rowan Greer has taught us anything about early biblical interpretation, it is the futility of holding ancient exegesis up against the standards of modern historical criticism, either by judging ancient readers by how closely they adhere to the "literal" or "historical" meaning or by characterizing the history of early interpretation as the search for an adequate method.[42] For ancient Christians, biblical exegesis was a thoroughly theological endeavor, guided by the community's faith and oriented to the needs of the seeking Christians. The Gnostics were no different.

In retelling the story of the flood, Gnostic writers reflected profoundly on the types of human beings that exist in the world and how acquaintance and ignorance have persisted throughout human history. Since the issues were complex, so were their diverse readings, and the Gnostics differed on such questions as who caused the flood and why, who was saved, and by whom and how. These variations reflected and shaped more fundamental differences on how Gnostics fit along the spectrum of contemporary biblically based religious groups, how human beings forgot their true spiritual origin, and why some now come to acquaintance and others do not. This diversity on questions of anthropology and soteriology does not mark the Gnostic school of thought as uniquely disorganized or speculative among the literary, social, or theological movements within Christianity, as the diversity within the literatures we call "Pauline" or "Valentinian" or "monastic" attest. Rather, like these other subgroups, the Gnostics' exegetical decisions were guided by certain fundamental theological commitments that bound them together and set them apart from other Christians, most prominently that, despite the feverish efforts of the demonic rulers of this world, the ultimate God has managed to preserve the divine essence present in humanity and, in the final days, has sent a savior to call human beings back to acquaintance with their true home. No biblical story exemplified that gracious divine care as much as that of Noah, the ark, and the rescue of "the immovable race."

Notes

1. James L. Kugel and Rowan A. Greer, *Early Biblical Interpretation* (LEC; Philadelphia: Westminster, 1986), 202. For their criticisms and suggestions I am grateful to Bert Harill and to the graduate students in my course on Gnostic religion and literature at Indiana University, Bloomington, in Fall 1997.

2. The "Gnostics" spoken of in this essay include only the members of the early Christian school of thought who called themselves "Gnostics." For this methodological principle and a listing of the relevant evidence, see Bentley Layton, "Prolegomena to the Study of Ancient Gnosticism," in *The Social World of the First Christians: Essays in Honor of Wayne A. Meeks* (ed. L. Michael White and O. Larry Yarbrough; Minneapolis: Fortress, 1995), 334–50. I am not persuaded by the criticisms of this procedure made by Michael Allen Williams, *Rethinking "Gnosticism": An Argument for Dismantling a Dubious Category* (Princeton: Princeton University Press, 1996), 31–43. English translations of Gnostic writings and testimonia are taken from Bentley Layton, *The Gnostic Scriptures: A New Translation with Annotations and Introductions* (Garden City, N.Y.: Doubleday, 1987), sometimes altered.

3. Williams, *Rethinking "Gnosticism"*, 63–76.

4. The flood is mentioned briefly in a seventh source, *The Holy Book of the Great Invisible Spirit*, or *The Egyptian Gospel* (IV 72:10–12). I will not attempt to trace literary relationships of dependence among these flood retellings. For thorough efforts to chart such relationships among Gnostic sources, see John D. Turner, "Sethian Gnosticism: A Literary History," in *Nag Hammadi, Gnosticism, and Early Christianity* (ed. Charles W. Hedrick and Robert Hodgson; Peabody, Mass.: Hendrickson, 1986), 55–86; and Alastair H.B. Logan, *Gnostic Truth and Christian Heresy: A Study in the History of Gnosticism* (Edinburgh: T & T Clark; Peabody, Mass.: Hendrickson, 1996), esp. 29–69. The table and indeed this essay were inspired by Bentley Layton, review of G. A. G. Stroumsa, *Another Seed: Studies in Gnostic Mythology*, *RB* 94 (1987): 608–13.

5. See Jack P. Lewis, *A Study of the Interpretation of Noah and the Flood in Jewish and Christian Literature* (Leiden: Brill, 1968).

6. Most notably G.A.G. Stroumsa, *Another Seed: Studies in Gnostic Mythology* (NHS 24; Leiden: Brill, 1984).

7. Hippolytus, *Haer.* 9.12.23; Cyprian, *Ep.* 74.11; cf. Tertullian, *Bapt.* 8; *Idol.* 24; Lewis, *Interpretation of Noah and the Flood*, 161–66; H.S. Benjamins, "Noah, the Ark, and the Flood in Early Christian Theology: The Ship of the Church in the Making," in

Interpretations of the Flood (ed. Florentino García Martínez and Gerard P. Luttikhuizen; Themes in Biblical Narrative: Jewish and Christian Traditions 1; Leiden: Brill, 1998), 134–49.

8. Gerard P. Luttikhuizen likewise sees explaining "the supposed existence of different categories of human beings" as an important "story line" in Gnostic retellings of the flood, but his analysis is guided by the dubious agenda of determining "to what extent" this story line "was preprogrammed in the Genesis accounts" ("Biblical Narrative in Gnostic Revision: The Story of Noah and the Flood in Classic Gnostic Mythology," in Martínez and Luttikhuizen, *Interpretations of the Flood*, 109–23, esp. 115).

9. Cf. Logan, *Gnostic Truth*, 293 n. 10; Luttikhuizen, "Biblical Narrative in Gnostic Revision," 120.

10. The Gnostics considered here are identified by all their opponents as a group within Christianity, and all the relevant writings include references or allusions to Christian figures or texts (such as Christ or Paul). Most American scholars pose the question of Gnostic origins as a choice between "heterodox Judaism" and "Christianity," a choice resting on the questionable assumption that at this time there was an "orthodox Judaism" that could be easily distinguished from a "Christianity." See Karen L. King, "Rethinking the (Jewish) Origins of (Christian) Gnosticism" (paper presented at the colloquium "Rethinking the Origins of the Judeo-Christian Tradition," Trinity College, Hartford, Conn., June 1999).

11. Cf. Williams, *Rethinking "Gnosticism"*, 193–94.

12. For convenient lists of scholars on both sides of this issue, see James E. Goehring, "Libertine or Liberated: Women in the So-called Libertine Gnostic Communities," in *Images of the Feminine in Gnosticism* (ed. Karen L. King; SAC; Philadelphia: Fortress, 1988), 329–44, at 339 nn. 42–43. Williams doubts the report (*Rethinking "Gnosticism"*, 179–84).

13. See Jason David Beduhn, *The Manichaean Body* (Baltimore/London: Johns Hopkins University Press, 2000).

14. Layton, *Gnostic Scriptures*, 200.

15. Cf. Stroumsa, *Another Seed*, 84.

16. Anne McGuire, "Virginity and Subversion: Norea against the Powers in the *Hypostasis of the Archons*," in King, *Images of the Feminine*, 239–58, at 248.

17. The text is ambiguous about whether the attempted rape occurs before or after the flood, which is not narrated explicitly. But it seems clear in any case that Norea is not destroyed in the cataclysm.

18. McGuire, "Virginity and Subversion," 250.

19. Ibid., 250–51, 254–58.

20. Ross S. Kraemer, Response to McGuire, "Virginity and Subversion," in King, *Images of the Feminine*, 259–64, at 264.

21. The now classic study of Gnostic baptism is Jean-Marie Sevrin, *Le Dossier baptismal séthien: Études sur la sacramentaire gnostique* (Bibliothèque copte de Nag-Hammadi, Section "études" 2; Quebec: Les Presses de l'Université Laval, 1986).

22. Williams, *Rethinking "Gnosticism"*, 193–202.

23. Cf. *Gosp. Eg.* III 56:4–12; J. A. Loader, *A Tale of Two Cities: Sodom and Gomorrah in the Old Testament, Early Jewish and Early Christian Traditions* (CBET 1; Kampen: J. H. Kos, 1990).

24. Cf. A. F. J. Klijn, "An Analysis of the Use of the Story of the Flood in the Apocalypse of Adam," in *Studies in Gnosticism and Hellenistic Religions: Presented to Gilles Quispel on the Occasion of His 65th Birthday* (ed. R. van den Broek and M. J. Vermaseren; EPRO; Leiden: Brill, 1981), 218–26, at 222.

25. *Pace* Stroumsa, *Another Seed*, 85–86.

26. Luther H. Martin, "Genealogy and Sociology in the Apocalypse of Adam," in *Gnosticism and the Early Christian World: In Honor of James M. Robinson* (ed. James E. Goehring et al.; Forum Fascicles; Sonoma, Calif.: Polebridge, 1990), 25–36.

27. Martin, "Genealogy and Sociology," 29–31. Julius Caesar's adoption of Octavian is a famous example.

28. It is possible that this verse stands behind the "repentance" of Sabaoth in *The Reality of the Rulers* (95:13–15) (Williams, *Rethinking "Gnosticism"*, 74).

29. See Williams, *Rethinking "Gnosticism"*, 205–8, on the limited power of fate in the *Secret Book*.

30. Lewis, *Interpretation of Noah and the Flood*, 102–4.

31. The short version identifies the divine agent as "afterthought": "But the [greatness] of forethought produced the thought, that is, afterthought, and it appeared to [Noah]" (III 37:18–21).

32. Cf. Michael Allen Williams, *The Immovable Race: A Gnostic Designation and the Theme of Stability in Late Antiquity* (NHS 29; Leiden: Brill, 1985), 168–69.

33. Layton follows Codex III and so translates "they recognized" (III 38:5–6; *Gnostic Scriptures*, 50).

34. Logan, *Gnostic Truth*, 266–72.

35. Cf. Williams, *Rethinking "Gnosticism"*, 281 n. 79.

36. Logan, *Gnostic Truth*, 272.

37. Klijn, "Analysis," 224–25.

38. Luttikhuizen, "Biblical Narrative in Gnostic Revision," 113.

39. See David Brakke, "Canon Formation and Social Conflict in Fourth-Century Egypt: Athanasius of Alexandria's Thirty-Ninth *Festal Letter*," *HTR* 87 (1994): 395–419.

40. Kathryn E. Tanner, "Theology and the Plain Sense," in *Scriptural Authority and Narrative Interpretation* (ed. Garrett Green; Philadelphia: Fortress, 1987), 59–78.

41. Stanley Fish, "Normal Circumstances, Literal Language, Direct Speech Acts, the Ordinary, the Everyday, the Obvious, What Goes without Saying, and Other Special Cases," in *Is There a Text in This Class? The Authority of Interpretive Communities* (Cambridge, Mass./London: Harvard University Press, 1980), 268–92, at 277.

42. See esp. Kugel and Greer, *Early Biblical Interpretation*, 177–79.

The Insufficiency of Scripture

Adversus haereses 2 and the Role of Scripture in Irenaeus's Anti-Gnostic Polemic

RICHARD A. NORRIS, JR.

Book 2 of Irenaeus's *Adversus haereses* stands out in that work as something of an oddity if not an anomaly. Both in the logical and rhetorical form of its argumentation and, as I shall argue, in the subjects or issues with which it deals, it is set apart from the rest of the treatise. Furthermore, there is much of it that the reader—and I suspect not just the modern reader—simply does not know how to take. In the process of criticizing Valentinian myth, Irenaeus often seems to present alternatives to the views that he repudiates; but it is not always clear whether he intends these to be taken quite seriously, or whether, like some rhetorical juggler, he is simply tossing them up in the air in order to show how easy it is to find plausible contraries to his adversaries' beliefs. It is certain in any case that much of what he says in Book 2 is seldom echoed, much less explicitly resumed, in the later books of *Adversus haereses*. Book 2 appears, then, to be largely if not entirely self-contained— an enterprise separable and indeed separate from that of Books 3–5.

The question is *why* this is the case. If, considered as a refutation of Valentinianism (together with its parents, siblings, offspring, and first cousins), Book 2 is intended to be complete, an obvious issue arises. Why did Irenaeus go on to write three more books on the same subject? It might of course be the case that Irenaeus originally thought Book 2 was, or would be, sufficient for his purposes, but later changed his mind—perhaps because he had not realized how long it would take him to complete his project, or, alternatively, because his conception of the project changed, at least partially, as he wrote

Book 2. On the other hand, one might propose that Book 2 is indeed complete in itself but suggest, at the same time, that Irenaeus more or less consciously chose to refute his opponents in two different ways: that is, to employ two different modes of argumentation to the same point, thus demonstrating that the gnostic position could be demolished on the basis of almost any relevant set of premises. Finally, one might decide that it is a wrong critical perception to think that Irenaeus regards Book 2 as being "on the same subject" as the later books—that it is not merely in method but in matter that it differs from them; and on this hypothesis, which is the one to be argued here, one would of course have to specify what the subject-matter of Book 2 actually is, and how it differs from that of the other books of *Adversus haereses.*

First, however, it is important to note that the problem addressed here— that of the character and function of Book 2—has by no means gone unnoticed or unconsidered in the past. André Benoît has dealt with these matters explicitly and carefully. He sees in Book 2 the intended "rebuttal" (*anatropē*) promised by the original title of the work: *Exposure and Rebuttal of the "Knowledge" Falsely So Named.*[1] Book 2 constitutes in fact the "refutation properly so called," that is, one which is undertaken simply "by means of reason" or "good sense," and without reference to particular *theological* premises. In this book, Irenaeus tried "to show the internal contradictions of the gnostic systems at the level of formal logic."[2] However, Benoît notes, this form of refutation cost Irenaeus more space than he had expected. By the time he had reached the end of Book 2, moreover, he realized that his refutation was incomplete. He had omitted "the proof from the dominical scriptures."[3] "As if making an excuse for himself," then, "he announces a new book,"[4] which would adopt this very method of refutation. In the end, though, even this third book, which, writes Benoît, would constitute "a sort of appendix,"[5] proved insufficient, and Irenaeus went on to announce yet a fourth and a fifth, each of them an afterthought. The three closing books, then, "were not foreseen at the start and were nothing other than successive appendices."[6]

Benoît's analysis appears to combine the first two of the alternatives I have noted above. On the one hand, as I have indicated, it takes Book 2 to be the intended second part of Irenaeus's project, and therefore its (intended) completion. Book 1 was the *elenchos*, the exposure and indictment, and Book 2, the *anatropē*, the rebuttal. At the same time, however, this analysis recognizes that Book 2 is set apart not only by its aim (i.e., to rebut) but by its method (i.e., by its attempt to dispose of heresy, as brought to definitive focus in Valentinianism, solely by rational analysis of its inherent inconsistencies).

On these two assumptions alone, however, it would be impossible to explain why Irenaeus did not simply stop writing at the end of Book 2, since presumably he would have accomplished, at least in his own mind, what he had set out to do: he would have exposed what he took to be the plain rational absurdity of his opponents' position. In order to explain the presence of Books 3–5, then, it is necessary for Benoît to introduce a third assumption: namely, that "this proof *ex ratione* did not exclude other arguments: appeal to Scripture, to faith, to tradition."[7] Presumably the point of this proposition is not simply to record the truism that arguments from tradition and arguments from "common sense" can be logically compatible, or to notice that premises drawn from scriptural or traditional sources can function within arguments *ex ratione*. Rather, it is to state something about Irenaeus—that he waked up to, or came to believe, something that had not occurred to him before. What Benoît is suggesting, then, is one of two things. Either (1) Irenaeus had always intended some appeal to Scripture and to "the hypothesis of the truth" as a necessary part of his argument, so that the second and presumably final book of his work turned out to be methodically specialized only because he did not have sufficent space to introduce arguments from Scripture and "the faith"; or (2) by the time he was finishing Book 2, Irenaeus realized that his refutation was not actually complete and needed supplementation by a different order of argument, i.e., argument from Scripture and "the faith."

The choice between these alternatives is not easy to make, for what they differ about is the question of the degree to which, from the beginning, Irenaeus was guided by an *explicit* intent to go beyond the sort of argument to which he largely confines himself in Book 2. On the other hand, the choice between these alternatives is hardly a lively issue, since the conclusion to which they lead is the same: namely, that to one degree or another Irenaeus was never very clear in his conception of how he would go about his task. The proposition that Books 3–5 are afterthoughts implies that he had not, in his mind, analyzed with any care what was involved in a debate about the sorts of issues that were at stake between him and his opponents.

There is of course a certain plausibility about this position. No one who reads the *Adversus haereses* can doubt that Irenaeus is, as a writer, unusually susceptible to the lures of attractive side-issues. Furthermore, his way of organizing his polemic is an odd one. In part it is a topical organization, focused around central *issues* (e.g., the unity of the Christ), and in part it is methodological, focused around particular *bases of argument* (e.g., common sense or Christian tradition) or *ranges of evidence* (e.g., the teachings of the apostles); and this procedure, needless to say, is more likely than most to nurture repetitiousness. For all that, Irenaeus never works without a clear outline in mind. Benoît himself demonstrates this when he shows how the structure of Book 2 reproduces in a certain way that of Book 1; and the work of Bacq on Book 4 offers a perceptive demonstration of the care and subtlety Irenaeus can employ in carrying out a particular, and complex, line of argument.[8]

One is bound, then, to be somewhat sceptical about Benoît's hypothesis regarding the manner in which *Adversus haereses* was written, and in particular about his view that Books 3–5 represent a series of afterthoughts. It has been pointed out by several students of Irenaeus that the project of countering Valentinian exegesis is one that is called for not merely by Irenaeus's announcements at the end of Book 2, but by the very accusations he brings against his opponents in the preface of Book 1,[9] and by the care he takes in the body of Book 1 to reproduce samples of Valentinian exegesis, and not least the Ptolemæan reading of the Johannine prologue (cf. *Haer.* 1.1.3; 3.1–6; 8.1–5). Furthermore, a reading of Books 3–5 makes it clear that their basic purpose is not so much direct rebuttal of "gnostic" theses as it is presentation and defence of Irenaeus's own position. They are meant to set forth a "reading"— the correct one, to be sure—of the Scriptures. It is scarcely possible, then, to picture the content of Books 3–5 as "appendices" or afterthoughts. Their business is of the essence of Irenaeus's project from the start.

If that is the case, however, it becomes necessary to reconsider the place and character of Book 2. If Books 3–5 are, in their overall structure, part of Irenaeus's original plan, then the same must be said of Book 2 more or less as it stands; and this means that one must give an account of Book 2 that explains not just why it seems, at least for the most part, to confine itself to arguments based solely on "reason"—or better, perhaps, on logical, philosophical, and critical commonplaces of Irenaeus's time—but also what the topic or issue is for this book. I have already noted that the business of each of the other books of *Adversus haereses* is conceived both in terms of an issue or issues and in terms of a basis or method of argument. The question, then, is whether Book 2 is to be envisaged as dealing with a particular issue as well as proceeding by an appropriate method.

In the past, this question has tended, at least tacitly, to be answered in the negative. It has normally been suggested, along the lines of Benoît's analysis, that Book 2 undertakes a global refutation of Gnosticism and, accordingly, that it is distinctive not in what it talks about but only in the way it talks. There are, however, reasons to think that this may not be the case.

These reasons are closely involved with Irenaeus's conception of the nature of his opponents' "heresy," and to this matter we now turn.

It is notorious that Irenaeus tries to trace all heresy back to a single root: the teaching and person of Simon Magus. The section of Book 1 in which this hypothesis is developed,[10] however, appears to be one that Irenaeus has taken over from Justin Martyr's *Syntagma*. Justin had evidently pictured his heretical tradition as constituted by a "succession" of teachers and disciples; and Irenaeus, in this section of Book 1 but not elsewhere, follows his example. The notion of a heretical succession of teachers and schools (in which even Marcion is included) is one that grew naturally out of Justin's analogy between the disintegration of philosophy after the days of Plato and Pythagoras and the rise of heresy among the Christian churches—the analogy that gave "heresy" its very name. Furthermore, Irenaeus seems quite happy with this theory as he reproduces it in *Adversus haereses* 1.23–28. It reinforces his idea that there is a unity of sorts about the phenomenon of heresy, even though, as he keeps telling his readers, heretics are forever engaged in an obsessive search for novelty and hence can never quite settle on a clear and uniform teaching.

As a matter of fact, though, *Adversus haereses* 1.23–28, with its echoes of Justin and his theories, is subordinated in the design of the book to Irenaeus's treatment of another set of opponents, who were the primary focus of his attention: that is, the teachers whom he calls "disciples of Valentinus." In the foreground of this group he places "the people who are active in teaching even now," whom he identifies as "the circle around Ptolemy," and whose doctrine he describes as a "blossom of the school of Valentinus" (*Haer.* 1.pref.2). To this particular group he dedicates slightly less than a third of Book 1. He then turns to the "school" as a whole, beginning with Valentinus himself (1.11.1), and ending with an extended treatment of Marcus the Magician—all with the professed aim of showing that his opponents "do not say the same things with regard to the same subjects but contradict themselves both with regard to matters of substance and with regard to names" (1.11.1). Only at this point does he introduce the materials he has inherited from Justin's *Syntagma*, no doubt with the aim of suggesting that these Valentinians of his day also fit into Justin's scheme. In fact, however, he makes a bad job of showing this; for he traces the roots of Valentinianism back to "the so-called gnostic *hairesis*" (1.11.1) to which, as it turns out, he can assign the names of no identifiable teachers. Rather, he simply asserts that the "Simonians—i.e., the teachers on Justin's succession-list of heretics—gave rise to "a multitude of gnostics, sprung up from the earth like fungi" (1.29.1). Irenaeus had evidently become acquainted with some "gnostic" writings or traditions, among them a version of the work we know as *The Apocryphon of John*, and he took these to manifest the immediate sources of Valentinianism. To be sure, they did not fit very well between Justin's "Simonians" and Valentinus; nor did Irenaeus know of any *hairesis*, in Justin's sense, from which these stemmed; nor could they be labeled with the name of a "father of the discourse" (to use another phrase of Justin's).

These difficulties, however, did not trouble Irenaeus at all; for while he agrees with Justin that there is a genuine unity to be discerned in the whole phenomenon of heresy, and while he is obviously delighted to think that a figure as despicable as the Simon Magus of Acts 8 should be the sole historical source of it, he himself has a more useful way of figuring this unity. The essential clue to Irenaeus's own method lies in the very structure of Book 1, in which Justin's genealogy of sects is sandwiched between the two parts of Irenaeus's own genealogy of Valentinianism (which, unlike Justin's, is set out from present to past). Irenaeus in fact considers that the Valentinian tradition, especially as represented by the Ptolemaeans and Marcosians, is the paradigm case of heresy. Indeed he asserts at the opening of Book 4 that "their doctrine is the epitome of all the heresies."[11]

What this implies, of course, is that even though the various heretical teachers regularly differ from one another in their insatiable search for novelty, there are nonetheless certain fundamental theses or attitudes on which all are agreed; and this judgment does not exclude Marcion, even though Irenaeus is well aware that in many respects Marcion does not fit the Valentinian pattern. Irenaeus, then, is committed to the view that all heresy has a single basic form, one that reproduces itself in a number of otherwise discordant embodiments. And in Book 2 he informs us what this common element is, when he observes that

> almost all the heresies, numerous as they are, affirm that there is one God, but they alter him by their unsound teaching [*per sententiam malam*], being ungrateful to the One who made them, just as the Gentiles are by reason of their idolatry. Then too they despise God's handiwork [*plasma*], taking a stand against their own salvation. . . . These folk shall rise up in the flesh, though they like it not, that they may acknowledge the power of the One who raises them from the dead. (2.22.2)

The two essential points, then, on which the heretics agree is (a) their refusal to acknowledge that the Creator—in the Valentinians' Platonic language, the Artisan or "Demiurge"—of the visible cosmos is the one real and ultimate God;[12] and (b) their refusal to acknowledge that "flesh"—which is what Irenaeus means by "God's handiwork"—is susceptible of salvation.

With this account one can usefully compare Justin's observation that the heretics "teach people to blaspheme the Maker of the universe, and the Christ he prophesies as coming, and the God of Abraham and Isaac and Jacob" (*Dial.* 35.5). Irenaeus's statement, as just quoted, sums up this three-fold characterization of heretical teaching under a single head concerning the Demiurge, and then adds to it a second gravamen having to do with the salvation of the flesh. This procedure, however, does not imply any serious disagreement with Justin. Irenaeus seems in practice to acknowledge that Justin's three-point elaboration of the accusation regarding the Demiurge is correct. In effect if not consciously, he employs the latter to define the very program of *Adversus haereses* 3–4. It is impossible not to notice that the three final books of the grand treatise follow roughly the program suggested by Justin's summation of heresy, but with Irenaeus's important addition. Book 3 addresses the question of the ultimacy and uniqueness of the Creator God, and then turns, at chapter 16, to the unity and divine dignity of the Demiurge's Messiah, "the Christ he prophesies as coming." Book 4 takes up the issue of the identity of "the God of Abraham and Isaac and Jacob" with the Father of Jesus Christ, and of course Book 5 concerns itself with the resurrection of the flesh (which cannot be divorced from eschatology in general). This analysis, though, still leaves Book 2 unaccounted for.

The fact is, however, that Irenaeus has yet another problem with his opponents, and one which is just as important in his own analysis of heresy as are the items he specifies in *Adversus haereses* 2.22.2. He voices constant complaints about the manner in which they "falsify the words of the Lord" in the Gospels (1.pref.1), about their habit of focusing on "parables" (i.e., difficult and obscure passages in the Scriptures), whose sense they can twist to their purposes, and about their addiction, as he sees it, to numerology. It is apparent from these complaints about Valentinian exegesis that he and his opponents read and interpret roughly the same set of Scriptures. The substantive issue between them is not *what* writings are to be consulted but *how* they are to be interpreted.[13] He notes with particular irritation that they practise a type of source-criticism, arguing that different passages in the Old Testament come from different authorities,[14] that the apostles taught different doctrines to different categories of individuals (3.5.1), and that "even the Lord himself sometimes spoke words deriving from the Demiurge, sometimes from the Midst, and at other times from the Highest [*a summitate*]" (3.2.2).

The Valentinians for their part asserted that the key to their exegesis—to its contents and presumably to its method—was to be found in an oral tradition they had received, one that Paul himself alludes to when he speaks of a "wisdom not of this aeon" that is conveyed "among the perfect"[15]—and clearly only among the perfect, an epithet the Valentinans applied to themselves. Thus Irenaeus, when he attempted to criticize Valentinian teaching, found himself, at least initially, in a difficult situation. He was clear enough in his own mind about what he took to be the basic errors of his heretics, and he was no doubt aware that these errors laid claim to some sort of scriptural, and hence exegetical, basis; but he had little clue to the principles according to which this exegesis proceeded—i.e., of the exact content of the "secret" oral tradition.

It is therefore understandable that Irenaeus took great pride in his acquisition of a relatively exact knowledge of the content of this secret tradition, and that he saw the great merit of his treatise *Adversus haereses* to lie in its use of this knowledge for the rebuttal of his adversaries. His predecessors in the struggle against heresy—a category in which he no doubt includes Justin—"were unable satisfactorily to gainsay the disciples of Valentinus because they were ignorant of the latter's *hypothesis*" (4.pref.2), he observes; but he for his part had read "the commentaries [*hypomnēmata*] . . . of the disciples of Valentinus and met with certain of them," and hence he was in a position to "reveal the things that have hitherto been kept secret" (1.pref.2). This moreover is exactly what he does in Book 1. He sets out what his reading in Valentinian sources had taught him about their *hypothesis* (i.e., their great narrative of creation and restoration in its several "inconsistent" versions) and the exegeses by which it was supported.

What is of interest here, however, is not the content of this tradition, nor the question whether Irenaeus had correctly understood his opponents, but quite simply what immediate conclusions his knowledge of this secret tradition induced him to draw about his heretics and their teaching. His first perception was simply that this *hypothesis* was, on the face of it, *different from*, and to that extent inconsistent with, the story told by the Scriptures. Indeed he thought that most of it was simply idle speculation about matters with which the Scriptures did not, at least explicitly, concern themselves.[16] Hence he adjudged Valentinian efforts to discover allusions to their overworld in the Scriptures to be nothing more than attempts to "adapt" the scriptural story to a "fiction" that in fact had nothing to do with it. The most notable example of this procedure seems to have been, for him, Ptolemaean exegesis of the Johannine prologue, where, he suggests, his adversaries retain the "names" but not the story-line (*hypothesis*) of the original, and thus distort the meaning of the text.[17] When, in Book 1.1–7, he relates the content of the Ptolemaean myth, he conveys this judgment by the simple rhetorical device of segregating the exegeses on which the myth is (allegedly) based from the narrative itself.

Consonant with this procedure were the Valentinian attempt to discover a "God beyond God"[18] and their contention that as "spirituals" (*pneumatikoi*) they were members and products of the spiritual overworld—both of which Irenaeus took to be manifestations of sheer arrogance and elitism, not least because they claimed, on this basis, to be superior in nature to the only God the Scriptures or the baptismal catechesis and confession recognized, i.e., the God named as Creator in Genesis 1. Hence Irenaeus diagnosed them as suffering from a prideful lust for *hyperbainein*—for "transgressing" the limits of the human condition, and for "going beyond" the only God and the only cosmos there actually is. Finally, but not least, Irenaeus saw his adversaries as practising a kind of systematic hypocrisy. They used the same language as ordinary Christians, but they *meant* something different by it.[19]

All of these criticisms play, in fact, on a single theme that represents a third basic characteristic of heresy as Irenaeus came to understand it (in spite of the fact that he plainly does not see Marcion as playing the same game). If the Valentinians denigrated the Creator God, demoting him to the rank of a mere artisan and denying him any real power of origination, and then repudiated the salvation of this Creator's "handiwork" (*plasmatio, plasma*), including, as Irenaeus saw it, themselves, that was, in the end, because they envisaged a hierarchy of orders of reality—or, to put it another way, because they reduplicated the visible cosmos in their spiritual *plērōma*. This circumstance explains not merely their belief in a "God beyond God," but also their *hyperbainein*, and their annoying habit of using ordinary Christian language and then explaining what it meant in a totally different idiom with a different set of references. It is precisely this duplication—a better word here, I think, than "dualism"—of worlds, of Gods, and of languages that Irenaeus repudiates.

One must read Irenaeus's little methodological discourse in *Adversus haereses* 2.25–28 in this context, I think. Here he develops a polemic based in part, as Schoedel has shown, on the methodological canons of the empirical school in medicine and of the philosophical *hairesis* of the Sceptics,[20] and in part on Paul's remarks to the effect that "We know only in part" and that

"Knowledge puffs up, but love builds up" (1 Cor 13:9). In this discourse, he takes his opponents to task for basing their doctrine on inquiries into ultimate causes—questions that go beyond the capacity of any creature. Indeed he gives examples of such questions, every one of which, as he sees it, the Valentinians pretended to answer. "Before God made the world, what was he doing?" (2.28.3) is one such question—an old Epicurean chestnut. Another asks "whence . . . or how God 'put forth' matter" (2.28.7). Others—closely related to each other—concern the "births and prolations of God himself, and his Thought, and his Word, and his Life," and the question on which Irenaeus expends most of his outrage: "How . . . was the Son 'put forth' by the Father?" (2.28.6). The answer to such questions, he thinks, is plain enough: "God knows." And this of course implies, "Human beings do not."

The apparent simplicity of this answer, however, is deceptive. When Irenaeus says, "God knows," the God he refers to is, among other things, the Creator and Lawgiver whose self-revelation to Moses is set out (as Irenaeus's opponents would have agreed) in the Pentateuch; and hence "God knows but we do not" means roughly the same as "the Scriptures (not to mention the Rule of Truth) have nothing to say on this matter." Thus in response to the question about what God was up to before he made the cosmos, Irenaeus observes: "That this world was made by God in an act of production and has a temporal beginning—this the Scriptures teach us. But what God brought about before this is not conveyed in any Scripture. Therefore the answer [to this question] is God's business [*subjacet . . . Deo*]" (2.28.3).

There is a whole class, then, of speculative questions, questions about ultimate causes, to which the human intellect cannot discover answers. Nor is there any evidence that Irenaeus thought this "cannot" a merely temporary or adventitious one, ultimately to be overcome. His view seems to be that there is always an unfathomable "more" to God, no matter how advanced an individual (or society or "kind") may be. It is this conviction that makes him sceptical of claims to a knowledge about God and God's doings that goes beyond what is conveyed in the Scriptures—and more than that, critical of persons who claim to have achieved such a knowledge. He regards such claims not merely as unjustified, therefore, but as arrogant; and he charges that his opponents "keep back nothing for God"[21]—it being of course understood that "God" always refers to the Demiurge, the God of Moses.

Adversus haereses 2.25–28 is, therefore, what one might call an epistemological attack on the Valentinian overworld. Irenaeus of course attacks this same enemy morally, as one might expect, by alleging that the whole idea of such an overworld is nothing more than a fictional product of unabashed pride, of an addicted taste in *hyperbainein*, the transgression of human limits. What must be clear, however, is that Irenaeus regards "the mystery of [the] *plērōma*" as what, in a computer age, might be called virtual reality; and this is not a mere rhetorical strategy but something of which he is thoroughly convinced. The Scriptures and the Rule of Truth set forth the divine *oikonomia* (or *oikonomiai*): that is, the history of God with humanity, from creation to the final perfection and setting-right of things. They do not, however, answer questions that go beyond these limits. One can therefore, on the basis of the Scriptures, ask and argue about, i.e., inquire into, the divine *oikonomiai*. One can even ask what God it is of which the Scriptures speak, and whether the Lord and his apostles speak of the same God as did Moses. One cannot, however, on that basis speculate about some "God above God," or answer questions that in effect require knowledge of what went on "before" the starting-point of the biblical narrative, for the simple reason that these are matters concerning which the Scriptures say nothing. There are some issues regarding which the *data* of Scripture are indecisive.

Here, I think, lies the solution to the problem of Book 2. Valentinian exegesis, as its proponents themselves insisted, presupposed an esoteric tradition whose content was not conveyed, save partially and by way of hints, in their ordinary exchanges with other Christians. But when the content of this tradition did become known, it seemed apparent to Irenaeus both that it was not as a matter of fact, and that in principle it could not be, derived from reading and interpretation of the Scriptures. It came from somewhere else— perhaps, Irenaeus thought, from the lucubrations of philosophers, themselves no doubt deceived by demons. At any rate it represented in his eyes a product of speculation that transgressed the limits of creaturely knowledge and ventured into matters properly reserved to God.

This very conclusion, however, created a twofold problem for Irenaeus. To begin with, if he was correct in his judgment, then the content of this esoteric tradition, or at any rate the greater part of it, could not be refuted, in the strict sense, by resort to scriptural exegesis, for the perfectly good reason that it addressed and answered questions that neither Moses nor the other prophets—nor for that matter the Lord and the apostles—ever dealt with. To be sure, it was possible and indeed necessary to offer a more correct reading of the Scriptures, one that accorded with the Scriptures' own *hypothesis*. Such indeed was the business of the greater part of his argument, carefully set out in Books 3–5 and organized, in a rough way, around the items of contention noted earlier. Irenaeus firmly believed, for example, that the Scriptures were explicit and unambiguous in their affirmation that the Creator

God of Genesis 1 is the only God there is;[22] and even in Book 2, he entered
zestfully into the business of showing that Valentinian, and especially Marco-
sian, numerological speculations about the significance of the number twelve
or of the name "Jesus" were flawed in—among other things—their handling
of scriptural data.[23]

Such arguments, however, which draw in one way or another on scriptural texts, and attempt to show that Valentinian teachings are inconsistent
with them, are not typical of Book 2; and there was, as I have already suggested, a good reason for this apparently odd circumstance—one that brings
to light a second dimension of Irenaeus's problem. It had to be shown not
only that the content of the Valentinian *hypothesis* did not square with the
subject-matter of the Scriptures, but also—and without reference to the
Scriptures—that the gnostic *hypothesis* was false. It was all very well to observe and protest, as Irenaeus did, that the greater part of the gnostic myth,
in any of its several forms, could only be derived from the Scriptures by exploitation of obscure and ambiguous passages; but such protestation would
in the end accomplish little or nothing, since Valentinian teachers had a perfectly plausible justification for this procedure. His opponents insisted, says
Irenaeus, that "the Lord taught these things in secret, not to everyone, but to
certain disciples who were able to take them in." If, though, the Lord taught
them in secret, and then only to selected followers, one would not expect this
esoteric message to be conveyed openly in the Scriptures. Thus, Irenaeus
notes, "They get to the point of asserting that it is one [figure] who is proclaimed as God, and another 'Father' who is referred to by the parables and
riddles [*aenigmata*]" (2.27.2). Irenaeus no doubt saw in this statement a nice,
even epigrammatic formulation of a manifest absurdity. Why after all would
the Scriptures convey not one message but two different and inconsistent
messages? To him this question was merely rhetorical; but the great gnostic
myth, the *hypothesis* of his adversaries, spun out a view of the state of cosmic
affairs that made the idea of a double message imbedded in the Scriptures
seem perfectly plausible. In other words, Irenaeus was put in the position of
having to defend his way of reading the biblical books—and, of course, to do
so without assuming what he had set out to prove. Thus he had to provide a
rebuttal of the gnostic myth that did not rely upon the Scriptures read as he
customarily read them.

Hence—or so it seems to me—Irenaeus in Book 2 had a special *aim* and
treated of a special *subject;* and that is the essential point to see. His ultimate
aim, direct or indirect, was to legitimate his own way of reading the Scriptures, as the one message of the one Creator God; and his *subject* can be

identified by noticing what issues he deals with and what issues he ignores—and the delicacy with which he distinguishes them.

Thus on the one hand he does not deal with issues that are tied to the exegesis of texts that both parties to the argument understand in the light of their plain sense—texts, that is, where the issue or question is (a) one that Irenaeus acknowledges as real and licit, and (b) one for which the plain sense is the starting-point or occasion of the debate. Thus, for example, Irenaeus reserved discussion of Matt 11:27, which for his opponents intimated that "the Father" was unknown to anyone before Christ, until Book 4.[24] Similarly, he postponed consideration of 1 Cor 15:50, a crucial verse in view of his own insistence on salvation of "the flesh," until Book 5.[25] In these cases, presumably, he saw himself dealing with texts and topics that spoke directly of the divine *oikonomia* of creation and salvation and where, therefore, the exegesis of his adversaries could not easily be dismissed as extra-scriptural speculation, even if such speculation influenced it. In Book 2, by contrast, his only strictly exegetical discussions focus, as I have indicated, on the Valentinian use of numbers in Scripture to intimate events in, or structures of, their overworld. Such exegeses have nothing to do with the divine *oikonomia;* and Irenaeus, accordingly, deals with them not by offering an alternative, correct interpretation, but simply by questioning their consistency, whether with themselves, with gnostic myth, or with biblical data.

The bulk of Book 2, however, is not devoted to exegetical questions at all. Its central argument scrutinizes the Ptolemæan account of the *plērōma*, of its generation, and of the structure of the visible cosmos, as well as the Ptolemæan eschatology.[26] At no point in this argument are the Scriptures adduced for the resolution of any question: Irenaeus proceeds entirely by a method that seeks to exploit internal tensions and inconsistencies in the gnostic myth itself. Even though he believes that the Scriptures explicitly assert that the Creator is the sole God, he refuses to appeal to them to make this point: his subject-matter is not scriptural doctrine but the esoteric teaching of the Valentinians (as he understood it), and he wants his criticisms to arise out of that teaching itself. At certain points, needless to say, the topics dealt with touch directly on matters that are relevant for an understanding of God's cosmic housekeeping. Valentinian eschatology, for example, with its doctrine of the three "substances" and their different fates, is directly relevant to gnostic understanding of a passage like 1 Cor 15:44–49; but Irenaeus treats it, in Book 2, without reference to that or to any of the other Pauline texts on which it is based.[27] The argument is conducted solely on the ground of alleged inconsistencies in the Valentinian position. Only at one point does

Irenaeus's argument appear to violate the principle on which Book 2 is composed. In countering the gnostic contention that "spiritual" persons are superior to the Artisan God himself, who is merely "psychic" in nature, Irenaeus draws upon scriptural passages that seem to him to show that this allegedly "psychic" deity is in fact the creator of spiritual beings, and thus above them in the scale of being (see *Haer.* 2.30.6–8).

There is, then, a distinctive subject-matter for Book 2, and one to which Irenaeus never returns after his argument there is completed. That subject-matter is the Valentinian or gnostic myth of cosmic origins and restoration inasfar as it is (a) independent of any basis in plain statements of Scripture, and at the same time (b) presupposed by Valentinian scriptural exegesis. The point of Book 2, therefore, is not, as has often been asserted, to refute Valentinianism as such *sola ratione.* Its aim is rather to isolate the mythic *hypothesis* of Irenaeus's opponents and to render it thoroughly implausible, so that Valentinian exegesis of "plain" passages in the Scriptures would be bereft of the theoretical framework that might have rendered it convincing. In other words, Book 2 is a preliminary, ground-clearing operation. The method that it follows, moreover, is dictated by this subject-matter and this aim. In Irenaeus's view it was neither possible nor useful simply to adduce scriptural testimony with view to the rebuttal of this Valentinian *hypothesis;* for on the one hand he is certain that the Scriptures have nothing whatever to say about most of the questions the myth addresses, and on the other he acknowledges that the plausibility of Valentinian exegesis—not all of which, as he well knows, had addressed obscure or ambiguous passages—depends on the truth of the myth. Hence he adopts a method whose aim or effect, if it were employed successfully, would be simply to show the incoherence of his opponents' *hypothesis.*

As Aristotle had recommended for such purposes, Irenaeus deals preponderantly in enthymemes: arguments whose premises are accepted not because they are proven but because the parties to the debate agree upon them (if only for the sake of the argument). One of his favorite rhetorical devices is the dilemma, as Reynders pointed out,[28] for this form of argument admirably serves his purpose of demonstrating that the gnostic *hypothesis* is not a true *mythos* (i.e., as Theon says, "a false account portraying truth") but a simple fiction, and an unpersuasive fiction at that. He is of course not always fair to his opponents, and where a position of theirs is of uncertain bearing, Irenaeus can be counted on to put the worst possible interpretation on it; but this, as Cherniss has pointed out in connection with Plutarch's anti-Stoic polemics,[29] was standard procedure in philosophical debate.

Thus a rhetorical purpose is implicit in the very structure of *Adversus haereses*. The method and matter of Book 2 are calculated precisely to isolate or segregate the Valentinian *hypothesis* as an account that has two characteristics: first, that its basis is non-scriptural; and second, that what it talks about is unreal. In later books, as I have indicated, he will deal with particular scriptural texts that might be taken openly to countenance Valentinian teaching, or at any rate certain aspects of it. Thus he goes to great pains in Book 5 to explain the sense in which, in the Pauline writings, body, soul, and spirit are taken as elements in the makeup of a human being; and as he does so, his reader is aware both that he is responding to Valentinian exegeses of the Pauline texts he treats (see above), and that the Valentinian theory of the three "natures" is lurking somewhere in his mind. Nevertheless he never mentions that theory in his exegetical discussion in Book 5, nor does he allude to such exegetical issues when he takes the theory up in Book 2. Thus it is part of his "way" with his gnostics to segregate the esoteric *hypothesis* handled in Book 2 from gnostic readings of exoteric scriptural texts; and he accomplishes this by dismissing the former on non-scriptural grounds.

This implies, however, that the "rebuttal" contained in Book 2 of *Adversus haereses* not only is not, but was never intended to be, a complete refutation of the teaching of Irenaeus's opponents. Book 2 is there because Irenaeus discerned—or thought he discerned—that the gnostic *hypothesis* laid out in Book 1 was *other* than that of the Scriptures: "other" in the sense of having another set of agenda than that of the Scriptures, and one that the Scriptures simply did not address. For just that reason it had to be refuted—or at any rate dismembered—without reference to the Scriptures: and this in order that the scriptural *hypothesis* itself could be exegetically articulated in opposition to Valentinian interpretations of individual passages. The presence of Book 2 attests the necessity Irenaeus discovered and faced to step outside the scriptural language-game in order to affirm it; and in that sense it is a confession of the insufficiency of the Scriptures.

NOTES

1. André Benoît, *St Irénée: Introduction à l'étude de sa théologie* (Paris: Presses Universitaires de France, 1960), 152–53.

2. Benoît, *St Irénée*, 155–56, 161.

3. *Haer.* 2.35.4.

4. Benoît, *St Irénée*, 156.

5. Benoît, *St Irénée*, 156.

6. Benoît, *St Irénée*, 158.

7. Benoît, *St Irénée*, 156.

8. P. Bacq, *De l'ancienne à la nouvelle alliance selon saint Irénée* (Paris: Éditions Lethielleux, 1978).

9. *Haer.* 1.pref.1: "falsantes verba Domini, interpretatores mali eorum quae bene dicta sunt effecti."

10. But see also the preface of Book 2, where the point is reiterated emphatically.

11. *Haer.* 4.pref.2: "in primo libro . . . in quo et ostendimus doctrinam eorum recapitulationem esse omnium haereticorum." Cf. *Haer.* 2.31.1, where Irenaeus asserts that once the Valentinians are refuted, "the whole multitude of heretics are overthrown."

12. What Irenaeus means by "altering God" can be ascertained by reference to *Haer.* 2.26.3 *ad fin.*, where he speaks of one who "by the knowledge he thinks himself to have discovered alters God himself and elevates his own thought [*sententiam*] up above the greatness of the Maker." This is an elaborate way of saying that the ultimate God of the Valentinian *hypothesis* (a) is no more than an idea in the mind of the gnostic believer, but (b) is responsible, in that character, for the denigration of the Creator (who in actuality is the only God there is).

13. Marcion of course is accused of "mutilating" the Scriptures (*Haer.* 1.27.4, cf. 3.11.9), but Marcion is a special case. The only accusation Irenaeus can bring against the Valentinians on this score is that "they set forth writings of their own and boast of having more gospels than there are"—a charge that he supports by noting their use of a work called (blasphemously, he thinks) "The Gospel of Truth" (*Haer.* 3.11.9). Nevertheless he offers no evidence that they appeal publicly to such a work to ground their teaching, and one is bound to suspect that this charge is brought merely to lend credence to his all-too-neat hypothesis that some heretics admit fewer, and others, more gospels than there are. From a Valentinian point of view, it was surely Irenaeus who supplemented the accepted list of ecclesiastical books, with works like the Acts of the Apostles and the so-called Pastoral Epistles.

14. See *Haer.* 4.35.1, and compare the argument of Ptolemy in his *Letter to Flora.*

15. 1 Cor 2:6. Compare the reference to "the apostolic tradition, which even we have received by succession," in Ptolemy, *Flor.* 33.7.9.

16. Irenaeus believed that there is a limited sphere within which human inquiry can properly and effectively work ("quae . . . dedit in hominum potestatem Deus et subdidit nostrae scientiae": *Haer.* 2.27.1); and this sphere embraced (a) "things that we can observe" and (b) "whatever there is in the Scriptures that is plainly and unambiguously said" (2.27.1). Clearly the Valentinian *hypothesis* spoke of matters that satisfied neither of these criteria.

17. See *Haer.* 1.9.2: "Et unumquodque eorum quae dicta sunt auferentes a veritate et abutentes nominibus, in suam argumentationem [Gk. *hypothesin*] trans-

tulerunt." They keep the names, then, but change their referends to make them fit an unintended story-line.

18. They "draw" people "on the pretext of *gnōsis* away from the one who established and ordered this universe, as if they had something higher and nobler to show than the one who made heaven and earth and all that is in them" (*Haer.* 1.pref.1).

19. " . . . similia quidem nobis loquentes, dissimilia vero sentientes" (*Haer.* 1.pref.2).

20. W. Schoedel, "Theological Method in Irenaeus (*Adversus haereses* 2.25–28)," *JTS*, n.s. 35 (1984): 31–49.

21. *Haer.* 2.28.4: "nihil Deo reservetis." It is ironical that Irenaeus should bring this charge against teachers who held that even the Aeons of the spiritual overworld (with the exception of Intellect/Truth) must remain ignorant of the ultimate God.

22. See *Haer.* 2.28.1 ("Habentes . . . in aperto positum de Deo testimonium"), summing up the argument of 2.27.2.

23. He points out, for example, that there is no real analogy between the "fall" of the "twelfth apostle" (Judas) and that of the twelfth aeon of the Valentinian Dodecad (Sophia); and that it is implausible to take Luke 4:19 ("a year of the Lord's favor," cf. Isa 61:2) to mean that Jesus' ministry lasted exactly one year and that he therefore died in the "twelfth month."

24. See *Haer.* 4.6.1–7; cf. 4.2.2. The question here was in part 1 of the actual text of Matthew's Gospel.

25. See *Haer.* 5.9–11. 1 Cor 15:50 reads: "Flesh and blood can never inherit the kingdom of God."

26. This argument opens at 2.1.1 and closes at the end of 2.30, but it is interrupted twice—by an excursus on the nonbiblical sources of Valentinian teaching (2.14), and by Irenaeus's little treatise on theological inquiry (2.25–28), which argues that such inquiry should be governed by a trustful love of God and a recognition of the limitations of human knowledge. It takes up again at chapter 29 (on the Valentinian eschatology); Irenaeus's attack on the view that the Demiurge is "psychic" by nature (2.30) seems to be an elaborate footnote to 2.29.

27. See, for example, Rom 7:22; 1 Cor 2:13–15.

28. B. Reynders, "La polémique de saint Irénée," *Revue de théologie ancienne et médiévale* 7 (1935). See also P. Perkins, "Ordering the Cosmos: Irenaeus and the Gnostics," in *Nag Hammadi, Gnosticism, and Early Christianity* (ed. Charles W. Hedrick and Robert Hodgson, Jr.; Peabody, Mass.: Hendrickson, 1986), 221–38.

29. See Plutarch, *Mor.* 13.2.

Zoological Marvel and Exegetical Method in Origen and the *Physiologus*

ALAN SCOTT

Origen claims that without a sound knowledge of the "natures of animals" (Wis 7:20) Jesus never would have called Herod a fox, nor would other sinners be referred to in the Bible as a "brood of vipers," "horses," "senseless beasts," or "deaf adders."[1] We are told by his student Gregory Thaumaturgus that Origen was interested in natural phenomenon (*physiologia*), which would include teachings about what we would call the life sciences (*Or.* 8), and his scattered but numerous references to the animal kingdom influenced the depiction of beasts in Jerome, Ambrose, Basil, and the early Byzantine tradition.[2]

Even more important in shaping attitudes toward animals in the Middle Ages and beyond was an anonymous book called the *Physiologus*. Whereas some sciences (e.g., astronomy) made genuine progress in the Hellenistic era, zoology stagnated. It was a period in which observation of animal behavior and real insights about their nature became rare, and interest in the bizarre more pronounced. Increasingly Hellenism inclined to "paradoxography," the "love of exotic subject matter and fabulous natural history."[3] A variety of writers solemnly described animals that fell in love with humans, rivers that turn cattle white or black, flying snakes, birds that can count, and so forth. These colorful stories became part of the literary discourse of their day, where they were frequently yoked to a philosophical purpose, either to demonstrate some aspect of contemporary debate (usually over Stoic doctrine), or to draw an edifying moral.

In the early Christian era, when so much of classical culture was brought to bear on theological issues and on the exegesis of scripture, it was perhaps inevitable that the exposition of fantastic beasts for moral purposes would spawn a Christian equivalent. The *Physiologus* was the work created after the example of pagan paradoxography, claiming that the proper understanding of the marvelous properties of beasts showed how nature itself contained clues to mysteries exposed in scripture and Christian theology.

The date of the *Physiologus* is uncertain, but there are good reasons to think that it was written in Egypt.[4] There are clear parallels to Origen in the text,[5] and it is likely that the *Physiologus* has used Origen as a source, and must therefore have been written not in the second century (as some scholars had thought), but sometime after the middle of the third.[6]

Though the *Physiologus* seems to have been written in the wake of Origen's theology, it nevertheless represents a new and very different approach to the allegorical understanding of nature and scripture. The *Physiologus* does not follow Origen's lead in Christian allegory, but, in its own primitive way, goes off in a new theological direction, and it would have many imitators in the medieval period.

Origen's interest in the animal marvels is twofold. First, like Philo before him, he inherits a theological debate between Stoics and Skeptics where the issue is what animal behavior tells us about providence. Second, as a matter of practical exegetical interest, he frequently found it necessary to say a few words about the various exotic beasts which are named in the pages of scripture.

Most of Origen's philosophical consideration of the animal kingdom occurs in the fourth book of his *Contra Celsum*, where Origen responds to Celsus' optimistic assessment of animal reason. Origen (like his Jewish predecessor Philo)[7] generally takes the Stoic view that zoological wonders are signs of divine providence rather than bestial intelligence. This is true, e.g., of the filial piety of the stork (*Cels.* 4.98), the pharmaceutical abilities of snakes and other creatures (*Cels.* 4.87),[8] or the care ants take in choosing for winter storage fruits with good shelf life (*Cels.* 4.83).[9] The following points are at issue; in the first four Origen is adopting a Stoic position:

1) Were beasts created for humanity? This is what Origen affirms against Celsus, who argued that animals seem to have a better time of it.[10]

2) Are beasts fundamentally different from human beings? This too Origen believed, since only humanity had been made in God's image.

3) Are they rational? Origen opposed this, claiming animals acted in accordance with their own nature, while rational beings acted on the basis of the reason which they shared with their Creator.[11]

4) Can they be regarded as moral agents? Since he assumed animals were not rational, Origen had to deny this.[12]

5) Are some beasts given the power of foreknowledge so as to be useful in divination? Origen disagreed with this view, here switching sides in the debate and adopting existing Academic arguments against the Stoic position.[13]

Origen also considers the nature of various beasts within the context of scriptural exegesis, where Origen either discusses a creature mentioned in the Bible, or uses a fact (real or imagined) about the animal kingdom to illuminate an exegetical point. Apart from his apologetic work *Contra Celsum*, this is Origen's more primary and typical concern. Sometimes he discusses the nature of a beast as part of his exposition of a passage; on other occasions he more ambitiously hopes to show how a seemingly chance reference to beasts in a passage in fact discloses theological secrets of scripture.

Exegesis along these lines informs us that just as there is one bee who is king of the other bees (the Greeks did not know it was a queen), so there is one Lord Jesus Christ who is the leader of all the prophets (*Hom. Isa.* 2.2; cf. Prov 6:8 [LXX]). Fish without scales or fins are unclean (Lev 11:9–10) because without them they must swim near the mud of the bottom, and so it is that the saint who has "scales" and "fins," i.e., who has put off his old garments and gone on to better things, escapes the mud of skepticism and attains the "net" of faith (Matt 13:47) (*Hom. Lev.* 7.7). Standard associations of animals were also useful: the lion fears no beast but all are subject to it; so too all things are subject to the perfect Christian who thus is the lion of Num 23:24 (*Hom. Num.* 16.8). The sheep, then as now a symbol of abject servility, symbolizes bestiality and the lack of intelligence (*Comm. Jo.* 10.142). The sacrifice of the goat (Lev 1:10), a proverbially lusty animal, symbolizes the way in which rational individuals overcome their own licentiousness (*Hom. Lev.* 2.2).

An exegetical problem which Origen faced was that many nonexistent animals appeared in the pages of the Septuagint. The Hebrew word *reem*, "wild ox," was unknown and had been translated *monokerós*, "unicorn" (e.g., Ps 21[22]:21). *Layish*, an uncommon word for "lion," became in Greek translation the mythic "ant-lion" (*murmēkoleón*, e.g., Job 4:11).[14] Similarly the legendary basilisk, which killed opponents with its deadly glance, pops up in various passages (being, anticlimactically, merely a Hebrew adder), and so is treated quite seriously by Origen.[15] The translators of LXX perhaps did not think it necessary to expend much energy on these out-of-the-way corners of scripture, but they did not reckon on Origen's microscopic analysis of the text, which attempted to leave nothing unexplained.

When faced with some exegetical puzzle which requires secular learning, Origen will usually defer to the opinion of pagan experts. In his discussions of the natural world he often quite openly is relying on sources, though unfortunately (unlike Clement) he generally does not tell us who they are. Scholars in this era tended to copy down stories about the world of natural history from their sources almost without alteration,[16] and by continuing this practice Origen (like all the writers of this period) often looks ridiculous. For example, the popular tale that stags draw out snakes by their breath and eat them, being impervious to their venom, becomes one of his stock examples.[17] In his diatribe against Celsus he gives the griffin (with the elephant) as an example of how an animal can be larger, stronger, and live longer than a human being, and yet be inferior.[18] Like other Christian apologists he uses the example of the vulture's parthogenesis to defend the Christian doctrine of the virgin birth.[19] Similarly, since the worm was thought to reproduce asexually, Ps 21:7 [22:6] ("but I am a worm and no man") is said to refer to Jesus' birth (*Hom. Luc.* 14). When Celsus passes along fantasies about the animal kingdom, Origen in fact usually is content to let them stand, and to argue the philosophical issue involved rather than the alleged marvel. As it turns out both writers are limited by the curses of ancient science: a scholastic tendency to accept written authority, and the practice of subordinating observations about the natural world to the immediate demands of philosophical/theological argument.

In this subject as also in his edition of the *Hexapla*, however, Origen often showed considerable critical abilities, voicing the same sort of reservations that were being raised by pagan contemporaries. Along with the luxuriant growth of paradoxographical literature, some protests against it also were made throughout the Hellenistic era,[20] and Origen shared some of this spirit. Like many in antiquity, Origen had reservations about the story of how the phoenix places its dead father in the shrine of the sun (*Cels.* 4.98),[21] and he dismissed Celsus' claim that ants carry on conversations with each other and that birds had religious gatherings (4.84, 89). He reports that his opponent Celsus said that elephants were capable of taking oaths, and Origen says he has never heard of such a thing (4.98).[22] Discussing scriptural impossibilities he says that the goat-stag (*tragelaphos*) of Deut 14:5 (LXX) does not exist, and that a griffin (*grups*, Deut 14:12, Lev 11:13 LXX) has never been caught (*Princ.* 4.3.2).[23]

The overall effect of his zoological errors is, of course, lessened by the secondary place such observations have for him. For Origen, zoological references have a limited objective: either answering pagan critics (especially

Celsus) in the cause of Christian apologetic, or interpreting difficult passages of scripture. The natural world is the background, not the foreground. He makes his share of mistakes, but the effect is less glaring since his focus is elsewhere.

We are in a different world when we come to the *Physiologus*. The *Physiologus* was translated, re-edited, and recast in a bewildering variety of ways. Sbordone identified three major recensions (primitive, and two medieval editions), and even in the oldest recension there are five separate text types, whose interrelationship is now apparently impossible to sort out.[24] One of the complicating factors in editing it has been its tremendous popularity, especially in the medieval period, when it was translated into nearly all the European and Oriental languages.[25] It apparently began with forty-eight chapters: forty-one about beasts and fishes, one about plants (the mythical peridexion), and six about stones, but the number and content of chapters varied considerably throughout the medieval period.

The chapters are all discrete and self-enclosed (their original sequence now appears impossible to determine; I follow the order in Sbordone's edition). There is a complete lack of internal reference; nothing in any one chapter picks up on anything before or builds up to another. The pattern of each chapter is unvarying and indeed monotonous: there is citation of scripture and a description of some marvelous creature, attributed (cryptically) to "the Physiologist," i.e., "the natural historian." This is followed by an allegorical interpretation, which in turn often invokes more scripture. Three random examples give the basic idea.

Physiologus chapter 5 quotes Ps 101:7[102:6], "I have become like an owl in the house." The natural historian said of the owl that it loves the darkness more than the light. Thus our Lord Jesus Christ loved us when we were in darkness, and it was we Gentiles who received adoption as sons (Gal 4:5). Because of this the Savior said, "Do not be afraid, little flock, because the Father is pleased to give you the kingdom of Heaven" (Luke 12:32).

In chapter 31, the natural historian says that the salamander quenches an oven by entering it. How then do some not believe that the three young men entered a burning fiery furnace without being harmed (Dan 3)? Furthermore, this also refers to the prophecy of Isaiah that you shall pass through fire and the fire will not harm you (Isa 43:2).

Finally, we are told (chap. 46) that the Indic Stone, when tied to a person with dropsy, absorbs moisture from him. Later, when put on the scale, a small stone will outweigh the sick individual's body; placed in the sun, the stone gradually sheds its foul waters. The stone refers to Christ, who was bound to our hearts through the cross and bore our iniquities; with his stripes we are healed (Isa 53:5).

The importance of the *Physiologus* in the Middle Ages was enormous, and some of its fantastic imagery found its way to writers such as Chaucer, Shakespeare, and Milton.[26] Though few of its claims are original, it helped popularize such familiar ideas as the phoenix which rises from its ashes, the siren which lures sailors to their doom, the half-human and half-horse centaur, and the unicorn which can be lured into a trap by a virgin (chaps. 7, 13, and 22), to name a few.

The *Physiologus* is virtually free from contemporary references (which complicates dating it), and possibly it was anonymous from its inception—already in the sixth century it is attributed to Ambrose,[27] and medieval guesses for its author include Epiphanius, Basil, and Solomon. It may well be an example of a literature welling up from the imagination of an entire community and tradition rather than a single author, which would help account for the impossibility of establishing a single critical text.

To say that the *Physiologus* represents the latest form of a much larger tradition is not, of course, to necessarily declare it a classic. Its imagery is grotesque, and in combining a rude literary style with a baroque vocabulary, it generally gets the worst of both worlds. Clearly it added nothing positive to zoology as a science. Indeed, as Klaus Alpers has observed, the *Physiologus* is not in the scientific tradition of Aristotle and Theophrastus at all, not even in the flawed manner of the paradoxographical literature, but rather belongs entirely to a biblical/typological tradition of interpretation.[28]

And even strictly within this biblical/typological tradition it is a disappointment. The theology of the *Physiologus* seldom rises above a vague praise of asceticism and an equally vague condemnation of undefined heresy. It not only lacks Origen's critical reservations—Origen is incomparably more learned and less naïve than the author of the *Physiologus*—but it also does not match his ability to genuinely illumine a biblical text. Furthermore, though Origen did not cherish the literal sense of a passage, he did respect it, and the sense that scripture can be profitably read at this level is not lost in him.[29] Allegory is the favored but not the exclusive approach for Origen, whereas in the *Physiologus* the pages of scripture serve as little more than a cipher. In fact, in the *Physiologus* it is clear that biblical passages have been chosen with paradoxographical interests in mind: finding the beasts comes first, aligning them with a passage of scripture is second. Origen in contrast is engaged in the honest toil of exegesis; he usually raises the subject of fantastic animals because it arises in a text he is explicating.

And yet there are some things the *Physiologus* does that Origen cannot do, making it, despite its glaring limitations, still somehow a compelling book. For one, it is a rare example from early Christian literature of a book that lends itself readily to illustration. It was accompanied by drawings throughout the medieval period and probably even earlier;[30] most of the modern translations continue this tradition. Like most Platonists Origen has little interest in discussing something that can be pictured. The author of the *Physiologus*, however, deserves comparison with the Gospels, Acts, and the book of Revelation for bestowing on Christian theology a work suited to the pictorial imagination.

The *Physiologus* is also interesting for the way it disengages allegory from the text of a canon and applies it to the natural world. It was preceded in this venture by the genius of Valentinus, who likewise saw the possibility of a wider theological application for allegory[31]—one of the few real parallels between the *Physiologus* and the world of gnosticism—and this is strikingly different from Origen's exegetical allegory. In Origen the feeling is present that every nuance and corner of scripture is full of significance. He believed that nothing he found in the Bible had come there by accident; everything had a secret meaning. In the *Physiologus*, this idea is applied not so much to scripture, but to nature as a whole. The author has the idea that nature is itself filled with theological meaning which can be discerned allegorically. This idea that nature might be interpreted in the same way as a book was not obvious to early Christian theology, and in fact a theology of the natural world was otherwise slow in developing. Innocent of the philosophical issues raised by the Stoics and their rivals, the *Physiologus* discovered another way in which nature could be related to theology. The medieval bestiary, which was to become a very robust genre, owes much to the approach we find in the *Physiologus* and less to Origen, even though Origen's exegesis of nature was more broadly influential, especially in the early Middle Ages.[32]

In the Bible creation is described as good, and though there are times in early Christian theology when we feel its beauty,[33] the gaze of Origen and of most of the theologians of that era is usually elsewhere.[34] The *Physiologus* did not have anything like Origen's learning or his exegetical insight, but the author does have a genuine sense of the created order's wonder and mystery often lacking in more intellectual contemporaries. His ways of expressing this mystery are crude and mythological, but it is a case of the duller student finding something that his more brilliant classmate missed. The *Physiologus* is not much read today (not even by scholars), but one can see why it had such power a millennium ago.

NOTES

1. *Comm. Cant.* 3; Luke 13:32; Matt 3:7; Jer 5:8; Ps 57(58):5; cf. also Clement of Alexandria, *Strom.* 4.3.12. Many thanks to Joy Shen for her help.

2. For the uses of animal imagery, see the references collected by Henri Crouzel in his chapter "Images bestiales," in *Théologie de l'Image de Dieu chez Origène* (Aubier: Éditions Montaigne, 1954), 197–206. Focusing on accounts of how vipers were born, Ursula Treu, "Ottergezücht," *ZNW* 50 (1959): 113–22, shows how closely patristic writers follow Origen; the influence on the *Physiologus*, though eventually considerable, for the most part is later.

3. Michael J. Curley, *Physiologus* (Austin: University of Texas Press, 1979), xvii; cf. P. M. Fraser, *Ptolemaic Alexandria* (Oxford: Clarendon, 1972), 685. See in general K. Ziegler "Paradoxographoi," *PW* 18.3 (1949): 1137–66. A. Westermann's preface to his edition of the *Paradoxographoi* (London: Black & Armstrong, 1839) is still worth reading. In addition to Westermann, relevant texts are edited by A. Giannini, *Paradoxographorum Graecorum reliquiae* (Milan: Istituto Editoriale Italiano, 1965).

4. Fritz Hommel, *Die aethiopische Übersetzung des Physiologus* (Leipzig: Hinrichs, 1877), xv–xvi.

5. Fr. Lauchert cites many paradoxographical parallels, *Geschichte des Physiologus* (Strassburg: Karl I. Trübner, 1889), 71–72. Note also the close exegetical relationship between *Physiologus* 15 ("On the Fox") and Origen, *Comm. Cant.* 3, where clearly one is copying the other: in both the foxes which damage the vineyards in Cant 2:15 are tied in with Luke's description (13:32) of Herod as a fox; both strain to interpret Jesus' saying that "foxes have their holes and birds have their nest but the Son of Man has no place to lay his head" (Matt 8:20) as a reference to the supposedly scheming scribe who was pretending to wish to follow Jesus—hardly an interpretation which two exegetes would arrive at independently.

6. See by the present author, "The Date of the *Physiologus*," *VC* 52 (1998): 430–41.

7. See esp. Philo's *De Animalibus*, extant in Armenian; *Philonis Alexandrini De Animalibus* (ed. and trans. Abraham Terian; Studies in Hellenistic Judaism 1; Chico, Calif.: Scholars Press, 1981). Philo opposes especially the Academic tradition of Carneades.

8. Cf. Georgius Tappe, *De Philonis libro qui inscribitur Alexandros* (Göttingen: Dieterich, 1912), 15–16.

9. Urs Dieraurer, *Tier und Mensch im Denken der Antike* (Amsterdam: Grüner, 1977), 242.

10. *Cels.* 4.78; cf. [Origen] *Fr. Ps.* 1 (PG 12, 1089c).

11. *Cels.* 4.85, 98; cf. Philo, *Anim.* 92. See further Richard Sorabji, *Animal Minds and Human Morals: The Origins of the Western Debate* (Cornell Studies in Classical Philology 54; Ithaca, N. Y.: Cornell University Press, 1993).

12. *Comm. Jo.* 20.363; *Princ.* 3.4.3; *Cels.* 4.81, 92; *Fr. Ps.* 118 (SC 189, 364).

13. See Henry Chadwick, "Origen, Celsus and the Stoa," *JTS* 48 (1947): 37.

14. See P. Ansell Robin, *Animal Lore in English Literature* (London: John Murray, 1932), 6; Florence McCulloch, *Mediaeval Latin and French Bestiaries* (UNC Studies in Romance Languages and Literatures 33; Chapel Hill: University of North Carolina Press, 1960), 83.

15. *Hom. Luc.* 31; cf. also *Hom. Jes. Nav.* 11.6. There is a long exposition in *Fr. Jer.* 25, but its authenticity is suspect.

16. See, e.g., Terian *Animalibus* 55–56.

17. *Hom. Cant.* 2.11; *Comm. Cant.* 3; *Hom. Jer.* 18.9; *Comm. Matt.* 11.18; *Cels.* 2.48. See in general H.-Ch. Puech, "Le Cerf et le serpent," *Cahiers archéologiques* 4 (1949): 17–60.

18. *Cels.* 4.24. Griffins and elephants are often cited together: see Lucian, *Dial.* 15.4; Jerome, *Pelag.* 1.19; Priscian, *Solutiones ad Chosroem* (92,6 Bywater).

19. *Cels.* 1.37; cf. the *Geoponica* 14.26.2. Even Galen accepted the parthogenesis of some birds; see Robert M. Grant, *Miracle and Natural Law* (Amsterdam: North-Holland, 1952), 13.

20. E.g., Andreas, a physician in the time of Ptolemy IV, wrote a book against miracle-mongering, Athenaeus 7.312e (cited by Paul Pédech, *La Méthode historique de Polybe* [Paris: Les Belles Lettres, 1964], 393); so too Pliny denied that hyenas change their sex and did not believe in griffins and sirens, Pliny *Nat.* 10.136 (cited by Guy Serbat, "Pline l'Ancien: État présent des études sur sa vie, son oeuvre et son influence," *ANRW* 32.4:2106), or that amber was made from lynx urine, *Nat.* 37.52–53.

21. Cf. R. van den Broek, *The Myth of the Phoenix* (EPRO 24; Leiden: Brill, 1972), 360 n. 2.

22. Origen here may have misunderstood Celsus; in the original story the elephants probably only understood oaths made by their drivers. See further Chadwick's note in his translation (p. 261).

23. Aelian *NA* 4.27 says that it is not possible to catch a mature griffin, but that young ones can be taken into captivity. Origen elsewhere admitted the griffin: see n. 18 above.

24. That being so, more recent scholars have published the oldest text types synoptically: see D. Offermanns, *Der Physiologus nach den Handschriften G and M* (Meisenheim am Glan: Hain, 1966), and D. Kaimakis, *Der Physiologus nach der ersten Redaktion* (Meisenheim am Glan: Hain, 1974).

25. On medieval versions, see Nikolaus Henkel, *Studien zum Physiologus* (Hermaea 38; Tübingen: Max Niemeyer, 1976), 21; Max Goldstaub lists the various Oriental versions, *Der Physiologus und seine Weiterbildung* (Leipzig: Dieterich, 1899–1901), 342. The most important are the older Latin and Syriac versions, and the Ethiopic.

26. See F.N.M. Diekstra, "The *Physiologus*, the Bestiaries, and Medieval Animal Lore," *Neophilologus* 69 (1985): 142–55, and Robin, *Animal Lore*, passim.

27. In ps.-Gelasasius *Decretum Gelasianum* 225.

28. "Untersuchungen zum griechischen Physiologus und den Kyraniden," *Vestigia Bibliae* 6 (1984): 48. See also Patricia Cox, "The *Physiologus*: A Poiesis of Nature," *CH* 52 (1983): 443.

29. See e.g. Manlio Simonetti, *Biblical Interpretation in the Early Church* (trans. John A. Hughes; Edinburgh: T&T Clark, 1994), 44.

30. The single oldest ms. of the *Physiologus* is an illuminated Latin translation (ms. 318 in the Bern Burgerbibliothek, facsimile edition in Christoph von Steiger and Otto Homburger, *Physiologus Bernensis* [Basel: Alkuin, 1964]), which dates from the Carolingian Renaissance. Helen Woodruff argues that its illuminations are based on an older Greek model dating from the fourth to sixth centuries, "The *Physiologus* of Bern," *The Art Bulletin* 12 (1930): 237–41.

31. See David Dawson, *Allegorical Readers and Cultural Revision in Ancient Alexandria* (Berkeley: University of California Press, 1992), 4.

32. See Treu, "Ottergezücht."

33. See D.S. Wallace-Hadrill, *The Greek Patristic View of Nature* (Manchester: Manchester University Press, 1968); Mabel Gant Murphy, *Nature Allusions in the Works of Clement of Alexandria* (Washington, D.C.: Catholic University of America Press, 1941); Sister M. Theresa, *Nature Imagery in the Works of St. Ambrose* (Washington, D.C.: Catholic University of America Press, 1934).

34. Hal Koch writes, "nie findet man eine Spur davon, daß die Schönheit order Zweckmässigkeit der Welt ihn [sc. Origen] wirklich ergriffen hat," *Pronoia und Paideusis* (Berlin/Leipzig: W. de Gruyter, 1932), 42.

Porphyry of Tyre's Biblical Criticism

A Historical and Theological Appraisal

MICHAEL B. SIMMONS

Porphyry of Tyre: A Pagan Polymath

Porphyry of Tyre (234–305), originally called by the Semitic name Maichos after his father, was the greatest anti-Christian writer in antiquity. He has been accurately described as the best scholar of his age and as one who possessed an encyclopedic knowledge of religious traditions and philosophical doctrines.[1] Born in Tyre, Porphyry ca. 250 came to Caesarea in Palestine, where he studied under Origen,[2] and it was at his school that he learned the Hebrew OT, the allegorical exegetical method of the Alexandrians, the prophetic books of the Bible, and the Gospels and Epistles of the NT, all of which he later vehemently vituperated in several published works. He might have been a believer who turned against the faith because Christian youths assaulted him.[3] From Caesarea he went to Athens to study philology and philosophy under Longinus, and by 263 he moved to Rome, where he became Plotinus'disciple and eventually edited the *Enneades*.[4] Such works as the *De antro nympharum, Epistola ad Anebontem Aegyptium,* and *Philosophia ex oraculis* derive from this period.[5]

Because of Porphyry's severe depression, Plotinus advised him to go to Lilybacum, Sicily (268). There Porphyry heard of his master's death in 270 (*Vit. Plot.* 11). During his stay in Sicily he also traveled in North Africa (*Abst.* 3.4.7). He returned to Rome and supervised the Neoplatonic school there with considerable success, Iamblichus numbering among his famous disciples.[6] Apparently late in life he married a Jewish widow with seven children.[7] He appears to have had a significantly direct influence upon the Diocletianic Persecution (303–5).[8] Around the age of sixty-eight he had a highly mystical experience, and he died a few years later ca. 305 (*Vit. Plot.* 23). He was greatly respected by scholars in his day (cf. Libanius, *Or.* 18.178: the "old sage" from Tyre), and was still revered in North Africa when Augustine was living (*Civ.* 10.29).

Porphyry was a polymath who wrote from sixty-six to eighty-one works.[9] In this essay I shall focus on *Contra Christianos* (*Christ.*), *De philosophia ex oraculis* (*Philos. orac.*), and *De regressu animae* (*Reg. an.*). *Christ.* in fifteen books was a systematic attack upon Christian scripture, which provoked written responses from (e.g.) Methodius of Olympus, Arnobius, Eusebius, Apollinaris, and Philostorgius.[10] Imperial legislation also condemned Porphyry. Constantine's Edict of 333 refers to the Arians as "Porphyrian."[11] In February 448 an edict of Theodosius II and Valentinian III ordered the burning of all copies of the *Christ.*[12] Only fragments found in Christian writings have survived. *Philos. orac.* was a collection of oracles which offered a Chaldaean-Neoplatonic soteriology,[13] and the *Reg. an.* was a philosophical work describing the soul's return to God.[14]

Porphyry of Tyre: Imperial Propagandist

Diocletian, the emperor responsible for the greatest persecution of the Christians in Roman history, was a highly superstitious believer in oracles. He reportedly received "many omens of future rule" during his military career, and perhaps the report is true that a Druidess prophesied his ascending to the purple (*Script. Hist. Aug.* 12.1; 14.2–3). A more reliable source reveals the appointment of "overseers of animals" responsible for the organization of sacrificial sites in Egypt immediately before the imperial visit there in 298.[15] His reputation as "a searcher into futurity" was widely known throughout the empire,[16] and it was a sentiment shared by many during the period.[17] A "conservative" like Diocletian, who upheld the traditional religion of Rome and persecuted anyone who did not, could justify his imperial policies and subsequently control the masses during a delicate transition (the Tetrarchy) if he could convince them that the gods which once made Rome great now supported him. And because the Romans did not have a canon of scripture perceived as divine revelation and universally binding on everyone, one effective way to offer proof of the gods' approval of imperial policies was acquired through oracles.

During the winter of 302–3, Diocletian and Galerius held a conference to decide whether a persecution should be launched against the Christians. The anti-Christian governor of Bithynia, Hierocles, attended the meeting (Lactantius, *Mort.* 16; *Inst.* 5.2), and it is very possible that Porphyry, who by this time had acquired fame throughout the empire for his writings against the Christians (cf. Eusebius, *Dem. ev.* 3.3), also participated. Oracular revelation of the third century had developed a close affiliation with pagan philosophy,[18] and Porphyry believed that the greatest expression of piety came by honoring the gods according to ancestral customs (*Marc.* 18). Christianity was contrary to the laws of the Roman Empire, a conviction shared by Diocletian, who would surely have seen Porphyry as an invaluable ally in the persecution:[19] he is undoubtedly the "priest of philosophy" who wrote three books against the Christians and regularly dined in Diocletian's palace.[20] The three books refer to *Philos. orac.* Finally, the remark in *Marc.*, written just before the outbreak of the persecution, that he was away in the "east" because of business with the Greeks, suggests that Porphyry did attend the conference.[21] Could the ecstatic experience that he had around this time (*Vit. Plot.* 23) have produced an oracle conveying the gods' approval of the persecution? He is on record for saying that the gods' blessings had disappeared from the world since Jesus began to be worshipped.[22]

The oracle of Apollo that defined Christianity as an "incurable weakness" and the crucifixion of Jesus as a just verdict[23] might have encouraged Diocletian to consult the oracle of Apollo at Didyma, which responded that "the just upon the earth" had hindered the prophetic spirit and were releasing evils upon humanity.[24] "Apollo" that year at Didyma might very well have been a priest-philosopher who had been reading Porphyry's book on oracles.[25] There was growing tension between pagans and Christians during this time on the subject of oracular revelation.[26]

It is reasonable to suggest that Porphyry, the premier theologian on oracles in the empire who was offering the only sure hope of salvation in the *Philos. orac.* (see Eusebius, *Praep. ev.* 4.7), and the leading anti-Christian author in the world, was invited to the conference of 302. Didyma was chosen because it would have served both emperor and philosopher in four ways. (1) Didyma had a reputation for upholding ancestral religious customs.[27] (2) Owing to the decline (if not demise) of Delphi by this time,[28] Didyma was now the most prestigious oracle site and, according to Porphyry, still active (*Philos. orac.* in Eusebius, *Praep. ev.* 5.16). (3) Didyma had a rich tradition of being associated with Roman emperors and therefore possessed a pro-Roman political posture.[29] (4) Didyma by this time was concerned not only with cultic matters, but also with "the formulation of explicit pagan theology."[30] Didyma was evidently the perfect place for uniting the forces of Diocletianic imperial policies and Porphyrian anti-Christian propaganda.

A Philosophical Paradigm for a Neoplatonic-Chaldean Anti-Christian Soteriology

Porphyry was indeed a polymath and a propagandist, but he was foremost a philosopher, a fact that scholars often overlook. Throughout the twentieth century he was given many labels: a Neoplatonic philosopher (Bidez); a pagan believer (Nilsson); a controversialist (de Labriolle); a scientific theologian (Raeder); a historian (den Boer); a pagan evangelist (Jerphagnon); and a biblical critic (Beatrice). Most recent studies have focused upon the fragments of the *Christ.* in order to analyze Porphyry's exegetical method of biblical criticism and his sources,[31] and often they encounter insurmountable problems.[32] One scholar has even called him the precursor of the nineteenth-century higher criticism of the Tübingen School.[33]

A new method for Porphyrian studies is needed. For we may rightly ask whether we are missing the main point of Porphyry's anti-Christian argument when we restrict ourselves to his exegetical and historical method found in a few fragments representing a tiny percentage of his works, and preserved by his worst enemies. Rather, we should focus upon the theological and philosophical presuppositions which form the rational basis of his polemics. Until we begin to look upon Porphyry not from the perspective of his Christian adversaries, but from the viewpoint of pagan religion and philosophy of the later Roman Empire, whose two main contributors, at least for Porphyry, were Neoplatonism and Chaldaean theology, then we will continue to misunderstand this all too enigmatic and often confusing thinker, whose writings are indispensable for a clear understanding of the Diocletianic period. Simply stated, our knowledge of Porphyry will always be fragmentary as long as we focus upon the fragments (i.e., of the *Christ.*) without placing them in the larger conceptual context of his pagan religious philosophy.

Porphyry was possessed of a very orderly mind that demanded logical organization, coherence, and precise expression.[34] He is justifiably called "the first systematic theologian in the history of thought."[35] It was he who encouraged Plotinus to "organize his doctrine," which led to the *Enneads* (*Vit. Plot.* 18), the coherent system of Plotinus' Platonism. We need only read Eusebius, *Praep. ev.* 4.7, who quotes from the first book of *Philos. orac.*, to realize just how precise and systematic were Porphyry's writings. In the sections below I argue that Porphyry developed his anti-Christian argument according to a distinct conceptual paradigm that combined Neoplatonic metaphysics with Chaldaean theological beliefs. The system that finally evolved was structured according to a small number of supplementary themes—of which a representative number will be given below—which gave order and coherence to the paradigm as a whole; but these in turn were based on *one* principal doctrine, soteriology, which permeates the anti-Christian works and represents the great theme of Porphyry's argument against Christianity.

History and Time

The philosophical basis of Porphyry's historical method of biblical criticism is often overlooked. Neoplatonism posited that reality in its perfect form is beyond the world of becoming. The philosopher must flee the physical world of the senses to penetrate the depths of intelligible reality (cf. *Vit. Plot.* 16). Because God is absolutely transcendent, the Christian doctrines of incarnation, atonement, crucifixion, and the resurrection were ludicrous to Porphyry.[36] This was due not so much to a conflict between a historical hermeneutic and a prophetic-eschatological interpretation,[37] as to the belief that historical method could serve his overall anti-Christian religious philosophy.[38] For we must keep in mind that Porphyry was an excellent historian[39] whose magisterial knowledge of the Christian interpretation of history was used to show the utter absurdity of the belief that God had not only acted in history, but had become a man with a physical body in order to do it. This idea conflicted with Porphyry's very "spiritual" religion, which affirmed the need for inner purity through meditation and philosophical inquiry.[40] What were some of the critical issues? First, Porphyry aimed a major criticism at the Christians' "mindless and unexamined faith"[41] in contrast to reliance upon reason. This point is very important for Porphyry, who believed that Christ, contrary to Christian belief, was at best a misguided mortal condemned by right-thinking judges (Augustine, *Civ.* 19.23). He never claimed to be God: this erroneous idea was made up by his disciples (Augustine, *Cons.* 1.1.1; 1.7; 1.31.48). The Christian view of history is therefore based upon a lie (*Cons.* 1.34.52). Another point of contention was the belief, held by (e.g.) Augustine, that a divine purpose and providential plan permeates human history. The idea of God acting in history was ridiculous to Porphyry, who believed in a cyclical pattern of history predetermined by *heimarmenē*.[42] This is the main *philosophical* reason why the Christian interpretation of OT prophecy was unacceptable: it was a literary invention *post eventum*, devoid of all historical truth.[43] Nor did Porphyry allow the Christians to employ an allegorical interpretation of scripture.[44]

Restricting himself (and his adversaries) to a literal interpretation of scripture enabled Porphyry to show the inconsistencies and incongruous explanations given by Christian exegetes.[45] The Bible is full of foreign fables and heathen customs;[46] its books were written by pseudonymous authors after the events they claim to predict.[47] Jesus himself was also inconsistent and hence untrustworthy.[48] Peter and Paul, leaders of the church, are criticized for the sharp dissension that occurred between them,[49] and they are accused of fabricating doctrines not taught by Jesus.[50] Even the story of the resurrection was the result of the apostles' ignorance.[51] Miracle stories are also based on the lies of the disciples, who are often called magicians.[52] Porphyry further rejected the historical proof of Jesus' ministry because of the uniqueness of his miracles: Apollonius and Apuleius had performed them as well.[53] It is no wonder that he repeatedly attacked OT prophecies in the *Christ.* and made the accusation that the gods have withdrawn their blessings since Jesus began to be worshipped. By using pagan prophecy (oracles), Porphyry could even turn the argument around and say that Peter used sorcery to prove that Christianity would exist for 365 years, and then come to an abrupt end.[54]

One of the more weighty arguments of Porphyry against Christianity concerned theological disagreements about time. What has happened, he asks, to the souls who lived before Christ came to offer the only way to God?[55] The transcendent God of Neoplatonism did not act within the progressive sequence of temporal events because "the material universe is the only complete manifestation of God on the level of space and time."[56] The "inner cosmos" of the soul is in no way separated from its possessor in space and time, and the individual must therefore escape this sensible realm—*omne corpus esse fugiendum ut anima post beata permaneret cum Deo* (Augustine, *Civ.* 10.29)—in order to apprehend intelligible reality. And this can be accomplished by turning inward to the nontemporal "interior present." [57] Let the *nous* follow God, Porphyry advises his wife Marcella, by reflecting him in its effort to resemble him. The soul should be subject to the intellect, and the body should be totally separated from, and dominated by, the soul. As long as the soul is cleansed of its passions, the intellect is free to contemplate intelligible reality (*Marc.* 13; *Abst.* 1.32.2). Only then can the philosopher die to the things of the world (*Abst.* 11.61.8). Detachment from the lower, material realm thus causes a permanent inactivity in the *nous*, which takes place when the philosopher constantly turns his thought to the intelligibles (τὰ νοητά) and abstains from sensations that would otherwise awake the passions in the soul (*Abst.* 1.32.2). Because the temporal realm, so attached to the physical laws and ever-changing processes that characterize the World of Becoming, can never provide ultimate truth and reality, only a highly mystical union with God can offer a hierarchical ascent to intelligible reality. Time, perceived as a process within the natural order of things, even temporal experience per se, is of little value for achieving this goal of Neoplatonic, and specifically Porphyrian, soteriology: mystical union with the One is timeless. For these reasons Porphyry made fun of Christian, and especially Pauline, eschatology.[58] Rejecting the orthodox Platonic doctrine of the transmigration of souls into animal bodies and denying the Christian belief in the resurrection of imperishable bodies, Porphyry believed that souls will live forever, not only without earthly bodies, but without bodies of any kind (Augustine, *Civ.* 13.19). Eschatology for him basically meant that God sent the soul into this world in order that it might realize its evils and quickly return to him after being purified and liberated by philosophy (*Civ.* 10.30). Following Plotinus, who criticized the Gnostics for dishonoring the heavenly bodies which were thought to be living deities (*Enn.* 2.9.5.23), Porphyry describes eschatological doctrines like the resurrection as absurd because it implies that God interrupts the eternal and logical order of his own universe.[59] Like the great macrocosm (the living universe), the microcosm, the human soul, has no end but only a liberation from the chains that have kept it bound to this transitory, temporal realm (*Civ.* 12.19).

But how does all of this relate to prophecy, something in which Porphyry certainly believed? The answer is that oracular revelation, to the degree that it relates to time, does not in any way imply that the gods themselves change or that they change in a causal sense the sequential continuum of temporal events. Rather, prophecy denotes *a divine revelation of things that have already been predetermined by fate* (Eusebius, *Praep. ev.* 6.1). The power of the prophetic faculty tells only what has been already appointed and fixed for each person (*Praep. ev.* 3.11.9–16). The gods, who are ordinarily subordinated to fate (*Praep. ev.* 6.1–3; cf. 5.7–8), have given to humanity the gift of theurgy in order to break its bonds.[60] Where does this leave the Christians' claim to divine truth derived from biblical prophecy? In *Philos. orac.* the Hecatean oracle subjected Christ and his disciples to the fates and thereby classified both among the uninitiated masses who had to acquire salvation through

Chaldaean theurgical rites. Hecate's remark that Christ was "devout and in heaven, like the devout ones" (Augustine, *Civ.* 19.23) betrays Chaldaean soteriological influence, which taught that the souls of the uninitiated ascended only to the sphere of the astral deities, and not to the highest (Noetic) realm where the Supreme Deity exists.[61]

Ontological arguments also played an active role in the conflict between paganism and Christianity during the period. Porphyry's early works, still under Plotinian influence, convey the concept of a very transcendent One who is beyond being.[62] He is incorporeal, immobile, indivisible, and has no need of external things (*Abst.* 11.37.1). He is the Father over all beings,[63] who is yet simple, pure, and self-sufficient (*Abst.* 1.57.3). Without shape or intelligible form, the One is enthroned above intellect and intelligible reality (*Vit. Plot.* 23).

During his later literary career Porphyry, under the influence of Chaldaean theology, modified his concept of divine reality, and therefore the One became much less transcendent.[64] We can give three reasons for this change. First, Porphyry stressed, to a greater degree than did Plotinus, humanity's need of divine aid in the soteriological process.[65] Second, although a few souls can apprehend intelligible reality by philosophical inquiry, most of humanity, who are unable to grasp the doctrines of Neoplatonism, must rely upon theurgy, which purifies the lower part of the soul—not the intellectual/spiritual part—and provides communion with the ethereal gods.[66] Third, Porphyry rejected Plotinus' belief that a part of the soul eternally remains in the intelligible realm.[67] But we must remember that he never abandoned the Neoplatonic doctrine of divine impassibility, and this eventually became the conceptual basis of his philosophical arguments against Christian doctrines such as those of the incarnation and the crucifixion.[68]

Revelation

Although the NT canon had not yet been defined, Christians by the late third century nonetheless had formulated the widely held belief that their scriptures were divine truth because they had been accurately revealed by the OT prophets many centuries before Christ. Under the direct inspiration of Yahweh's spirit, the prophets had predicted many things about the birth, ministry, and death of Jesus Christ. Thus everything in the NT about Jesus is reliable and true. What God had revealed in the OT prophets was fulfilled in the NT: biblical revelation is true because it has been given to human beings by God for their salvation. In responding to this central (and very successful) teaching of the Church, Porphyry developed a major part of his anti-Christian argument, which was based upon the following three premises.

The first major premise was a systematic and meticulous attack upon OT prophecies. Augustine informs us that Porphyry developed his argument according to three principal criticisms (*Civ.* 10.32). He begins by noting that the prophecies concerned merely *worldly matters,* a logical vituperation from a philosopher of his caliber. One example is the story of Jonah's living in the whale's belly. This, he says, is utterly improbable and highly incredible, and if it has a figurative meaning, a precise explanation must be given.[69] We recall here that Porphyry was thoroughly acquainted with the Alexandrian (allegorical) exegetical method, which he may have learned from Origen, and often used it against the Christians of his day.[70] The second principal criticism was that the prophecies concerned *only this present life.* Thus, in response to Porphyry, who argued that Moses did not predict *anything* regarding the divinity of Christ, Christian writers reacted with a detailed argument of their own based on the antiquity and precise details of the prophecies about Christ that had already been fulfilled many years before.[71]

The final and principal criticism in this category was that *the prophecies were not given by men of standing.* The prophets of the OT and the apostles of the NT were therefore unreliable witnesses, and the latter were especially guilty because they misconstrued the so-called prophecies of the OT to suit their own purposes.[72] Frequently Porphyry accuses the apostles of stupidity because of their inaccurate biblical references.[73] Porphyry also stresses the disunity and dissension between Peter and Paul, owing to a strong hostility he felt toward the leaders of the early Church.[74] If they were not in agreement, did not practice what Jesus had taught, and even fabricated stories and doctrines about Jesus of which he was totally ignorant and which he would have never condoned, how could the NT claim the status of divine revelation?[75]

The second major premise of Porphyry's argument related to revelation concerns the belief that Plotinian Neoplatonism was itself divinely inspired. Any philosopher who followed Plotinus' teachings could be assured that he was basing his life on revelation which had been given by the gods. Hence, the master had as his guardian spirit a god and not the usual *daimon,* as in the case of Socrates (*Vit. Plot.* 10); he manifested great spiritual discernment (11); he was able to prophesy how children's lives would be in the future (11); and he wrote under the inspiration and supervision of the gods (23).[76] And evidently the revelatory torch was passed to his disciple: Porphyry was called by his master an expounder of sacred mysteries (*Vit. Plot.* 15).

But only an elite few were philosophers, and that brings us to the third (and final) major premise of Porphyry's argument about revelatory truth. The gods have given their truth to the masses (that is, non-philosophers) in the form of oracles, and as we shall see in more detail in the next section, Porphyry collected many of these oracles, a good number of which possessed anti-Christian pronouncements, and published them under the title *Philosophia ex oraculis*. What was the gist of the position taken by the great polymath in the work? Accentuating the incurability of the dreaded Christian disease, the oracles proclaimed the insanity of Christianity's doctrines and the mere mortality of its founder, Christ (Augustine, *Civ.* 19.23). Fate decreed, therefore, that the Christians could not know the gods: they were incapable of receiving true revelation from them, and they would be terminated in exactly 365 years.[77]

Soteriology

In his *Epistula ad Anebonem,* Porphyry investigated the possibility of a universal way for the liberation of the soul and concluded that if it existed, it was still unknown to civilization.[78] Augustine further informs us that in book 1 of *Reg. an.* Porphyry said that such a universal way had not been discovered in all of his research, neither in philosophy, the moral teachings of the Indians, Chaldaean theology, nor in his study of history (*Civ.* 10.37). Because soteriology is *the* central theme of his anti-Christian writings and it represents the conceptual basis of the philosophical paradigm mentioned above, the desire to find an exclusive way of salvation for all people was a major concern of Porphyry, and it appears that he edited the collection of oracles for the *Philosophia ex oraculis* to offer this *via universalis* as *the only sure source of the soul's salvation* (Eusebius, *Praep. ev.* 4.7). As expressed in the preface to *Philos. orac.,* the purpose of the work as a whole was indeed soteriological.

Porphyry further informs the reader that the book will prove the excellence of the gods, encourage theosophy, and explain how divination can be useful for purification and contemplation. What is not mentioned is the manner in which Porphyry used the oracles to attack Christian soteriology, especially the incarnation, the deity of Christ, and the crucifixion. And although the very poignant, anti-Christian character of the *Philos. orac.* has already been established by modern scholarship, its soteriological importance has gone relatively unnoticed. Porphyry was frustrated that paganism did not offer a universal way of salvation, while at the same time Christianity claimed to have discovered it in Jesus Christ. So he appears to have constructed one in the *Philos. orac.*, and it is now necessary to see how it formed the basis of the philosophical paradigm noted earlier in this essay. What are the salient features of this central theme? The first is the superiority of reason over religious faith, which was the foundation of the ignorant Christians' religion.[79] Faith was ludicrous because, as we have already noted, the philosopher did not have the slightest need of theurgical purifications (Augustine, *Civ.* 10.27). But only a few reach God by virtue of the intellect (10.29). The rest of humanity relies upon theurgy: it is not the intellectual part, however, but the *vehicle* or lower part, that is purified (10.9). Although the soul once purified in this way has communion with the ethereal gods, it cannot return to the Father (10.9).

The absolute necessity for the soul to flee bodily sensations and passions was another emphasis in Porphyrian soteriology, and a major reason why he found the doctrine of the incarnation so repulsive: *omne corpus esse fugiendum ut anima post beata permaneret cum Deo* (*Civ.* 10.29). The soul could not fully be saved (liberated) until it was separated from the body. This is orthodox Platonism. For the Christians the fall of humanity resulted from sin in the soul; for Porphyry, sin resulted from a privation of good brought about by the fall of the soul into matter (*Abst.* 111.27.5). In order to be like God (111.26.13), the soul must be set free from slavery to the body and servitude to the passions (111.27.11). The very thing by which humanity was saved according to Christian teaching, the human body (of Jesus), was the very thing from which humanity must be liberated according to Neoplatonic soteriology. It is no wonder that Augustine in Book 10 of the *City of God* often refers to Porphyry's hatred of the incarnation and the passion of Christ.

Assimilation to God is a spiritual process which necessitates the practice of virtue. By this the individual can make his spirit like the Being with whom he is co-natural (*Marc.* 16). In a passage reminiscent of Pauline theology (1 Cor 13), Porphyry says that four elements are necessary to develop a proper relationship with God: faith, truth, love, and hope (*Marc.* 24). The only salvation is conversion to God. As we have already noted, human beings have a greater need of divine assistance in Porphyrian soteriology than they do in the Plotinian system.[80] We thus become like God by (1) living according to the *nous* and (2) overcoming corporeal sensations and the soul's passions (*Abst.* 1.46.2).

It should not surprise us, therefore, that Porphyry abhorred the biblical doctrines of incarnation, the deity of Christ, the crucifixion, and the atonement; that he dedicated himself to demonstrating the falsity of the scriptures; that he attempted to offer a *via universalis salutis animae* in the *Philos.*

orac.; or that he wrote a book proving, he believed, that the gods revealed through oracles that Christians worshipped a dead, misguided mortal and were thus fated never to receive the gifts of the gods (*Civ.* 19.23). Whether the resident of the Roman Empire was an erudite and cultured intellectual who could achieve salvation through philosophy, or whether he was a member of the uninitiated masses who relied upon theurgical rites; both could conclude, after becoming familiar with the teachings of Porphyry, that Christianity was essentially anti-salvific.

Conclusions

I have argued that a new methodology in Porphyrian studies is necessary for an understanding of the great polymath's anti-Christian argument. An integrated and comprehensive analytical method must be devised in order to see how the fragments of works like the *Christ.* and the *Philos. orac.* fit into the larger philosophical and religious context of his writings as a whole. As noted above, if we continue to focus almost exclusively on the fragments preserved by his enemies, our knowledge of Porphyry the polymath, the propagandist, and the philosopher will be fragmentary. This essay is only a small step toward the formulation of the proposed methodology. I have also suggested that Porphyry probably worked in close association with the official imperial policies of the Diocletianic Persecution. My final conclusion concerns the conceptual paradigm according to which Porphyry constructed his anti-Christian argument. Although I have identified a number of its basic themes (e.g., on history and being), this list is not exhaustive. But the very heart of Porphyry's argument, and the foundation upon which all other themes are based, is the synthetic Neoplatonic-Chaldaean soteriology which he constructed, whose purpose was twofold: (1) to offer the way of salvation to the pagans; and (2) to prevent people from believing in Christ as the only savior of mankind.

NOTES

1. E.R. Dodds, *Pagan and Christian in an Age of Anxiety* (Cambridge: Cambridge University Press, 1965), 126. Cf. A. Meredith, "Porphyry and Julian against the Christians," *ANRW* 23.2:1119–49; R.J. Hoffmann, *Porphyry's* Against the Christians:

The Literary Remains (Amherst, N. Y.: Prometheus, 1994), 157; and generally, P. Frassinetti, "Porfirio esegeta del profeta Daniele," *Rendiconti classe di lettere e scienze morali e storiche* 86 (1953): 194–210; and C. Evangeliou, "Porphyry's Criticism of Christianity and the Problem of Augustine's Platonism," *Dionysius* 13 (1989): 51–70.

2. Eusebius, *Hist. eccl.* 6.193; Porphyry, *Vit. Plot.* 3, 14, 20.

3. Socrates, *Hist. eccl.* 3.23.37; cf. my *Arnobius of Sicca: Religious Conflict and Competition in the Age of Diocletian* (Oxford Early Christian Studies; Oxford: Clarendon, 1995), 218–19.

4. Eunapius, *Vit. Soph.* 456; Porphyry, *Vit. Plot.* 4, 19–21.

5. Joseph Bidez, *Vie de Porphyre* (Ghent: E. van Goethem, 1913), 29–36.

6. See Simmons, *Arnobius*, 218–20.

7. Simmons, *Arnobius*, 218–20; cf. T. D. Barnes, "Porphyry against the Christians: Date and Attribution of Fragments," *JTS*, n.s. 24 (1973): 424–42, at 432.

8. Lactantius, *Inst.* 5.2; cf. Bidez, *Vie*, 116; Henry Chadwick, *The Sentences of Sextus* (Cambridge: Cambridge University Press, 1959), 66; Robert L. Wilken, *The Christians as the Romans Saw Them* (New Haven: Yale University Press, 1984), 136; Simmons *Arnobius*, 24–27.

9. There is no consensus on the exact number: Simmons, *Arnobius*, 219.

10. Simmons, *Arnobius*, 221.

11. Socrates, *Hist. eccl.* 1.9.30; *Cod. Theod.* 15.5.66.

12. *Cod. Theod.* 16.6.66; *Cod. Just.* 1.1.3.

13. Simmons, *Arnobius*, 216–303; P.F. Beatrice, "Quosdam Platonicorum Libros," *VC* 43 (1989): 248–81, although I am not convinced that the *Philos. orac.* and *Christ.* are the same work.

14. E. Teselle, "Porphyry and Augustine," *AugStud* 5 (1974): 113–47.

15. In two letters dated 23 September 298 from the Strategus of the Panopolite nome: P. Beatty, Pap. Pan. 1, col. 14.380–84, found in T.C. Skeat, *Papyri from Panopolis in the Chester Beatty Library Dublin* (Dublin: Hodges, Figgis, 1964); on Diocletian's fascination with oracles see also Zosimus, *Hist. nov.* 2.12, 36–37; Simmons, *Arnobius*, 41.

16. Lactantius, *Mort.* 10.1; cf. Simmons, *Arnobius*, 32–46.

17. Eusebius, *Praep. ev.* 4.19, refers to "those prognostications about uncertainties at which the multitudes marvel." On Maximinus' rescript (312) and his devotion to oracles, see Eusebius, *Hist. eccl.* 8.14.8–9, and S. Mitchell, "Maximinus and the Christians in A.D. 312: A New Latin Inscription," *JRS* 78 (1988): 105–24, at 120, showing that the upper classes were associated with Theotecnus' oracles of Zeus at Antioch.

18. Cf. Mitchell, "Maximinus and the Christians," 120; Robin Lane Fox, *Pagans and Christians* (New York: Knopf, 1987), 196–200.

19. Cf. Simmons, *Arnobius*, 32–45; on Porphyry's belief that Christianity is illegal, see *Christ.* frag. 39 (Eusebius, *Hist. eccl.* 6.19.7).

20. See my argument in Simmons, *Arnobius*, 24, 222–23; cf. Lactantius, *Inst.* 5.2.

21. Chadwick, *Sentences*, 142; Simmons, *Arnobius*, 24, 221.

22. Eusebius, *Praep. ev.* 5.1; Augustine, *Cons.* 1.33.51; Arnobius, *Adv. nat.* 1.1.

23. Augustine, *Civ.* 19.23, quoting an oracle from *Philos. orac.*

24. Eusebius, *Vit. Const.* 2.50; Lactantius, *Mort.* 11; see Simmons, *Arnobius*, 41.

25. Suggested by Fox, *Pagans and Christians*, 595.

26. Eusebius, *Hist. eccl.* 6.19.7; 8.5–9; 8.14.5; 9.2.1–2; 9.3; *Praep. ev.* 4.19; 5.16; *Vit. Const.* 2.4; 2.29; Lactantius, *Mort.* 11; Zosimus, *Hist. nov.* 2.7; 2.10; 2.12; Porphyry, *Vit. Plot.* 22; Pap. Pan. 1, col. 14.380–84: *Script. Hist. Aug.* 12.1; 14.2–3; Augustine, *Cons.* 1.15.23; *Civ.* 10; 19.23. The use of oracles by pagan emperors (Julian) was still remembered in John Chrysostom's day (*Bab.* 2).

27. Cf. J. Fontenrose, *Didyma: Apollo's Oracle, Cult, and Companions* (Berkeley: University of California Press, 1988), 99; cf. p. 203: oracle no. 8 (early third cent.); p. 180: oracle no. 2; p. 204: oracle no. 30 (AD 285–305).

28. See Fontenrose, *Didyma*, 20–22.

29. Cf. Fontenrose, *Didyma*, 20, 105, 170; David Potter, *Prophets and Emperors* (Cambridge: Harvard University Press, 1994), 98–99; 169.

30. Mitchell, "Maximinus and the Christians," 120. For the revival of oracular revelation in the third century AD and its affiliation with pagan philosophy, see Fox, *Pagans and Christians*, 196–200.

31. Cf. W. den Boer, "A Pagan Historian and his Enemies: Porphyry against the Christians," *CP* 69 (1974): 198–208; P. M. Casey, "Porphyry and the Origin of the Book of Daniel," *TS* 27 (1976): 15–33 (arguing that Porphyry used a Syrian Christian exegetical tradition); and Arthur J. Ferch, "Porphyry: An Heir to Christian Exegesis?" *ZNW* 73 (1982): 141–47 (arguing that Porphyry did not use Christian sources for his biblical criticism).

32. E.g., P. F. Beatrice, "Pagans and Christians on the Book of Daniel," *StPatr* 25 (1993): 27–45, arguing that Porphyry's source for interpreting Daniel was Josephus, but even Beatrice notes the "profound differences" between the two (p. 45).

33. den Boer, "Pagan Historian," 203.

34. See P. Hadot, "La metaphysique de Porphyre," in *Porphyre: Huit esposes suivis de discussions* (ed. J.-H. Waszink; Geneva: Fondation Hardt: 1966), 125–64, at 162.

35. Peter Brown, *Augustine of Hippo: A Biography* (Berkeley: University of California Press, 1967), 91. Cf. the remarks of Al-Qifti Ta'rikh al-Hukama in A. Smith, *Porphyrii Philosophi Fragmenta* (Stuttgart: Teubner, 1993), 10 (frag. 4T).

36. See den Boer, "Pagan Historian," 207; Robert M. Grant, "Patristica," *VC* 3 (1949): 225–29; Casey, "Porphyry and the Origin," 30.

37. Beatrice, "Pagans and Christians," 38.

38. Cf. den Boer, "Pagan Historian," 200.

39. Cf. Brown, *Augustine*, 316, calling Porphyry a much better historian than Augustine.

40. E. Evrard, "Le maître de Plutarque d'Athenes et les origenes neoplatonismes Athenien," *L'antiquité classique* 19 (1960): 391–406, at 400.

41. See E. A. Judge, "Christian Innovation and Its Contemporary Observers," in *History and Historians in Late Antiquity* (ed. B. Croke and A. M. Emmett; Sydney: Pegamon, 1983), 13–29, at 17.

42. den Boer, "Pagan Historian," 207; Casey, "Porphyry and the Origin," 32; Wilken, *Christians*, 147.

43. den Boer, "Pagan Historian," 200.

44. G. Binder, "Eine Polemik des Porphyrios gegen die allegorische Auslegung des Alten Testament," *ZPE* 3 (1968): 81–95, at 83; den Boer, "Pagan Historian," 15; and Porphyry in Eusebius, *Praep. ev.* 3.7.1; 3.7.2–4; 3.9.1–5; 3.11.1–2, clearly revealing Porphyry's own allegorical interpretation.

45. *Christ.* frag. 39 (Eusebius, *Hist. eccl.* 6.19.4).

46. *Christ.* frag. 39 (Eusebius, *Hist. eccl.* 6.19.8–10).

47. *Christ.* frag. 43A (Jerome, *Comm. Dan.* pref.).

48. *Christ.* frags. 44, 70 (Jerome, *Pelag.* 2.17; *Comm. Matt.* 24.16–17).

49. *Christ.* frags. 21C, 22 (Jerome, *Comm. Gal.* 2.11–12, 5.10).

50. *Christ.* frag. 21A (Jerome, *Comm. Gal.* pref.).

51. *Christ.* frag. 14 (Jerome, *Comm. Matt.* 27.45): " . . . discipulos Christi ob imperitiam super resurrectione domini interpretatos."

52. *Christ.* frags. 2, 4, 6, 11, 55 (Jerome, *Pamm.; Tract. Ps.* 81; *Comm. Matt.* 9.9; *Comm. Dan.* 1.1; *Qu. hebr. Gen.* 10).

53. *Christ.* frag. 4 (Jerome, *Tract. Ps.* 81).

54. Augustine, *Civ.* 18.53–54, on which see Henry Chadwick, "Oracles of the End in the Conflict of Paganism and Christianity in the Fourth Century," in *Mémorial André-Jean Festugière: Antiquité païenne et chrétienne* (ed. E. Lucchesi and H. D. Saffrey; Geneva: Cramer, 1984), 125–29.

55. *Christ.* frag. 81 (Augustine, *Epist.* 102.8); cf. frag. 82; Simmons, *Arnobius*, 62–64, showing Arnobius' response to Porphyry.

56. A. H. Armstrong, "Man in the Cosmos: A Study of Some Differences between Pagan Neoplatonism and Christianity," in *Romanitas et Christianitas* (ed. W. den Boer et al.; Amsterdam: North Holland, 1973), 5–14, at 7.

57. Armstrong, "Man in the Cosmos," 8.

58. *Christ.* frags. 91–92 (Augustine, *Epist.* 102).

59. *Christ.* frag. 92 (Augustine, *Epist.* 102.2).

60. Ruth Majercik, *The Chaldaean Oracles: Text, Translation, and Commentary* (Leiden: Brill, 1989), 106–7; Eusebius, *Praep. ev.* 6.4.

61. For Chaldaean soteriology, see now Majercik, *Chaldean Oracles*, 21–46.

62. J. M. Rist, "Mysticism and Transcendence in Later Neoplatonism," *Hermes* 92 (1964): 213–25, at 223; and Porphyry, *Sent.* 10, 12, 15, 26.

63. *Abst.* 1.57.3; cf. P. Hadot, "Fragments d'un commentaire de Porphyre sur le Parmenide," *REG* 74 (1961): 410–38, at 423.

64. Rist, "Mysticism and Transcendence," 223–24.

65. Porphyry, *Reg. an.* in Augustine, *Civ.* 10.10; cf. Andrew Smith, *Porphyry's Place in the Neoplatonic Tradition: A Study in Post-Plotinian Neoplatonism* (The Hague: Nijhoff, 1974), 104; Simmons, *Arnobius,* 30–32.

66. Simmons, *Arnobius,* 264–303.

67. R. Berchman, "Arcana Mundi between Balaam and Hecate: Prophecy, Divination, and Magic in Later Platonism," in *SBL Seminar Papers, 1980* (SBLSP; Atlanta: Scholars Press, 1980), 107–85, at 147.

68. *Reg. an.* in Augustine, *Civ.* 10.28–29; *Abst.* 1.45.4; 11.43.3–4.

69. *Christ.* frag. 46 (Augustine, *Epist.* 102.30).

70. Meredith, "Porphyry and Julian."

71. *Christ.* frag. 38 (Theodoret, *Graec. Affect. Cur.* 7.36); for the Christians see Eusebius, *Dem. ev.* pref.; 1.1; 1.6; 2.2; 4.15; *Praep. ev.* 4.6; *Hist. eccl.* 6.19.4; and Augustine, *Cons.* 1.20.28.

72. *Christ.* frag. 5 (Jerome, *Comm. Joel.* 2.28–30).

73. *Christ.* frags. 9–10, 19 (Jerome, *Comm. Matt.* 3.3; *Tract. Ps.* 87; *Comm. Gal.* 1.1).

74. *Christ.* frags. 21B, D (Jerome, *Epist.* 112; *Comm. Isa.* 15.54).

75. *Christ.* frags. 20, 37 (Jerome, *Comm. Gal.* 1.16; 5.12).

76. Potter, *Prophets and Emperors,* 166.

77. Chadwick, "Oracles of the End."

78. Pierre Hadot, "Citations de Porphyre chez Augustin," *REAug* 6 (1960): 205–44, at 240.

79. *Christ.* frag. 3 (Jerome, *Comm. Matt.* 21.21); Augustine, *Civ.* 19.23; Eusebius, *Praep. ev.* 4.6–8.

80. Smith, *Porphyry's Place,* 104; cf. *Marc.* 24.

Paradoxes of Now
and Not Yet

The Separation between the Church and the
Kingdom in John Chrysostom, Theodore,
and Augustine

ARTHUR BRADFORD SHIPPEE

Some phrase like "now and not yet" is often used to capture the early Christian paradox of how one was to experience in this world the eschatological world of the Kingdom of God.[1] A precise balance between the two poles of the paradox was not maintained, however, but tended to be tipped either to the "now" or the "not yet," and the eschatologies of the Antiochenes John Chrysostom and Theodore of Mopsuestia and of Augustine differ here. Nor is this a theoretical or obscure difference, for it is manifest in their catechetical material, with all the popular currency that suggests. After examining these cases in particular, we will turn to the question of how the Augustinian and Antiochene variations on this eschatological theme emerged in their own age and how they played out in later ages.

The elements of the contrast between the traditions can be called, especially for John, a partly or semi-realized eschatology, and, for Augustine, a two-age future eschatology. John's catechumens were given to understand that baptism and the church were actual, if partial, experiences of the kingdom of God, so that the Christian life was a form of the angelic, heavenly life. Augustine's catechumens were given to understand that their present earthly life and future heavenly life were distinct experiences.

John Chrysostom

The goal of John's catechesis[2] was for his catechumens to appreciate the greatness of the gift of baptism. He wanted them to think of baptism as honorable and desirable, and he wanted them to be happy about the gift they would soon receive. John gained his goal by drawing on traditional Christian imagery which also had vivid secular connotations, for it was through these secular connotations that John evoked the frame of mind and emotional state within which one was to perceive baptism and the new Christian life. For example, John used the traditional imagery of the bride of Christ and the wedding feast,[3] but he spoke as if he were giving an epithalamium celebrating a very advantageous wedding. Proclaiming this a time of longing, joy, and celebration, John praised the bridegroom's high birth and wealth, as well as his love for such a bride. So great a marriage should be every young woman's desire, since she gained great riches and appeared very beautiful in her new dress. John excited his audience with the attractions surrounding a wedding and its feast, and so he led them to appreciate baptism in the same enjoyable ways.

The semi-realized nature of his eschatology is seen clearly in John's other major set of imagery, built around the traditions of the Easter celebration of Christ's victory. This was the time when the catechumens came before God in baptism, putting on Christ and becoming soldiers of Christ and citizens of the heavenly Jerusalem. The secular parallels used by John are the imperial victory and advent, and the appointment into a high office in the imperial hierarchy which was bestowed by the emperor in person. By modeling baptism and the Christian moral and sacramental life on the secular institutions of the imperium, John presented them both as proper objects of one's highest ambitions and as direct experiences of the heavenly kingdom. As people were ambitious to take part in the imperial services, so Christians were to be ambitious to take part in the kingdom of God. To clarify this compact statement, let us turn to a brief sketch of the imperial presence and hierarchy in order to illuminate some examples of John's use of this imagery; from this a sense of John's realized eschatology will emerge.

The late antique Roman government[4] was made up of the civil and military services, each referred to as a *militia*. The two services' lines of command met only in the office of the emperor. The imperium was the guarantor of the whole of the government's authorities, and the personal presence of the emperor was central to the imperium.[5] All the higher and many lower offices were in theory imperial appointments, and those elected took the signs of their office directly from the emperor's hand. Cities, on the other hand, would meet an emperor either through his state visit, the imperial *adventus*, or through sending an ambassador to him. These meetings were opportunities for benefactions, either tax abatements or some other largesse.

The view of the imperial office was shaped by the ideology of Rome's eternal victory, and the celebration of the imperial advent was a prime vehicle of propaganda whose practice and meaning were clear to all.[6] A delegation would come to meet the emperor and escort him into the town; leading citizens would host him, which was a signal honor; individual and general benefactions would be distributed; and games would be held in his name. It was a complex exercise in patriotism, patronage, and the formation of society.

As the government became more centralized and bureaucratized, careers in the imperial hierarchy came to be a premiere source of social advancement and enrichment. Here again the office and person of the emperor were paramount, since all offices depended upon the imperial authority and their holders served at the emperor's pleasure. The authority of a prefect or governor was an extension of the imperial authority, deputed to them and publicized by the presence of imperial portraits.[7]

That even rather minor offices were awarded publicly by the emperor shows that direct access was the prime channel of power and honor. The act of meeting the emperor, the increasingly ceremonial *adoratio purpurae*,[8] marked one's right to stand before him with *parrēsia*, the ability to express one's opinions openly; it was therefore not a sign of servility but of standing, a public acknowledgment by the emperor of one's right to take part in affairs.

Let us see how John appropriates this imagery. For John, the best part of baptism was gaining the immediate presence of the triumphant, ruling Master,[9] itself as greatly desirable as access to the emperor was in society. As with the emperor, the Master's approach was a festal day, on which he handed out great benefactions.[10] In baptism, as in an imperial audience, one approached the Master directly to receive this great honor, and once admitted, like an emperor's friend, one was to ask him for other boons, too.[11] These gifts were the most helpful aspects of an emperor, and they were superbly available to one being baptized at Easter.[12] Baptism itself was pictured by John as an election to a high office in the imperial hierarchy, an office that both conferred honor and imposed responsibilities.[13] The authority of the office, however, guaranteed one's freedom to carry out those responsibilities. In this way, the Christian life became, like Paul's life and career, an active one of doing those good deeds which one can.[14] The Christian life was social, and it was carried out in the church and in the world in the same manner that it would be in the heavenly Jerusalem.[15]

The picture that emerges from these passages is clear. The guiding metaphor was the system of imperial benefactions. The best time for distributing royal gifts was during the imperial advent celebrating victory. One especially honored by the emperor would host him at home—imagine the preparations!—and be considered among the emperor's friends. One elected to a high office received the tokens of office directly from the emperor's hands, and when admitted to adore the purple and greeted with an imperial kiss, he was sure to gain favorable consideration from the emperor. He would also gain authority and respect in society, allowing him the freedom to act.

Such, then, was Christianity. Easter was the great imperial advent, when the honor of baptism was handed out. One must be prepared to host Christ in one's soul. In baptism, one met Christ immediately and could ask him for boons. The office and honor received by the neophyte allowed him, in fact they authorized and required him, to act freely and morally among people, avoiding sin and doing good deeds. This activity was understood as one's duty as a citizen of the Jerusalem above, ruled by the victorious risen Christ. In describing the most solemn moments of baptism, John had recourse to the most solemn moments of a royal audience, the crowning object of ambition in his society.

This complex of imagery dramatically implies a realized eschatology. The election, office, and citizenship were all heavenly, but they were immediately possessed by the Christian, and they were to be lived out here below. Both worlds existed in the church and in the believer's Christian life, and these were John's concern throughout the catecheses.

Theodore of Mopsuestia

John's friend and colleague in Antioch, Theodore, used eschatological teachings in his catecheses[16] which were similar to John's, if more muted; in fact, there are more similarities, small and large, between the two catechists than is often recognized. We can begin to see the social and semi-realized eschatology they share by comparing two texts which show common language, imagery, and context. First, from John:

When you go down into the bath of those waters, remember my worthlessness.... Remember me after it is well with you.... All of you now have great confidence [*parrēsia*] in approaching the King; we are sending you to Him as public ambassadors in behalf of human nature [*presbeis hyper tēs physeōs tōn anthrōpōn*]. You bring to Him no crown of gold, but a crown of faith. He will receive you with abundant good will; ask Him, then, in behalf of the common mother of us all, that she be neither in tumult nor disturbed. . . . For all of you have great confidence in approaching the Master, and He will receive you with a kiss. (P.-K. 3.9 [31])

In this Holy Thursday sermon, John has been describing the actions of baptism in a rather disconnected way, one by one, and this observation falls between explanations of the immersion itself and the sacred kiss. The *inclusio* of *pollē parrēsia pros* ("great confidence in approaching") sets off this unit, giving us a miniature portrait of the baptizand's meeting the universal Emperor in baptism as one met the worldly emperor in the rite of *adoratio*. The anthropology is manifest: one gained in baptism a freedom to act for the good of others. As an ambassador greeted so intimately was sure to have his petition granted, so the new Christian was to exercise his new freedom in moral and social ways with every hope of success.

Theodore in his first homily on baptism says:

And He [Jesus Christ, the assumed human being] became for ever immune from death. . . . . He ascended into heaven and became for ever beyond the reach of . . . Satan . . . and . . . dwelt in heaven and possessed a close union with the Divine nature. From the fact that the man who was assumed from us had such a confidence (with God), He became a messenger on behalf of all the (human) race so that the rest of mankind might participate with Him in His great change. (W. S. 6.2.22)

This passage is part of a description of the human condition from our first fall through Christ's saving works, and the description is set within a broad discussion of the performance of the sacraments, especially of baptism.[17] Theodore's typical emphases are here, especially the focus on the assumed Jesus Christ and the close union with God. What is important for us is the last sentence and its anthropology. "Confidence" translates *parehseya*ʾ, a transliteration of *parrēsia*, which was certainly the underlying Greek word. A word used frequently by both Theodore and John in their catecheses, *parrēsia* was the confidence that a trusted, intimate subordinate has with his master. Mingana translates ʾ*yzgada*ʾ *chalph gens* as "messenger on behalf of the race," but the first word should be translated precisely as "ambassador."[18] The picture, then, was this: Jesus was humanity's ambassador to the court of God, where his good relationship with the King of all ensured that he would strike a favorable deal on humanity's behalf.

The correspondences between the two passages are quite exact. We have the common vocabulary and imagery of the ambassador who can petition confidently for a favorable decision from the King. We have the common context of describing the performance of baptism and understanding it as moral and social. And we have the *parallel* situation between Theodore's assumed human, who in resurrection came before God, and John's baptized humans, who in baptism, the type of resurrection, came before God.[19] For both John and Theodore, baptism was a heavenly experience, involving one in activities of the kingdom of God.

This parallel between John's baptizand and Theodore's Jesus suggests that we can approach Theodore's anthropology through his Christology, since the anthropology is the most individual part of his Christology. Theodore's Christology focused on the roles of both God and the assumed human, and therefore on the relationship between them. The divine Word initiated this relationship, to which the human being's will responded with a free and rational obedience. The free subordination of the human being to the Word allowed the assumed Jesus to retain an active human will while sharing in the divine prerogatives in a unique way through the incarnation.[20]

Because the anthropology of Theodore's Christology explained human reason as the capacity for moral discernment and choice, we find a soteriology that was strongly moral in character and also strongly social in character. The freedom gained by a Christian in baptism was a freedom to act, namely, to do good to and among others in the context of the church community. It was also a freedom gained in the economy of the incarnation and resurrection. In other words, the human ability to do good in the present was an honorable authority deputed by means of baptism and the sacraments, and these rites were efficacious because God had established Jesus Christ's rule in the Kingdom of Heaven.[21]

One can, therefore, call Theodore's anthropology a sociology, since it described not the ideal human being but the ideal of humanity. The triumphant Lord, that is, the assumed Jesus, ruled in a Kingdom of Heaven that was a city populated with angels and people. In the world, human participation in that other-worldly Kingdom was located concretely within the church, in one's active participation in both the sacramental life and the moral life.[22]

So, in Theodore as in John, one sees a typology between the societies of church and heaven, where participation in the church was a participation in heaven, although this way of life was perfected only in the resurrection.[23] Theodore drew on the Old Testament for this typology, of course, so that the related forms of church and kingdom were foreshadowed in the history of Israel; yet, while the church and Israel looked alike because both mirrored the kingdom, the relationship of church to kingdom was much the closer.[24] Whatever the particular differences between the catecheses of John and Theodore, and they are many, as a cursory reading shows,[25] still there emerges from both a semi-realized eschatology which saw the church as sharing in the imperial pattern of Christ's kingdom.

Augustine

Augustine's catechumens[26] received a much different view of the relationship of the present life to the future life. They learned that the Christian life was an extension of the earthly past, while heaven's rest was a future hope. For example, baptism was a crossing of the Red Sea; so, although the Egypt of sin was destroyed, this present life was still a desert sojourn one must endure until the final crossing of the Jordan into the promised land and the heavenly Jerusalem, the land of the living. The sacramental elements were like the miracles of manna and the water from the rock. Although heaven-sent, their function was earthly, for they were not the heavenly banquet, but rather they served to sustain one while in the desert.[27] While the desert sojourn of this life was distinct from the old life in captivity to sin, it was in the same order. The next world was in a different order.

Discussion of the Lord's Prayer also covered different types of nourishment, divided between the two worlds.[28] The daily bread one asked for was not part of one's heavenly reward, but rather it was like the box lunch which a worker needed while toiling in the vineyard. It fed the soul, but it was only food and not itself a reward. A worker was owed both food in this age, lest he grow faint, and wages due when the job was done, in which he could then delight. These wages were eternal life, contracted in this age but paid only in the next.

The ethical life, Augustine told his catechumens, was the imitation of the humble, earthly life of Jesus.[29] It was constituted, therefore, by deeds of this world, not of that heavenly world characterized by contemplation and rest.[30] This is very different from John's message, where the believer's good deeds were the civic duties of a citizen of heaven.[31] For John, there was a heavenly ethic, which one was to follow on earth; for Augustine, this claim simply would not make sense.

Outside of his catechetical material, Augustine worked out many details of his eschatology in *De civitate Dei*, especially in Book 20, in the exegesis of passages from the Apocalypse. As we have seen in the catechetical material, the church was relatively closer to this world than to the next. While there was change from the old world, the more significant change would be after the trials of the end time and Christ's return. God's justice did currently rule, but this justice was largely hidden for the time being, even from the pious (*Civ.* 20.2).

The picture is laid out clearly in *Civ.* 20.7–9. Christ's millennial reign was in fact in progress (20.7), as the functioning of the church shows: there were the sacraments and penance, and the martyrs and saints governed even now before the resurrection (20.9). This government was very different from the final kingdom of God, however. The devil may have been bound, but he was still potent,[32] and the devil's party, tares among the wheat, was hidden from sight (20.7). Augustine, in a way strikingly different from the Eastern traditions, looked with dread toward a final time when the devil, unbound, would persecute God's church with unequaled fierceness (20.8). In fact, the devil was bound only to allow the church some time to take root among the peoples, so that the faithful among them might be brought into it in time (20.7).

In the interim, the kingdom of Christ was present in the millennial reign, but in a limited way, since there was still the conflict with the devil and with lusts (20.9). After the final trial and the general resurrection, the saints will reign in peace without an enemy, as all tears will have been wiped away (20.9). Then the contemplation of God will be undistracted. Throughout these sections, while Augustine affirmed that both the church militant and the church triumphant are the kingdom, he emphasized how different the experiences of the two will be. The current kingdom looked very much like the world around it, sharing its problems; the future kingdom will look very different, being untroubled and contemplative.[33]

In both these contexts, namely, the catechesis for the general public and *Civ.* for a more restricted audience, a consistent picture emerges: heaven was not experienced in the present age in any significant way. One heard about heaven and hoped for it, but one lived in a world far distant from it and far more akin to the old world. The contrast between these elements in the eschatologies of John and Augustine is quite stark, divided sharply between the partly (almost wholly) realized eschatology of John and the strongly future or two-age eschatology of Augustine. For both, the life of the church was an interim age between Egypt and the promised land, but for Augustine it still largely conformed to the past, while for John it largely conformed to the future.[34]

Origins of the Eschatological Distinction

In earlier patristic writers there tended to be a rough balance between the two poles of the paradox of now and not yet, perhaps tipping toward the "not yet." For instance, while one may expect Origen to have shown a realized eschatology akin to, say, John Cassian's, the shape of his discussion of the *epiousios* bread of the Lord's Prayer more closely resembled Augustine's: it is something that the soul needs in this world rather than something that it will enjoy in the next.[35] It appears that the distinction under study emerged in the period of John and Augustine, which suggests that we seek its origins among the developments that followed Constantine's conversion and the peace of the church.

At this point we come to territory studied by Rowan Greer that is quite relevant.[36] For example, Greer's "marvelous paradox" of the early Christian experience of living as if aliens yet as if citizens[37] is analogous to the eschatological paradox of now and not yet, and he contrasts Tertullian's and Clement's uses of this theme in ways that foreshadow the later contrast of eschatologies. Here, then, we need only sketch some leading points.

The conversion of Constantine deeply shaped the Byzantine understanding of history and so of eschatology. The data of a Christian emperor and gradually a Christian imperium challenged the old ambivalence to the contemporary world. Eusebius began what became the Orthodox response by interpreting this change through the political prophecies in Daniel.[38] History, this reading suggested, had entered a new era in which the world's institutions themselves were brought under Christ's yoke. Many people had been converted, but now society itself was to be converted, and the world made safe for theocracy. For our purposes, a positive understanding of the Christianization of the government and society had two effects, individual and communal.

Discussion of how God ruled in the faithful soul is found in Clement and Origen and many others, but it was always qualified, for the Christian's citizenship was not yet complete. Under a Christian emperor, however, this language could be understood in a more concrete fashion, and there emerged more definite affirmations of the possibilities for true angelic citizenship in this world. The ambiguity between the realms remained in later sources, yet not so much in the quality of the experience as in its temporary character.

Under a Christian emperor, moreover, the social aspect of the Christian experience could be more concretely grounded in this world. As the institutions of the society were Christianized, the Christian's experience of society could be given more positive value, and a socially oriented typology between this world and the next could be fleshed out, bringing type and antitype into a more exact correspondence.[39] We see this process in Theodore and especially in John, for whom Antioch's ambitions hinted at the glories of the heavenly Jerusalem.[40]

Eusebian political eschatology did not flourish in the West, however, in part because the imperial office itself was never held in such respect as in the East. The old, rich families in the West valued their traditions and independence, and prejudices against royal power had long pedigrees. Nor was the reputation of the imperium helped by the political crises of the early fifth century. This is one factor that makes it no surprise to see in Augustine a "disenchantment with the myth of the Theodosian Christian Roman Empire."[41]

Besides this stance toward imperial history, Augustine's future eschatology is tied to his movement in the 390s away from the fairly confident Platonism of his earlier writings. This movement is a complex process, and different authors highlight different aspects.[42] Continued study of the Bible is a basic part of the picture.[43] Greer speaks of the social aspect of Augustine's experience in the life of the church with its cult of the saints, wherein God's miracles demonstrate God's sovereignty.[44] Brown speaks of a loss of confidence in the future and a new need to understand the past, seen in a yearning that is "Romantic."[45] Markus speaks of a loss of confidence in one's ability to conform to God's order.[46] Rist traces how various philosophical questions were worked out under the influence of various philosophical traditions.[47] All of these illuminate, but I would like to touch on a topic whose measure seems not yet fully taken, namely, the role of skepticism.

Skepticism had been the public philosophy of the New Academy until the break between Antiochus of Askalon and his teacher, Philo of Larissa, in 87–86 BCE. Antiochus's rejection of Academic Skepticism opened the way to the development of Middle Platonism, with its eclecticism and dogmatism. The Skepticism of Philo of Larissa and earlier Academics, however, remained influential in Rome, as Cicero is witness.[48] Augustine was deeply affected by skeptical arguments, and took care early in his Christian career to refute Academic Skepticism,[49] although skeptical concerns remain influential. For instance,[50] partly to answer skeptical objections, Augustine came to restrict "knowledge" to what was directly experienced physically and what was manifest intellectually; the rest of what one accepted and used in life was in the category of "belief," which was based on some "authority." But, because of the strange nature of time, any experience in the past was no longer directly known; rather, it was believed on the authority of one's memory. One knew the present, had beliefs about the past, and was ignorant of the future, and people were presently restricted to this "fragmented" point of view; in the next world the saved would regain the "synoptic" view of time as wholly present which God always enjoys.[51] This argument, however, with its flank defended against skepticism, resulted in stressing the difference between the believer's life here and the life with God. Temporal experience and knowledge, common to saints and sinners, was of a radically different order than the life with God.

It is significant that others besides Augustine were convinced by his arguments, which were departures from the commonplace; here too, perhaps, a widespread affinity for skeptical concerns provided a background that made Augustine's arguments plausible. A cautious approach, informed by skepticism, to what can be known of and in this world would be open to the two-age eschatology based on promise and hope that prevailed in the West after Augustine.

Whatever the precise balance of influences, it appears that the contrast between Eastern and Western eschatologies emerged clearly in the later fourth century, largely under three influences. The first two were a spirituality informed by Middle Platonism and a political and social eschatology emerging from Constantine's conversion, which came to shape Byzantine thought, and the third was Augustine's mature synthesis with its extensive revisions of earlier opinions, which came to shape Latin and medieval thought.

Results of the Eschatological Distinction

While I have emphasized the differences between Augustine and the Antiochenes, it would be easy enough to emphasize the similarities. To Augustine's disillusionment with the Theodosian myth, we can match John, who in the catecheses contrasted the dishonor of the contemporary state practices with the holiness of the Master's celebrations,[52] and whose life in Constantinople and dealings with the Empress Eudoxia show someone quite aware of the dissimilarity between type and antitype, although he would struggle to bring them into greater accord. Theodore, as I observed above, saw the dissimilarities when he compared the church either to the past or to the future, as if there were an unresolved conflict in his mind about where the church belongs, perhaps like Augustine's conflict in now allowing, now denying, that there was overlap between the population of the two Cities.[53] Without seeking to harmonize all their views, one can suggest that they represent variations on a theme, exploring the ambiguities inherent in an unstable balance between now and not yet.

I have emphasized the differences, however, because they show the historical directions that the two traditions would take. The differing imbalances, developing parochially, reinforced themselves, leading to increasingly different understandings until two quite distinct communities emerged, although neither had meant this difference to define itself against the other.

The contrast between Western and Eastern eschatologies, in fact, turns out to be one of the marks of the deep fissure that separates Catholic and Orthodox traditions, and many examples can be given. One finds the Western emphasis on "not yet" prominent in St. Benedict as well as in St. Bernard; one finds the Eastern emphasis on "now" prominent in John Cassian as well as in Maximus the Confessor;[54] and, for an extreme example, one can contrast Gregory Palamas's realism with Ulrich Zwingli's sacramental theology.[55] While the initial variations on the theme of now and not yet do not appear intentionally or necessarily exclusive, they developed to become one reason why a Reformed theology, for example, or even a Roman Catholic theology, can appear incomprehensible to an Orthodox believer. Both traditions can show that their eschatologies are biblical; the appropriation of that evidence in different ways for sixteen centuries, however, has produced what seem separate compositions.

To end with an unresolved tension, however, need not be negative, as Greer himself proposes while discussing the marvelous "paradox of alien citizenship." As there, so here too we can see "the value of the tension produced by attempts to live out the paradox. A dialogue is created, and it can be argued that the Church is strongest when the dialogue is full."[56] A dialogue requires that there be two points of view on a subject and that the distinctions between them be understood. Clarifying how the Eastern and Western variations relate to the theme of "now and not yet" facilitates the mutual understanding on which a full dialogue depends.

NOTES

1. Any critical handbook can guide one through the eschatologies of the NT. Both elements of the paradox seem present in Judaism, not only the common future eschatology, but also a partly realized eschatology, e.g., at Qumran: 1QH 3.19–36; 11.3–14; 1QSa 2.11–22. Technical support from B-Stamp Productions, 000122, is gratefully acknowledged.

2. Still standard for M. 2 (*CPG* 4464) is PG 49, and for *Hom. princ. Act.* 1–4 (*IpA, CPG* 4371) is PG 51. For W. 1–2, 4–7 (*CPG* 4465–66 and 4468–72) and P.-K. 4 (*CPG* 463) see Antoine Wenger, *Huit catéchèses baptismales* (SC 50; Paris: Cerf, 1957), and for P.-K. 1–3 (*CPG* 460–462) see Auguste Piédagnel, *Trois catéchèses baptismales* (SC 366; Paris: Cerf, 1990).

In work in progress I demonstrate a different ordering of John's catecheses than is usually given. P.-K. 1 was given about thirty days before Easter. M. 2, W. 1–2, and P.-K. 2–3 were given on Wednesday and Thursday of Holy Week; W. 4 and P.-K. 4 at the Easter vigil; W. 5 on Easter day (as were *CPG* 4341 and 4408); W. 6 and *IpA* 1 on Easter Monday; and W. 7–8 and *IpA* 2–4 through the rest of Easter Week.

A proposed standard for abbreviations and citations is given in my review in *JECS* 3 (1995): 72–75. For M. 2, I will use the section numbering in Paul W. Harkins, *St. John Chrysostom: Baptismal Instructions* (ACW 31; Westminster, Md.: Newman, 1963). For the others, the SC numbering should now be standard. For P.-K. 1–3, I add Harkins's numbers in parentheses.

3. W. 1.1. See also W. 1.1–18 and P.-K. 3.1–2 (1–10). W. 6.24 and *CPG* 4408 §5: Easter week is like the seven-day wedding feast.

4. Documentation for this summary: Arnold Hugh Martin Jones, *The Later Roman Empire: 284–602* (Oxford: Basil Blackwell, 1964; repr. Baltimore: Johns Hopkins University Press, 1986) (abbr. *LRE*), esp. chaps. 15 (Senate and *Honorati*) and 16 (Civil Service); J. H. W. G. Liebeschuetz, *Antioch: City and Imperial Administration* (Oxford: Clarendon, 1972), and "Government and Administration in the Late Empire (to A.D. 476)," in his *From Diocletian to the Arab Conquest: Change in the Late Roman Empire* (Aldershot: Variorum, 1990); and John Matthews, *The Roman Empire of Ammianus* (Baltimore: Johns Hopkins University Press, 1989) (abbr. *RE of A*), esp. chaps. 12, 16. This picture applies more to the East than the West in the fourth century.

5. The importance of his presence is seen in the events around the accession of Jovian or the usurpation of Procopius. See, e.g., Ammianus Marcellinus, 26.7–9, and Matthews, *RE of A*, 191–203.

6. See Sabine MacCormack, *Art and Ceremony in Late Antiquity* (Berkeley: University of California Press, 1981), and M. McCormick, *Eternal Victory: Triumphal Rulership in Late Antiquity, Byzantium and the Early Medieval West* (Cambridge: Cambridge University Press, 1986). Consider, e.g., Constantius's visit to Rome in 357 described in Ammianus, 16, and Matthews, *RE of A*, 231–34.

7. See Jones, *LRE*, chap. 16 on the service in general; letters, *probatoriae*, 378; *dignitates* were conferred by the emperor and the ceremony must have been frequent and lengthy, 337. Patronage: Matthews, *RE of A*, 46–47, 78–80, and index, *s.v.*, 573, on Ammianus, and 271–74; also Jones, *LRE*, 387–88; 329–30; Liebeschuetz, *Antioch*, 192–208. It was the overturning of the imperial statues, a treasonous act, that precipitated the crisis in Antioch in 387.

8. On *adoratio:* William T. Avery, "The *Adoratio Purpurae* and the Importance of the Imperial Purple in the Fourth Century of the Christian Era," *Memoires of the*

American Academy in Rome 17 (1940): 66–80; Matthews, *RE of A*, 244–47. The *adoratio*, a sign of favor, relieved fear of the autocrat; see Ammianus, 5.17–20, discussed in Matthews, *RE of A*, 37.

9. That is, *despotes*, John's regular title for Christ throughout the catecheses. This refers specifically to the divine and ruling Word, and the human Jesus is all but absent.

10. P.-K. 2.3 (5–7): baptism is performed now because "now our King has won the war against the barbarians. For even more savage than barbarians are all the demons." In celebrating this victory at Easter, it is customary, as in the secular world, that royal gifts be distributed, a simile equating baptism with appointment to high office and rank. As in the world, in this triumphal celebration, some (the baptizands) will wear shining robes, receive a reward, *timē*, from the King, and be the Master's partners, *koinones*, during the season. See P.-K. 3.4 (20); P.-K. 3.9 (30–31).

11. John began the P.-K. series addressing his class as people about to receive a great honor and office, *timē kai archē*. In W. 2.12, the Holy Week catechesis and exorcism made the heart worthy of the king's presence, *axian tēs tou basileos parousias*. In W. 2.29, those about to be baptized were about to approach the throne of the king who apportions gifts. They were to show ambition, *philotimia*, in their requests, asking for spiritual gifts worthy of the giver. They gained him as an ally who had given them confidence, making them friends.

12. P.-K. 2.3 (6–7). The celebrations put on by secular, *exothen*, kings were full of shame and dishonor, P.-K. 2.3 (6). This would include Theodosius the Great.

13. E.g., W. 1.44–45; W. 4.17–18.

14. E.g., W. 4.3–4; W. 5.22. W. 4 and 5 recall imagery in W. 1 and 2.

15. E.g., W. 4.3, 5. P.-K. 2.6 (14–15): in exorcism they were naked, like captives, but paradoxically this was heavenly, returning them to their homeland, the heavenly Jerusalem, and making them citizens above.

16. Theodore's catecheses, *CPG* 3852, edited and translated in Alphonse Mingana, *Commentary of Theodore of Mopsuestia on the Nicene Creed and Commentary . . . on the Lord's Prayer and on the Sacraments . . .* (Woodbrooke Studies 5–6; Cambridge: W. Heffer, 1932–33), cited by volume, sermon in that volume, and page. W. S. 6.2.26 is p. 26 of vol. 6, from the second homily. Also, Raymond Tonneau and Robert Devreesse, *Les homélies catéchétiques de Théodore de Mopsueste* (Studi e Testi 145; Vatican City: Biblioteca Apostolica Vaticana, 1949).

17. W. S. 6.2.20–22.

18. See Jessie Payne Smythe, *A Compendious Syriac Dictionary* (Oxford: Clarendon, 1903), and William Jennings, *Lexicon to the Syriac New Testament* (Oxford: Clarendon, 1926), *s.v.* Jennings cites four NT texts: Luke 14:32; 19:14 (translating *presbeia*); 2 Cor 5:20; Eph 6:21. In Greer's discussion of this text, *Theodore of Mopsuestia: Exegete and Theologian* (Westminster, U.K.: Faith Press, 1961), 74–75, we should understand the direction to be from us to God, which in fact accords better with Greer's overall analysis.

19. The exactness of the correspondence is illustrated by John's different treatment of the same rites in W. 2.29.

20. R. A. Norris, *Manhood and Christ* (Oxford: Clarendon, 1963), 201, 233–34; on reason, 129–32; Greer, *Theodore*, 51–53. Norris and Greer speak of Theodore's thought in general, but the points can be illustrated from the catecheses: e.g., the unique bond of the union and the deputed prerogative of worship appear in W. S. 5.6.64, 66.

21. Of freedom: W. S. 6.3.47: the linen orarium given at baptism was a sign of freedom; 6.3.35: the "law suit" of exorcism gained freedom from servitude; and 6.1.3: prayer was a freedom to act. Norris, *Manhood*, 165, cites similarly *In prim. ep. ad Tim.* 2.1 (*CPG* 3845). The church itself had the form of the resurrection under Christ the *princeps*, from *In ep. ad Col.* (*CPG* 3845), discussed by Greer, *Theodore*, 76. The whole picture is also strongly shaped by scripture, a point basic to Greer's analysis. On these points, see Greer, *Theodore*, 74–77, 84–85; Norris, *Manhood*, 129–32, 145–46. A deputed freedom: W. S. 5.1.19: the gift was far above humanity's nature. Also Greer, *Theodore*, 66–67, 76–77.

22. W. S. 6.2.23–24: populous city; 6.2.24–27: church as type; 6.4.51–52 and 6.5: sacramental life; 5.1.20: the blest in heaven will be rulers and warriors of righteousness; and in general 6.1: the Christian life of prayer and good works was modeled on the heavenly free life, which implied that the heavenly free life is active and social.

23. This is clear in Theodore, see next note, but John's focus was primarily on this world. For instance, the robes of John's neophytes could remain a brilliant white for days, years, and even throughout life, M. 2.10; *IpA* 1.5; W. 5.19–23. John knew that this was a practical impossibility, P.-K. 3.5 (23) and W. 2.19, but John all but ignored the next world to concentrate on present zeal and advancement.

24. Theodore distinguished the church's life from both the post-resurrection world and from the previous world, so one might call it a third age, or perhaps better, a state sharing in both ages. When Theodore looked back to Adam or to Moses, he saw a much lower state: W. S. 5.1.20–21; 6.2.21–22, 27–30: Adam in Paradise could not compare with the Lord ruling in heaven; 6.1.6: Moses' law of slavery; 6.2.18–19: law and temple a shadow; 6.5.79–81: the old sacrificial system; 6.3.41–42: Judaising was a service of Satan spread by the angels of Satan; W. S. 5.2.27: the doctrine of the Trinity was a newly revealed truth withheld from previous ages. (These passages show a fundamental difference from Pelagius's thought.)

The present state was good: W. S. 6.1.6: it was a gift of God to Christians higher than the law of Moses, because the first law gave birth to servitude, but Christians received the grace to call God "Father"; 6.1.7: Christians lived lives in harmony with the heavenly Jerusalem, fleeing worldly concerns, and God was "Father" because of the freedom, honor, and greatness acquired; 6.1.8: good deeds corroborated that one was a child of God, worthy of freedom, and so on throughout the homily. W. S. 6.2.17–19: the sacrament's power, difference between Israel and church, reality of Christ's work, etc.

But the present is distinct from the future. Theodore began this series, W. S. 5.1.19–20, with a new song, for "death and corruption have ceased . . . and the life of the new creature has been made manifest, a life which we hope to reach after our resurrection." The manifested life may be Christ's, in which humans will share later. Furthermore, both sacraments were symbols (of baptism, the beginning of homily 4, W. S. 6.4.49–50; of the Eucharist, the beginning of homily 5, 6.5.71–72), and the second birth and the grace of the Holy Spirit were in truth only available in the resurrection, being present here only in faith marked by the symbols of the water and the bread.

When Theodore contrasted the church and the sacraments with earthly things, they were all but in heaven; when he spoke of them directly, heaven receded to the future age. Theodore seemed to contrast the church to the old world in the earlier sermons, and the church to the kingdom in the later sermons, as if he meant to move his hearers' attention from earthly things to heavenly. In any case, however, the church's ties to heaven were much more important than the ties to Israel.

On the idea of the Two Ages, and some of its attendant tensions, see the discussions in Norris, *Manhood*, chap. 13, and Greer, *Theodore*, esp. 76–78.

25. Famously, John's Christology looks Alexandrine; but notice here how congruent their anthropologies are. Also, compare their uses of Jer 18:1–6 in W. S. 6.4.56–57 and P.-K. 1.14–15 (23–26), where the shared outline was developed differently by each.

26. Considering especially his *De catechizandis rudibus, Sermo de symbolo ad catechumenos,* and some of his Easter sermons, collected and translated in Philip T. Weller, *Selected Easter Sermons of Saint Augustine* (St. Louis: B. Herder, 1959).

27. This whole pattern is found in *Serm.* 353 (Weller no. 26) §2 and *Serm. Mai* 89 (Weller no. 16). The font is like the Red Sea: *Catech.* 20.34 and *Serm.* 213.8; this image is of course old and widespread. Contrast, however, John's discussion in M. 2.16; P.-K. 4.12, 15.

28. *Serm.* 56 on the Lord's Prayer (Weller no. 29) §10: the bread itself is the word of God distributed in the churches (how very Lutheran). *Serm. Guelf.* 9.4 (Weller no. 18); *Serm. Denis* 8 (Weller no. 25); *Symb.* 3.10; *Catech.* 17.26.

29. Example of the Lord, in cross and in humility: *Symb.* 3.6, 10; *Catech.* 19.33 (Abraham saw the future humility of the Lord); 20.36; 22.40; 27.55; *Serm.* 213.4. Toil and obedience of this world: *Serm. Guelf.* 9.4 (Weller no. 18). Rest and contemplation in the next world: *Catech.* 17.27; 19.31–33; 25.47; 26.52; 27.54. Christ's humility is a touchstone for Augustine.

30. *Catech.* 25.47: in the next world, one is made equal to angels to see the Trinity in fervent contemplation in heavenly silence. Also *Catech.* 27.54.

31. W. 7 was preached at a tomb of martyrs. In W. 7.3–4, John referred to the throng who gathered there to honor them, holding up their honor among people and *parrēsia* before the Master as objects worthy of zealous imitation. Their example should fire one's ambition to be equally successful.

32. John's devil was cowardly, and a good show of force drove him away, W. 2.23; W. 4.5; P.-K. 3.7 (27); P.-K. 4.11–12.

33. The stark difference between the two experiences of the kingdom is clear also in *Civ.* 20.17.

34. In passing, consider the role of memory. For Augustine, memory integrated one's self, including one's evil, into a whole. Robert Markus, *Conversion and Disenchantment in Augustine's Spiritual Career* (Villanova, Pa.: Villanova University Press, 1989), discusses Augustine's view of the self-shaping power of memory in his opposition to the perfectionisms of Manichaeism, Donatism, and Pelagianism. To his disenchantments with perfectionism, Markus adds those with Platonists' comprehensible cosmos and with the "Theodosian myth of the Christian Roman Empire" (p. 41).

John, to the contrary, urged his catechumens to forget the past like new brides, as Ps 45:11 instructs, W. 1.6–15. In joining a new household, they were to break with the old. John Cassian also counseled forgetting the past in *Conf.* 1.5, citing Phil 3:13–14. How different from the verse's use in Augustine, *Conf.* 9.10!

35. *Or.* 27.13, 7–9, where also he reported but rejects the idea that *epiousios* referred to "tomorrow's" bread requested for "today," which in fact was Cassian's view, *Conf.* 9.19–21. In *Or.* 25–26 Origen was ambiguous about the quality of the kingdom's presence. His position was of course rooted in the individual and spiritual.

36. Namely, in Greer's books *Broken Lights and Mended Lives* (University Park: Pennsylvania State University Press, 1986) and *The Fear of Freedom* (University Park: Pennsylvania State University Press, 1989).

37. Greer, *Broken Lights,* chap. 6.

38. Eusebius's point shaped his conception of church history, as *Hist. eccl.* 1. makes clear; it emerged from the panegyrical works on Constantine as well. Besides Greer's work, one can enter into the literature on this historical eschatology through the articles in Alexander Kazhdan, ed., *Oxford Dictionary of Byzantium* (4 vols.; New York: Oxford University Press, 1991), *s.v.* "Eschatology," etc. Central to Greer's *Fear of Freedom* are the post-Eusebian shift of emphasis from a theology of virtue to a theology of the sacred commonwealth and the development of a new Augustinian synthesis marked by grace and obedience. Robert A. Markus, *Saeculum: History and Society in the Theology of St Augustine* (rev. ed.; Cambridge: Cambridge University Press, 1988), similarly studies these shifting theologies and eschatologies from a complementary perspective.

39. These are central aspects of the theological changes studied in Greer's *Fear of Freedom,* e.g., 124.

40. For related points, see G. Downey, "Polis and civitas in Libanius and St. Augustine: A Contrast between East and West," *Académie Royale de Belgique, Bulletin de la Classe des Lettres* 52 (1966): 351–66.

41. Markus, *Conversion,* 41–42. Also relevant is the discussion of sin and society, 34–41, which talks about the limited order of this age. Markus, *Saeculum,* discusses Augustine's rejection of the Eusebian and older "apocalyptic" eschatologies in the process of his broader analysis of society, e.g., 56–63.

42. In particular I refer to Peter Brown, *Augustine of Hippo* (Berkeley: University of California Press, 1967), esp. chap. 15; Markus, *Conversion* and *Saeculum;* John Rist, *Augustine: Ancient Thought Baptized* (Cambridge: Cambridge University Press, 1994); and Greer, *Broken Lights* and *Fear of Freedom.*

43. The importance of *Div. Quaest. Simpl.* is widely noted, including by Augustine, *Retract.* 2.1 (27).

44. Greer, *Fear of Freedom*, 179.

45. Brown, *Augustine*, 156–57.

46. Markus, *Conversion*, 24–33, 41. This "disenchantment" with a Platonic confidence is tied to his "disenchantment with the myth of the Theodosian Christian Roman Empire" (pp. 41–42).

47. Rist, *Augustine*, esp. chap. 3, "Certainty, Belief, and Understanding."

48. On these points, see Paul Kristeller, *Greek Philosophers of the Hellenistic Age* (New York: Columbia University Press, 1993), and John Dillon, *The Middle Platonists* (Ithaca, N.Y.: Cornell University Press, 1977). Middle Platonism was eclectic in believing in a basic consensus of the early Academics, Peripatetics, and Stoics, exclusive of Skeptical and Epicurean ideas; Skepticism seems moribund in the East. The epistemological difference between Skepticism and the dogmatic claims of Middle Platonism resembles our distinction between eschatologies. In Middle Platonism, the goal of humanity was to become like god, *homoiōsis theōi.* This was the philosophy that Philo Judaeus found in the books of Moses and which underlay the theologies of Clement of Alexandria, Origen, and the Orthodox tradition in general. Orthodox theologians, of course, would insist that the soul's ability to know God directly is something given or returned to it through God's grace, a point separating them profoundly from both Plotinus and Pelagius.

49. Skeptical arguments helped lead Augustine from Manichaeism, *Conf.* 5.14.25. The refutation is found most obviously in *Contra academicos*, extensively dependent on Cicero. See also Rist, *Augustine*, 42–43, who notes that his refutation was aimed at "'global' [Skepticism], doubtful of *any* claim to knowledge" (p. 43).

50. The following is taken from Rist, *Augustine*, 73–85, "Time, Memory, and Illumination."

51. Rist, *Augustine*, 84–85.

52. P.-K. 2.3 (6).

53. Markus, *Saeculum*, 59.

54. For Benedict, see the Prologue to the Rule; for Bernard, see the homilies on the Song of Songs in P. Matarasso, *The Cistercian World: Monastic Writings of the Twelfth Century* (London: Penguin Books, 1993), 65–83. For Cassian, see *Conf.* 10–11; for Maximus on the Lord's Prayer, see G. E. H. Palmer, Philip Sherrard, and Kallistos Ware, eds., *The Philokalia* . . . (London: Faber & Faber, 1981), 2:285–305.

55. Generally, one can consult Aristeides Papadakis and Alexander Kazhdan, "Palamas" and "Palamism," *Oxford Dictionary of Byzantium*, 3:1560–62, and for Zwingli, Alister E. McGrath, *Reformation Thought: An Introduction* (2nd ed.; Oxford: Blackwell, 1993), 170–81.

56. Greer, *Broken Lives*, 160.

Vision of God and Scripture Interpretation in a Fifth-Century Mosaic

WAYNE A. MEEKS &
MARTHA F. MEEKS

Sometime in the reign of the iconoclastic emperor Leo V "the Armenian" (813–820), a monk named Senouphios "in the hills of Nitria in Egypt" heard a voice from heaven directing him to go "to the monastery in Thessaloniki called 'of the stonecutters' (Λατόμων)." Senouphios "had been begging God for a long time to be allowed to see him as he would come to judge the earth"; hearing this clear answer to his prayer, he set off at once with only his cloak and staff. After many adventures he arrived in the distant metropolis, only to be told by the monks that there was no image in Thessaloniki like the one he was seeking. Dejected by the thought he had been deceived by the Devil, the old monk returned to Egypt—only to have the heavenly oracle repeated more urgently. Once more he trudged the long way back to Thessaloniki. This time he was rewarded. As he sat alone one day in the sanctuary of the Stonecutters' Monastery,

> suddenly there was a storm and an earthquake and, moreover, thunder and such a disturbance that it seemed the very foundations of the sanctuary were shaken. And immediately the mortar and the brickwork with the ox hide that overlay the sacred representation of the Lord . . . were stripped off and fell to the earth. Those sacred features of Christ appeared, shining with fiery appearance like the sun in the midst of the cloud. When the

Apse Mosaic, Church of Hosios David (earlier Latomou), Thessaloniki. Photograph by John Dean, reprinted courtesy of Thomas F. Mathews.

old monk, standing in the midst of the sanctuary, saw this, he cried aloud, "Glory to you, O God, I thank you," and relinquished his blessed soul.[1]

The story of Senouphios's vision, the "Miracle of the Latomou," became an important part of Salonican lore. In the twelfth century a certain Ignatius, abbot of another monastery, wrote it down.[2] Sometime after 1430, when the Turks captured Thessaloniki, the monks abandoned Latomou Monastery[3] and it vanished from the records. After the restoration of Thessaloniki to Greek rule in 1912, Latomou was listed among the city's monasteries that no longer survived. The Suluca Mosque that stood in northeastern Thessaloniki was identified in 1917 as the former Church of Hosios David ("the Blessed David"), and in 1921 the building, now severely damaged, was reconsecrated to that local ascetic. Andreas Xyngopoulos, Superintendent of Byzantine Antiquities, explored the church. When he first examined the apse in March 1921 and saw a portion of the mosaic where the thick Turkish plaster had fallen, Xyngopoulos's astonishment must have approached that of Senouphios more than a millennium earlier. Fortunately, Xyngopoulos's soul was not required of him, and he conducted a detailed investigation of the mosaic and of the other features of the site. Charles Diehl recognized that the mosaic was exactly the one described vividly in Abbot Ignatius's "Edifying Account" and that the church must accordingly be that of the former Latomou monastery.[4] The date of the mosaic has been debated ever since its rediscovery, and no certainty has been achieved. However, most art historians place it sometime in the fifth century.[5]

The Image

What was this image that brought such rapture to the ninth-century monk and such excitement to art historians of the twentieth century? Still startling today in its sheer beauty, it obviously deserves Diehl's epithet, "un chef-d'oeuvre de l'art chrétien," and is remarkable not only for its location in a small, undistinguished building and for its early date, but also for its unusual combination of iconic motifs (see Figure).[6] A youthful, beardless Christ sits on a rainbow within a bright, circular *clipeus*, which is also streaked with multicolored clouds, their lines forming a counterpoint to the downward curve of the rainbow. His golden nimbus is inscribed with a cross in red outline. His hair, shoulder-length, repeats the circle of the nimbus in a mass around his roundish face; his expression is serene but somber. He wears a crimson *chiton* decorated with two full-length gold stripes, the left one visible only at the hem, just above golden sandals, and a purplish-blue *himation* that covers his left shoulder and arm and the lower part of his body. His right arm is extended, with the palm open, upward; the left holds an open scroll, on which is inscribed the slightly modified text of Isa 25:9–10: "Behold our God, on whom we put our hope, and we have rejoiced in our salvation, for he will give rest to this house."[7] The clipeus is translucent; through it we see parts of the wings of four creatures that support it: clockwise, beginning by the right hand of Christ, a human figure, an eagle, a bull, and a lion, realistically modeled. Each carries a large, red, jewel-encrusted book. The human figure wears a nimbus; the others do not. The wings are full of eyes, outlined in gold. The wings of the bull are divided by lengthwise lines into three segments each.

In rocky landscapes on either side of the Christ are two human figures in grayish-white *himatia* over blue-gray *chitones*. Both heads have nimbuses. On Christ's right stands an old man with long, pointed beard. He bows deeply from the waist, and his hands are thrown up close beside his face, each palm open forward and thumbs extended near his eyes. Opposite him sits a beardless man of uncertain age, legs crossed, right hand supporting his chin and left holding an open codex. His contemplative pose forms a stark contrast to the agitated stance of the other. The book's inscription reads: "This most honorable house [is] a life-giving, welcoming, nourishing spring for the souls of the faithful." The same text stretches, in large silver letters on a red band, along the lower border of the whole mosaic, with the dedicatory addition, "Having made a vow, I attained [the object of my prayer], and having attained, I fulfilled [my vow]. For her vow, whose name God knows."[8]

Just above the border inscription meanders a great, green river, extending from just below the feet of the left-hand seer to just below the seated figure on the right. Left of center, just beneath the lion, the conventional personification of the river strikes an unconventional pose. As green as the river and almost indistinguishable from its waves, this bearded figure reclines, visible only from waist up, and with staring eyes and upraised hand appears to react with terror to the vision above. The gesture resembles that of the human figure on our left; the river person could almost be taken as the seer's reflection in the water. Three large, colorful fish swim in the river. In the center, directly beneath Christ's feet, five spits of land divide the waters, four central streams that are marked off as if by islands from the main river.

Biblical Motifs

When Xyngopoulos first examined the small area of the mosaic visible to him in March 1921—the winged lion, the edge of the clipeus, and the upper half of the left-hand seer—he immediately judged that "the whole composition in all likelihood had as its theme the vision of the prophet Ezekiel, with the description of which (Ezek 1:4ff.) it agrees almost entirely. The old man beside the lion appears to be Ezekiel himself, seeing the vision."[9] Xyngopoulos held fast to this interpretation when he had completed the cleaning of the whole apse in 1929, reinforced now by his knowledge of the twelfth-century "Edifying Narrative," which identified the two seers as Ezekiel and Habakkuk respectively.[10] Moreover, a fourteenth-century icon in the National Archaeological Museum in Sofia, originally in the Poganovo monastery, clearly depends in some way on the Salonican mosaic and identifies "Ezekiel" and "Habakkuk" with labels.[11] Most commentators agree that Ezekiel's "Chariot" vision is constitutive, though the identity of the two seers, especially the "Habakkuk," is still debated. Nevertheless, there are obvious problems with the supposition that the mosaic *represents* Ezekiel's vision.

First of all, the "chariot" and its elaborately described wheels are missing from the Latomou mosaic, as indeed is a *throne* of any kind. Comparison with the depictions of the vision in the monastic chapels of Bawit, Egypt, otherwise strikingly similar, and with the Ascension in the Rabula Gospels Codex shows how these features could be emphasized if the text of Ezekiel were more in control of the image.[12] Second, the four living creatures that support the light-globe within which Christ sits are not the four-faced "tetramorphs" seen by Ezekiel and often represented in later Eastern Christian art (including the Rabula Ascension, which however shows only one of them), but the four symbols of the Evangelists, derived from the rewritten or revisioned apparition in Revelation 4. That symbolism—indeed any influence by the Apocalypse—is unusual in art of the early Eastern church, so that one reviewer categorically denied the possibility of their presence in Thessaloniki. They are, nevertheless, unmistakable.[13] The puzzle grows when we remember that the one direct quotation from scripture in the mosaic's inscriptions is neither from Ezekiel nor from Habakkuk, but from Isaiah— yet there is no feature of the composition that recalls Isaiah's great theophany (Isa 6:1–5). (The Poganovo icon "corrects" this anomaly by providing an Ezekiel quotation—but in the hand of the figure it labels "Habakkuk"!)

Before we can get further in understanding the biblical allusions in the composition, we must rid ourselves of the Western (and especially Protestant) assumption that early Christian art *illustrates* the Bible ("the Bible of the poor"). Christa Ihm has collected a half dozen examples of apse decorations that parallel the Latomou mosaic. She concludes "that none of the apse images follows a specific [biblical] report; rather each time motifs from Ezekiel are freely combined with others from Isaiah and John [of Patmos]."[14] She argues that the imagery is mediated by the liturgy, which had already merged the theophanies of Isaiah, Ezekiel, and the Apocalypse and freely varies their details—just as the iconography does.[15] This insight surely puts us on the right track. However, we may also doubt whether the function of the apse decoration was primarily to illustrate the liturgy any more than to illustrate the Bible. If illustration had been its central purpose, we would be hard put to understand the passion on both sides in the iconoclastic controversies. Rather, liturgy, art, and preaching worked together to mediate an experience of worship. Biblical motifs, if not always particular biblical narratives, richly inform all three. We can still see the tradition of biblical allusion alive in the language of Abbot Ignatius's twelfth-century "Edifying Narrative."

The legend of Senouphios may also contain a clue to the way we should understand the unique melding of motifs in our mosaic. What the aged monk prayed for above all else was *a vision of God*. There is, of course, a long biblical and post-biblical tradition about the possibility of seeing God and about what those ancient worthies who are said in the Bible to have seen the deity really saw. Before we consider the connection of that tradition with the Latomou mosaic, it will be useful to list the mosaic's most important motifs and the biblical texts that might have suggested each of them.

The *clipeus*, the translucent globe of light that surrounds the Christ, is a central feature of the composition. As the art historian Thomas Mathews points out, it is not at all like the Roman shield image, *imago clipeata*, which has given this motif its common designation among art historians. The earliest extant Christian example is on a mosaic in the Catacomb of S. Domatilla in Rome, dated by Mathews between 366 and 384. Because of striking parallels in earlier images of the Buddha, Mathews thinks the motif may have been borrowed from India or Central Asia.[16] Be that as it may, the form it takes at Latomou vividly recalls Ezekiel's initial vision, which was of "a great cloud" borne by a north wind, with "splendor (φέγγος) around it and fire flashing, and in its midst as it were an appearance of electrum in the midst of the fire and splendor in it" (Ezek 1:4 LXX).[17] After describing the appearance of the four animals, the prophet says further that "above their heads, the heads of the animals, there was something like a firmament (στερέωμα) like the appearance of crystal, stretched out above [or, upon] their wings above" (v. 22).

It is surely this description that, directly or indirectly, suggested to the artist the translucency of the globe, which he has produced by technically brilliant modulation of the colors of the tesserae.[18]

Fire and light typically accompany biblical theophanies; they are particularly associated with the "glory" of God, and Ezekiel summarizes his vision with the words, "this is the appearance of the likeness of the glory (δόξα) of the Lord" (v. 28, cf. 10:19). So in Israel's classic theophany, at Sinai, "The form of the glory of the Lord was like flaming fire (πῦρ φλέγον) on the brow of the mountain before the sons of Israel" (Exod 24:17 LXX). The Greek version of the theophany reported in the "Prayer of Habakkuk" (Hab 3) reduces the light imagery in comparison with the Hebrew original, but it retains the line "his brightness (φέγγος) is like light (φῶς)" (v. 4) and the consternation of sun and moon at the brightness of God's weapons (v. 11). Dan 7:9 compares the throne to a "flame of fire" (φλὸξ πυρός); a river of fire flows forth from before God (v. 10). John of Patmos sees a throne from which come lightning and thunder, but the constant flame now is confined to "seven lamps burning before the throne" (Rev 4:5). Of all these, Ezekiel's description has most in common with the mosaic.

At the center of Ezekiel's vision, as of the Latomou mosaic, is a human figure, which Ezekiel describes with great circumspection: "the likeness, as it were, of the form of a human person above" (ὁμοίωμα ὡς εἶδος ἀνθρώπου ἄνωθεν), upon "the likeness of a throne" that resembled "the appearance of sapphire stone," standing on the crystal firmament (v. 26). This corresponds to the description of the Sinai theophany in Exod 24:10, though there the throne is not mentioned, and the sapphire is a "pavement (ἔργον πλίνθου) like the appearance of the firmament of heaven for clearness." That God was seen as a human figure in the theophanies seems generally to be taken for granted, though seldom explicitly stated—after all, humans had been created "in [God's] image, according to [his] likeness" (Gen 1:26). Only later Jewish interpreters would find anthropomorphism a problem, the human figure in heaven a puzzle, and especially the two figures of Daniel 7 ("an Ancient of Days," vv. 9, 13, "like a human's son," v. 13), both enthroned, a dangerous notion. All these anomalies were welcome, of course, to Christian interpreters; Abbot Ignatius calls our composition θεανδρικός εἰκών, "a God-manly image." These are matters to which we shall return. The throne is visible in most of the biblical theophanies: beside Ezekiel and Daniel, Isa 6:1; 1 Kings 22:19; and throughout John's Apocalypse (cf. also Heb 8:1; 12:2). It is also a frequent motif in depictions of Christ in Christian art. But in Latomou there is no throne. Christ "perches on a most unsubstantial rainbow."[19] This

is one of the most original aspects of the Latomou composition, and it has
no precise counterpart in the biblical descriptions. The source is most likely
Ezek 1:28, which says that "the nature (στάσις) of the brightness around
[the human figure]" was "like the appearance of a bow (τόξον), when it is
in the cloud on a rainy day." This in turn clearly alludes to God's covenant
with Noah and his offspring: "I place my bow (i.e., the weapon of war) in the
cloud. It shall be a sign of the covenant between me and the earth" (Gen 9:13;
cf. vv. 12–17). In John's description of his vision, the allusion to the covenant
is obscured by his use of ἶρις instead of τόξον. The rainbow is now "around
the throne," and it also borrows from Ezekiel's throne "the appearance of em-
erald" (Rev 4:3).[20] In none of these instances is the figure *seated on* the rainbow.[21]

The four winged animals who bear the translucent aureole also recall
Ezekiel's vision (Ezek 1:5–11, 15, 19, 20, 22–24; cf. 10:8–22, where they are
identified as "cherubim"), but with significant differences, as we have already
noticed. In Ezekiel each creature has four faces, of man, lion, bull, and eagle
respectively. It is the Apocalypse that has revised this to four different creatures, one each like man, lion, bull, and eagle (Rev 4:6–8). In the Prayer of
Habakkuk (which is also one of the Odes of the Greek church), God is made
known "between two animals" (ἐν μέσῳ δύο ζῴων, Hab 3:2), recalling the
two seraphs of Isa 6:2. Psalm 67:11 LXX also speaks of God's ζῷα, which
dwell in his inheritance; this Psalm also speaks of God's "chariotry" with which
he appears at Sinai (v. 18).[22] The animals of Ezekiel's vision have each four
wings (Ezek 1:11), while Isaiah's seraphs have six, as do the creatures seen by
John of Patmos. The Latomou creatures have two.[23] The cherubim of the tab-
ernacle and of the Jerusalem temple also seem to have had only two wings
(Exod 25:20; 1 Kings 6:23–27; 2 Chron 3:11–12; we are not told whether the
cherubim on the walls of the new temple envisioned by Ezekiel had wings,
though they had each two faces, of a man and of a lion: Ezek 41:18–19). The
wings of the creatures on our mosaic are full of eyes, corresponding to Rev 4:8.
In Ezek 1:18 it is the backs (νῶτοι) that are full of eyes, while in Ezek 10:12 the
wings also are full of eyes, but so are backs, hands, and wheels. We may wonder whether these mysterious eyes were identified with the "eyes of the Lord"
that, according to 2 Chron 16:9, oversee the entire earth, and which are represented by the seven lamps on the golden lampstand in Zechariah's vision
(Zech 4:10).

At the center of the meandering water on the lower border of the composition, five irregular bars of land divide the flood into four small channels—
while the larger river goes on its way around them. The motif, found in many
examples in early Christian art, recalls the account in the creation narrative of

a river that flows from Eden and divides into four streams (Gen 2:10–14).[24] If we were not familiar with this motif, we would be tempted to count six rather than four streams here, for the large river does not so much divide into the others as contain them—as if two motifs were being merged. The upward curve of the river and of the five land spits, accentuated by the curve of the wings of lion and bull, suggests the shape of the hill from which the rivers flow in many other representations. But of course Christ does not stand or sit enthroned on a hill here, but above the mountainous landscape in his aureole. It is plausible that the artist has seen examples of the hill of paradise with its four streams and incorporates it here, but adapts it to a different schema in which the great river full of fish is the dominant feature. Those interpreters who take the mosaic simply to represent Ezekiel's first vision are content to regard this as the River Chebar (Greek Χοβαρ), scene of that vision (Ezek 1:1, 3).[25] But something more is going on here.

Several biblical texts take up the river image in eschatological contexts. In Zech 14:8, "living water" will flow from Jerusalem "in that day," in which "the Lord will become king over all the earth." In Joel 4:18, a spring (πεγή) will flow "from the house of the Lord." In Rev 22:1, "a river of the water of life, bright as crystal," flows "from the throne of God and of the Lamb" through the New Jerusalem. But perhaps closest to our scene is the river Ezekiel sees in his temple vision (Ezek 47:1–12), which has contributed to the final vision of John's Apocalypse as well. The water flows from "beneath the threshold of the temple (οἶκος)" (v. 1). It becomes a river too deep to cross (v. 5), which makes healthy all water it touches and makes alive every animal it comes upon (v. 9). Its fish are "a very great multitude, like the fish of the Great Sea" (v. 10). We remember the double inscription that describes this church itself (οἶκος) as "a life-giving, welcoming, nourishing spring."

There remains the peculiar personification of the river, the green, grimacing figure who emerges from the water just below the lion and mirrors the gesture of the prophet to the left. Of course the river god or personification is a familiar feature of Hellenistic and Roman art, and it was widely adopted by the early Christians. But one has only to compare, for example, the powerful, serenely seated figure of the Jordan in the Arian Baptistery of Ravenna to see how different this one is. As J.-M. Spieser says, "We are far from the Jordan, witness of baptism; on the contrary, we have an image of the Jordan as pagan divinity, indeed as a demon that turns away and flees before the conquering Christ."[26] Ihm points out that the Jordan could take on this "demonic" guise on the basis of Psalm 114:3 (LXX 113:3), "The sea looked and fled, the Jordan turned back."[27] The motif of hostile waters, ultimately derived perhaps from the common ancient Near Eastern myth of the chaos-dragon, appears also in the theophany report in the Prayer of Habakkuk: "Were you angry with rivers, Lord, or was your wrath against rivers, or your rage against sea?" (Hab 3:8). "You rode your horses into the sea, greatly troubling the water" (v. 15). On the other hand, the beneficent river Ezekiel saw flowing from the new Temple could also be identified with the Jordan, as in a fragment by Severus of Antioch (ca. 465–538) quoted by Neuss.[28]

Our survey of biblical passages to which the motifs of the Latomou mosaic might allude amply vindicates Ihm's observation that it does not illustrate a particular text. On the other hand, it is not a pastiche of the three great theophanies Ihm cites, Isa 6:1–5, Ezekiel 1, and Revelation 4. There are more features of the composition that recall Ezekiel's visions than any other, but elements of the Apocalypse are also undeniable, and there are more or less probable allusions to many other texts, most of them also theophanic. Yet, despite the quotation from Isaiah on the codex held by the prophet, there is no element of Isaiah's vision report that is recognizable here. Biblical allusions abound; they are combined with great freedom yet with compelling visual logic. We are presented, not with a copy of Ezekiel's vision or John's vision, but with an extraordinary artist's vision that certainly was intended to respond to the desire of worshippers, like the monk Senouphios, to see God.

Visualizing the Unseeable

When Moses asked the same favor as Senouphios, God replied, "You cannot see my face, for no human person shall see my face and live" (Exod 33:20). Yet other texts of the Bible seem to contradict this prohibition. Earlier in the same chapter we are told that "the Lord spoke to Moses face to face, as one would speak to his friend" (33:11; cf. Num 12:8; Deut 34:10), and Moses and his companions, including seventy elders, "saw the God of Israel"; "God did not lay his hand on the chief men of the people of Israel; also they beheld God, and they ate and drank" (Exod 24:10–11, NRSV). The Septuagint translators, doubtless troubled by the contradiction, emended the last-cited passage to read "they saw *the place where God stood*." But there were other perplexing passages as well; for example, both Isaiah and Micaiah said simply, "I saw the Lord, seated on his throne" (Isa 6:1; 1 Kings 22:19), and the Old Greek translators left the scandal unchanged.

We have noticed how circumspectly Ezekiel described his vision at the river Chebar, with his "as" and "likeness" and "appearance." Nevertheless, that description exercised a powerful and sometimes troubling fascination over subsequent generations of interpreters and, perhaps, mystics, creating the elusive "Merkava tradition."[29] What was the "likeness as of a human form above" that Ezekiel saw "on the likeness of the throne"? Was it the same as that enigmatic "one like a human son" that Daniel saw enthroned with "the one ancient of days"? What was a human figure doing in heaven? If God could not be seen nor imaged, what did those prophets and their predecessors see? We know something about the ways Jewish interpreters from antiquity to the early middle ages tried to solve those puzzles and others that arose from the theophanic texts. We know, for example, how Philo read the Pentateuch's reports of visions and descriptions of the Ark and the Cherubim. He found in them appearances, not of God himself, who revealed himself to Moses simply as "the One who Is," ὁ ὤν, but of God's Logos and his Powers.[30] We know that "the Lord" seen by Moses, Isaiah, Micaiah, and the others could be understood by some readers as the highest angel, the one of whom God said, "My name is in him" (Exod 23:20–21).[31] We know that sometimes that angelic figure could be identified as the heavenly counterpart of Israel, either seated on God's throne or engraved as an image on that throne.[32] We know that in later speculation this figure could become "the little Yahweh" or "Yaoel" or "Metatron," and we know that some rabbis worried over those who might think there were "two powers in heaven."[33]

For the careful reader of the biblical stories of God's appearances, there were at least three problems. One was that, though it was either forbidden or impossible to see God, nevertheless a number of important personages claimed to have done so. The second was the appearance of a human figure in heaven, sometimes apparently equated with God, sometimes alongside God. The third was that there was no consistency among the appearances: details of the heavenly scene vary wildly from one report to the next. In some circles the second problem could be construed as a solution of sorts to the first. One could not in fact see God; the "Lord" seen by Isaiah, Micaiah, and Moses was God's subaltern, the highest angel who bore God's own name. That solution, of course, created new problems for those Jews who wanted to assert a more absolute monotheism, and it further complicated the chimeric variation of the reported heavenly scene.

Christian interpreters early on discovered in the contradictions a christological opportunity. "No one has ever seen God," the Fourth Gospel affirms; "a unique one, also 'God,' who is in the bosom of the Father—he has brought out the knowledge [of God]" (1:18).[34] And that Gospel's Jesus could tell his disciple, "Whoever has seen me has seen the Father" (14:9). Even earlier, Paul had read the Genesis creation story in the light of Ezekiel's and Daniel's visions to identify the risen Christ with "the second Adam," "the man from heaven," "a life-giving spirit"—that same human figure that appeared in the theophanies.[35] Elements of the visions of Ezekiel, Daniel, Isaiah, and Zechariah blend freely together in John's description of his vision on Patmos (Rev 4–5). Once the sect of the followers of Messiah Jesus began in their practice to discover the impulse to worship Jesus (e.g., Phil 2:10–11), to expect from him forgiveness of sins (e.g., Mark 2:5–9), to anticipate his "day" of vindication before the world (e.g., 1 Thess 5:2), a day in which he would judge the world, as the Son of Man (e.g., John 5:27)—once, in short, their practice implied that functions and names of the risen Christ were also functions and names of God, then those most ambiguous and troubling accounts of theophanies in the Jewish scriptures became the most welcome grist for the Christian reinterpretive mill.[36] Justin Martyr found the preincarnate Logos—"another God"—not only in the theophanies, but in appearances of angels and archangels and in any odd-looking reference to the Lord that might be other than God the Father.[37] Many others would take up the same quest for visions of Christ in the scriptures that were coming to be known as "the Old Testament."

Though occasionally Ezekiel's vision played a key role in the christological development, on the whole it did not attract much attention among patristic writers—at least in the surviving remains. The story of the valley of dry bones (Ezekiel 37) was treated more often, as an obvious support for the belief in the resurrection of the dead. The chariot vision was usually assimilated in the West to that of Revelation 4, and, beginning with Irenaeus, the four creatures were taken to represent both the powers of God or Christ and the Gospels.[38] Origen, however, wrote a twenty-five-book commentary on Ezekiel, only small fragments of which survive, as well as a number of homilies, of which fourteen are extant in Latin.[39] One of Origen's interpretive moves was to make Ezekiel himself a type of Christ, so that the vision represents Christ's vision at baptism (and Chebar then is equated with the Jordan) of a greater baptism he must undergo "in the course of the aeons."[40] David Halperin has shown that, though most of Origen's allegory is quite unlike Jewish exegesis, it has important connections with the "Visions of Ezekiel" found in the Cairo Geniza. From the latter, along with fragments found in midrashic collections, Halperin reconstructs a cycle of synagogue homilies that he thinks were preached in Caesarea around the festival of *Shevu'ot* in the third century and were at the core of the developing "Merkava" tradition.[41] There is other evidence that Origen carried on an extensive, if partly covert, dialogue with the

Caesarean rabbis of his time, centering on the interpretation of scriptural texts.[42] If Halperin is right that Ezekiel's chariot vision was one of them, that dialogue marks an important intersection of Jewish and Christian readings of the theophanic texts. There appears, in the fragmentary remaining evidence, no direct road from that third-century dialogue in Caesarea to the fifth-century vision in Thessaloniki. There are enough clues, however, to enable us to surmise two parallel tracks: one leading on to further development of the merkava tradition into more speculative forms, including the so-called *Hekalot* texts, and its exploitation for magical and mystical aims; the other, to the manifestation of the heavenly Christ, borne on the chariot of the cherubim, to worshippers assisted by image, liturgy, music, and the transformation of the host at the climax of the Eucharist.[43] Both tracks were in fact multiple, with many local variations. What the Jewish and Christian tracks had in common was preoccupation with roughly the same set of problematical texts, together with a powerful drive to visualize what heaven was really like and what that vision promised for human hopes. "Behold our God," proclaims the Christ of Latomou, "on whom we put our hope, and we have rejoiced in our salvation, for he will give rest to this house."

The variety of the theophanic texts, which as we have seen is reflected in the ambiguity of reference of the Latomou composition and has thus led to such diversity in modern attempts to pin down just what that composition purports to image, has its own intentional meaning for the theological interpreters. In the fourth century Cyril of Jerusalem makes the point directly in a comment on John 1:18: "Having said, 'No one has ever yet seen God,' the Evangelist showed us that everything which the prophets spoke, such as Isaiah, that he saw the Lord sitting upon a throne, Ezekiel, upon the Cherubim, and Daniel, on a throne, and certain others of them about beholding him—all those things belonged to condescension, not as though the naked essence itself were seen. For if they had seen the nature itself they would not have beheld it in different forms; for it is simple, formless, uncompounded, unlimited, and neither sits nor stands. For all these attributes belong to bodies, and neither any of the angels nor of the archangels sees him, much less any human being."[44] Chrysostom appealed to Ezekiel's vision in his treatise "On the Incomprehensibility of God," presenting an opinion common among the Antiochene exegetes.[45] Irenaeus had already made a similar point two centuries earlier. None of the prophets, not even Moses, ever saw God "face to face." Rather, they saw only "economies [or, modes of accommodation] through which humankind would see God, as was said also to Elijah [1 Kings 19:11–12]," and "likenesses of the glory of the Lord" (*similitudines claritatis*

Domini = ὁμοίωμα δόξης Κυρίου, Ezek 1:28). After discussing the cases of Moses, Elijah, and Ezekiel, Irenaeus concludes, "And the Logos himself, revealer (ἐξηγητής, cf. John 1:18] of the Father, whose being is rich and manifold, was not beheld in a single form or a single character by those who saw him, but according to the accommodations of his activities."[46]

The Greek theologians understood that the incomprehensibility of God does not entail refusal to image him at all, for he has given us his own theandric image in Jesus Christ. That understanding is what the "iconodules" were defending in the great controversies of the eighth and ninth centuries. Rather, the very multiplicity and ambiguity of the images, even those in the Bible itself, teach us that the holy triune God transcends human power to perceive and to conceive, yet comes near to us "by condescension." When the theophanies of the Old Testament were read as visions of Christ, then, as Irenaeus observed, conceptions of Christ, too, became multiple and ambiguous. Thomas Mathews has sharply observed the polymorphic portrayals of Christ and offered a challenging interpretation. If the apocryphal acts and gospels could report different people seeing Christ in quite different forms— one, a child, another, an old man, another, a beardless youth—why could not the ambiguity of visual images serve the same ends? Mathews's conclusion to his chapter on "Christ Chameleon" deserves quoting at length:

> We who live in a post-Christian world think we have arrived at a certain objectivity about Christ. We have assigned him his place in history books and assessed his impact on the course of human development. The new converts of the fourth and fifth century did not find it so easy. To them he was still utterly mysterious, undefinable, changeable, polymorphous. In the disparate images they have left behind they record their struggle to get a grasp on him; the images were their way of thinking out loud on the problem of Christ. Indeed, the images are the thinking process itself.[47]

The most controversial aspect of Mathews's interpretation is likely to be his insistence that some of the early representations of Christ, including that in the Latomou church, are feminized or androgynous.[48] The case is very strong in many of the examples, over a considerable time period. Whether a fifth-century worshipper—or the anonymous woman who commissioned it—would have seen the Latomou Christ as feminine is less clear.[49] Still, Mathews has challenged us to see features of this portrait that have been obscured for us by a controlling tradition in art history that for half a century has insisted that the Christ of Byzantine apse mosaics is "the imperial Christ," modeled on features of Roman and Byzantine court portraiture. Mathews demonstrates that the "imperial mystique" was based on a series of mistakes and misreadings, some of them egregious. Art historians will probably continue to argue whether, after all, this motif or that may owe something to imperial portraiture, but Mathews's argument as a whole is impressive in quality of evidence and in clarity.[50] The Christ who meets us in the Latomou mosaic is not a stern warrior king, but a long-haired, gentle-faced, soft-featured youth, dressed, however richly, as a philosopher, who gestures as if to invite us to a discourse on wisdom. If he is not effeminate, he is certainly no model for royal *machismo*.

Nevertheless, there is something undeniably majestic about this gentle figure who stares so patiently at the viewer and holds out the message of hope, salvation, and rest. His are philosopher's robes, but what philosopher is this who wears crimson, gold, and purple, whose golden nimbus is set with a jeweled cross, and who sits on God's bow on the crystal, cloud-bedecked disk of light borne by the four divine beings of God's chariot? Here we see just that paradox of power-in-weakness that the apostle Paul already understood to be the center of the gospel. While the Western church took up Paul's chief focus of that paradox in the scandal of the cross, so that eventually the crucifix became its central image, in the East it was the Johannine notion of incarnation, the manifestation of the God-Man, that became the center of awe and contemplation. That is what the anonymous artist of the Latomou monastery tried to show.

We have not solved the puzzle of the two side figures in the apse. There are no exact parallels, to my knowledge, in extant early Christian or Byzantine art. I am inclined to agree with Spieser that they represent quite specific personages, and that absent some new discovery we shall never know who those personages were.[51] The attitudes of the figures, however, are quite clear. The posture of the "Ezekiel" figure is not that of the *orans*, though there is some superficial resemblance. Rather, as Xyngopoulos recognized from the beginning, everything about his stance expresses awe, awe engendered by the vision itself. And the other figure's posture is even easier to read, for it is the classic pose of the ancient philosopher, not as teacher, but as the θεωρητικός, deep in contemplation.[52] Whoever these figures were supposed to be in the fifth century, their reactions to the vision of the gentle but majestic, polymorphous but unmistakable, God-man were the reactions every worshipper ought to have when that figure came to meet them "on the chariot of the cherubim" at the climax of the Eucharist: awe and contemplation.

"The miracle of the Latomou" has repeated itself. It is nothing less than a miracle that this little gem of early Christian art has survived a millennium and a half, through iconoclasm, earthquake, war, and conquest, twice plastered over, twice recovered. The "rest" it promised to the little house in which it stands has at best been ironic, but Christian theology, when true to its roots, has always understood that the ἀνάπαυσις promised to the faithful is as paradoxical as the power of the gentle and suffering Christ. Perhaps the true miracle of the Latomou is that even in our cynical age this relic of an ancient faith can still evoke awe in the viewer and its mysteries can lay claim on our contemplation.

Notes

My late wife and I did the research for this essay jointly. Although she did not live to participate in the actual writing, I have been able to draw on many of the notes she had taken, as well as many conversations about the Hosios David church, which began when we first saw it in Thessaloniki in 1993. The finished essay is the poorer for want of her editorial skill, her art-historical judgment, and above all her extraordinary vision, but I hope it remains a fitting expression of the enthusiasm she shared with me for offering a gift to Rowan Greer, a friend of—can it be?—nearly forty years.

This essay also appears in Wayne A. Meeks, *In Search of the Early Christians,* ed. Allen R. Hilton and H. Gregory Snyder (New Haven, Conn.: Yale University Press, 2002).

1. "Edifying Account concerning the Divine-human Image of our Lord Jesus Christ, which was revealed in the Monastery of the Stonecutters in Thessalonica, composed by Ignatius, monk and Abbot of the Akapnios Monastery," in *Varia graeca sacra* (ed. Athanasios Papadopoulos-Kerameus; Zapiski Istoriko-filologicheskago fakulteta Imperatorskago S.-Petersburgskago Universiteta, 95; Saint Petersburg: V. F. Kirshbauma, 1909), 102–13; quotation from pp. 111–12, my translation.

2. See previous note. Papadopoulos-Kerameus found the story in two manuscripts, one in the Kosinitza Monastery, the other in Moscow. The latter is dated to the twelfth century (Venance Grumel, "La mosaïque du 'Dieu Sauveur' au monastère du 'Latome' à Salonique [découverte en août 1927]," *Echos d'Orient* 33 [1930]: 165). The legend itself is probably much older. Indeed, Deborah Mauskopf Deliyannis has argued that Agnellus of Ravenna, writing around 831, borrowed the story whole and transposed it to Classe in the time of Bishop Peter I (Deborah Mauskopf Deliyannis, "Agnellus of Ravenna and Iconoclasm: Theology and Politics in a Ninth-Century Historical Text," *Speculum* 71 [1996]: 571). This would put circulation of the tale very close to the reported events. (My thanks to Peter Brown for calling my attention to the Deliyannis article.) The second "iconomachy," explicitly mentioned in the "Edifying

Narrative," §9, is an important subtext of the legend. However, the legend explains the covering of the mosaic not as a reaction to iconoclasm, but as a means of hiding from the wicked emperor Maximian (AD 285–305) the image, which had miraculously appeared in the church that his daughter Theodora, new convert to Christianity, had constructed in the guise of a bath. Does this most improbable part of the tale also allude covertly to the iconoclasm controversy? The coincidence of name of Maximian's (step)daughter with that of the widow of Theophilus, who in the year 843 restored the icons after the second period of iconoclasm, must at least have been very welcome to the author. On the latter Theodora's role, see George Ostrogorsky, *History of the Byzantine State* (rev. ed.; trans. Joan Hussey; New Brunswick, N.J.: Rutgers University Press, 1969), 219–23.

3. Although the "Edifying Account" uses the plural, all other records report the monastery's name in the singular.

4. A. Xyngopoulos, "Τὸ Κεραμεντὶμ-Τζαμι Θεσσαλονίκης," Ἀρχαιολογικὸν Δελτίον 6 (1920–21): 190–94. He published a full report of his findings, after extended work on the site in 1927 and 1929, in "Τὸ Καθολικὸν τῆς μονῆς Λοτόμου ἐν Θεσσαλονίκῃ καὶ τὸ ἐν αὐτῷ ψηφιδωτόν," Ἀρχαιολογικὸν Δελτίον 12 (1929): 142–80. After cleaning of the mosaic was complete, in August 1927, it was described briefly, without prior knowledge of Xyngopoulos, by Jean Papadopoulos, "Mosaïque byzantine de Salonique," *CRAI* (1927): 215–18. Charles Diehl, in October of the same year, appears to have been the first to call attention to the significance of the "Edifying Narrative" (ibid., 256–61), as he insists in "A propos de la mosaïque d'Hosios David à Salonique," *Byzantion* 7 (1932): 333–34. The "Edifying Narrative" suggests that the church was once dedicated to Zechariah. However, the "Life of Joseph the Hymnographer" (early ninth century) by John the Deacon (date uncertain) reports that the original name of the monastery was "God the Savior," which would certainly accord with the apse mosaic and inscription, and that it was renamed "Latomou" from the miracle that occurred there (ἐκ τοῦ γεγενημένου θαύματος; cited by Grumel, "La mosaïque," 167, from *PG* 105:945b). Grumel goes on to guess that "Latomos" must have referred to some particular "stone-cutter," not a quarry as the "Edifying Narrative" says, and that the stone-cutter was Senouphios himself, whose skeleton he thinks was one found wearing "the iron belt of an ascetic" in the church (pp. 169, 173–75). But dates of the burials are uncertain, and nothing in the tradition connects Senouphios with quarrying or masonry. To compound confusion, the mosque into which the damaged church was converted after the fifteenth century also is known by various names in the modern literature, but that need not concern us here.

5. Xyngopoulos initially dated the mosaic to the fifth century, but that was contested by C. R. Morey, who argued for a seventh-century date: C. R. Morey, "A Note on the Date of the Mosaic of Hosios David, Salonica," *Byzantion* 7 (1932): 339–46. Morey's argument was vigorously refuted by Diehl in the same periodical ("A propos la mosaïque"). In 1964 Gerke published a detailed stylistic and compositional analysis, which argues persuasively for a date early in the fifth century, and that view has

won wide acceptance, though Spieser, insisting that the Latomou mosaic must be later than those of the St. George Rotunda, argued in 1984 for a date around the middle of the sixth century. See Friedrich Gerke, "Il mosaico absidale di Hosios David al Salonico," *Corso di cultura sull'arte ravennate e bizantina* 11 (1964): 179–99; J.-M. Spieser, *Thessalonique et ses monuments du IVe au VIe siècle: Contribution à l'étude d'une ville paléochrétienne* (Bibliotèque des Écoles Françaises d'Athènes et de Rome, 254; Athens: École Française d'Athènes, 1984), 157.

6. Diehl, "A propos de la mosaïque," 335. The color photograph is by John Dean and is reproduced here by the generous assistance and permission of Thomas F. Mathews.

7. ἰδοὺ ὁ θ(εὸ)ς ἡμῶν, ἐφ' ᾧ ἐλπίζομεν κ(αὶ) ἠγαλλιώμεθα ἐπὶ τῇ σωτηρίᾳ ἡμῶν, ὅτι ἀνάπαυσιν δώσει ἐπὶ τὸν οἶκον τοῦτον. Isa 25:9–10 reads: καὶ ἐρουσιν τῇ ἡμέρᾳ ἐκείνῃ Ἰδοὺ ὁ θεὸς ἡμῶν, ἐφ' ᾧ ἠλπίζομεν καὶ ἠγαλλιώμεθα, καὶ εὐφρανθησόμεθα ἐπὶ τῇ σωτηρίᾳ ἡμῶν ὅτι ἀνάπαυσιν δώσει ὁ θεὸς ἐπὶ τὸ ὄρος τοῦτο. The inscription omits the third verb in the series and substitutes "this house" for "this hill," equating the church with Mount Zion.

8. +Πηγὴ ζ[ω]τική, δεκτική, θρεπτικὴ ψυχῶν πιστῶν ὁ πα[νέντιμος οἶ]κος οὗτος. [εὐξαμ]μένη ἐπέτυχα καὶ ἐπέτυχο[ῦς]α ἐπλήροσα+ +ὑπὲρ εὐχῆς [ἧς οἶδεν ὁ θεὸς τὸ ὄνομα].

9. A. Xyngopoulos, "Κεραμεντὶμ-Τζαμι," 193, my translation; note his sketch in fig. 6.

10. A. Xyngopoulos, "Καθολικόν," 158–59; "Edifying Narrative," §6; Papadopoulos-Kerameus, *Varia graeca*, 106–7.

11. The Poganovo icon bears an inscription identifying its theme as "Jesus Christ in the Latomou Miracle" (ΙΣ ΧΣ Ο ΕΝ ΛΑΤΟΜΟΥ ΘΑΥΜΑ), so there can be no question of its ultimate source. At the same time, it differs from the mosaic in some ways: "Habakkuk" is here a bearded old man, not the "handsome youth" of the Latomos mosaic; he carries a scroll, not a codex, and its inscription is from Ezek 3:1 (!), υἱὲ ἀνθρώπου κατάφαγε τὴν κεφαλίδα ταύτην (T. Gerasimov, "L'icone bilatérale de Poganovo au Musée Archéologique de Sofia," *Cahiers Archéologiques* 10 [1959]: 279–88, quotation from 280). It also lacks the four streams of paradise and substitutes for the river a rocky pool with fish (cf. André Grabar, "À propos d'une icone byzantine du xive siècle au musée de Sofia," *Cahiers Archéologiques* 10 [1959]: 289–304). Noting that these variants agree both with the "Edifying Narrative" and with what remains of a third parallel pointed out by Gerasimov, a much-damaged fresco in a funeral chapel in Bačkovo, Bulgaria, Xyngopoulos thinks it more likely that the immediate prototype of icon and fresco was a miniature illustrating Ignatius's "Narrative" and probably contemporary with it, made in Thessaloniki (A. Xyngopoulos, "Sur L'icone bilatérale de Poganovo," *Cahiers Archéologiques* 12 [1962]: 341–50).

12. Jean Clédat, *Le monastère et la nécropole de Baouît* (Mémoires publiés par les membres de l'Institut français d'archéologie orientale du Caire, 12, 39; Cairo: Institut

français d'archéologie orientale, 1904, 1916; see especially Plates 59 and 90 in vol. 12. See also Jean Maspero, "Rapport sur les fouilles entreprises à Baouit," *CRAI* (1913): 287–301, and idem, *Fouilles exécutées à Baouît* (Mémoires . . . , 59; Cairo: Institut Français, 1931). The Rabula Codex, containing the Gospels in Syriac and dated AD 586, is now in the Laurentian Library in Florence. Its ascension scene is often reproduced, e.g., in André Grabar, *Christian Iconography: A Study of Its Origins* (The A. W. Mellon Lectures in the Fine Arts, 1961; Bollingen Series 35.10; Princeton: Princeton University Press, 1968), Pl. 1.

13. Edmund Weigand, in a review of a 1930 article by V. Grumel and the 1927 notes by Papadopoulos and Diehl, insists that "die griechische Osten hat sich aber in Übereinstimmung mit seiner ablehnenden Haltung gegenüber der Johannesapokalypse auch die abendländische Deutung der τέσσαρα ζῷα als Symbole der Evangelisten lange nicht zu eigen gemacht" (*ByzZ* 31 [1931]: 194–95). He vigorously reiterates his position two years later in reviewing Xyngopoulos's major publication of the site and a debate by Morey and Diehl about its date (ibid. 33 [1933]: 212); he does not explain why Ezekiel's four creatures should have only one face each and be carrying books. At the opposite pole, James Snyder, "The Meaning of the 'Maiestas domini' in Hosios David," *Byzantion* 37 [1967]: 143–52, insists that the whole vision is based primarily on Revelation 4–5, not on Ezekiel (p. 150). Snyder points out that Thessaloniki's connections with the West were strong; it was the seat of the Roman vicariate in the East from the time of Pope Damasus (fourth century; p. 152). N. Thierry, "Apocalypse de Jean et l'iconographie byzantine," in *L'Apocalypse de Jean: Traditions exégétiques et iconographiques IIIᵉ–XIIIᵉ siècles* (ed. Yves Christe et al.; Actes du Colloque de la Fondation Hardt 29 février–3 mars 1976; Geneva: Librairie Droz, 1979), 319–39, denies any significant influence by the Apocalypse on Byzantine art, but he does not discuss the Latomou mosaic.

14. Christa Ihm, *Die Programme der christlichen Apsismalerei vom vierten Jahrhundert bis zur Mitte des achten Jahrhunderts* (Forschungen zur Kunstgeschichte und christlichen Archäologie, 4; Wiesbaden: Franz Steiner Verlag, 1960), 45, my translation. The Latomou mosaic is the earliest of the examples of the "Liturgical Maiestas" schema of apse decoration, one of the eight in Ihm's taxonomy. Other examples are paintings in two of the chapels of the Apa Apollo monastery in Bawit, Egypt; two frescoes in the Jeremiah monastery in Sakkara, a village west of Memphis in Lower Egypt; the apse fresco of the David-Garedja Cave Church in Dodo, Georgia; and S. Miquel in Egara (Tarrasa), Catalonia (pp. 43–44; descriptions in her catalogue of extant monuments, pp. 192, 199, 204, 206–7).

15. Ihm, *Programme*, 47–51, following the earlier suggestion by Wilhelm Neuss, *Das Buch Ezechiel in Theologie und Kunst bis zum Ende des XII. Jahrhunderts, mit besonderer Berücksichtigung der Gemälde in der Kirche zu Schwarzreindorf: Ein Beitrag zur Entwicklungsgeschichte der Typologie der christlichen Kunst, vornehmlich in den Benediktinerklöstern* (Beiträge zur Geschichte des alten Mönchtums und des Benediktinerordens, 1–2; Münster: Aschendorff, 1912), 82–84.

16. Thomas F. Mathews, *The Clash of Gods: A Reinterpretation of Early Christian Art* (Princeton: Princeton University Press, 1993), 117–18 and fig. 92 on p. 122.

17. All translations of biblical passages are my own unless otherwise noted and, for the OT, follow the LXX.

18. For descriptions of the mosaic technique, see especially Xyngopoulos, "Καθολικόν," 161–71, and Gerke, "Il mosaico."

19. Mathews, *Clash of Gods*, 118.

20. The rainbow reappears around the head of the "strong angel" of Rev 10:1.

21. Ihm, *Programme*, 45, finds the source of the Latomou rainbow in Isaiah, presumably thinking of Isa 66:1, "Heaven is my throne," but that does not really explain the motif. Neither τόξον nor ἶρις occurs in Isaiah at all. Another instance of Christ seated on a rainbow, within a *mandorla* filled with stars, is an icon from Mt. Sinai, probably from the seventh century: Georgios A. and Maria Soteriou, Εἰκόνες τῆς Μόνης Σινα (Collection de l'Institut Français d'Athenes; Athens: Institut Français d'Athenes, 1956–58) l:fig. 8, discussed 2:23–25; also reproduced in Grabar, *Christian Iconography*, fig. 287. Both the surrounding rainbow, incorporated into the mandorla around Christ, and the rainbow throne figure in the fresco of the Last Judgment in the parecclesion of the monastic church of the Savior in Chora in Constantinople (now the Kariye Museum in Istanbul). The fresco is generally dated to the fourteenth century. In the West the rainbow throne shows up occasionally in the middle ages: in the dome of San Marco, Venice, ca. 1200; in an illuminated Psalter of Shaftesbury Abbey, twelfth century (now in the British Museum), which has Christ and the Father sitting together on the rainbow; and in a relief on the bronze door of Saint Sophia in Novgorod, dated 1151–54. For the latter two, see Gertrud Schiller, *Ikonographie der christlichen Kunst* (Gütersloh: Gütersloher Verlagshaus, 1966–70) vol. 3, figs. 677 and 710. David J. Halperin, *The Faces of the Chariot: Early Jewish Responses to Ezekiel's Vision* (TSAJ 16; Tübingen, J. C. B. Mohr [Paul Siebeck], 1988), 250–61, observes that some rabbis had qualms about mention of the rainbow in Ezek 1:28. This, he argues, stems from an earlier, Palestinian synagogue tradition identified with R. Joshua b. Levi, which identifies the rainbow as a visible manifestation of God and prescribes a blessing to be spoken when seeing one. R. Joshua taught that when one sees a rainbow, one ought to fall on one's face as Ezekiel did (*b. Ber.* 59a, cited by Halperin, 255).

22. On the importance of this psalm in rabbinic speculation about the *merkava*, see Halperin, *Faces of the Chariot*, 16–18. The word "chariot" does not in fact appear in Ezekiel's description of his vision, but the LXX inserts it in the retrospective note in 43:3, and Sirach 49:8 calls his vision ἅρμα χερουβιν. The phrase "chariot of the cherubim" also appears in 1 Chron 28:18. God is often said to be "seated upon the cherubim," 1 Sam 4:4; 2 Sam 6:2; 2 Kings 19:15; 1 Chron 13:6; Ps 79:2 [80:1]; 98 [99]:1; Isa 37:16; Dan 3:55.

23. James Snyder, "The Meaning," finds six wings on each of the Latomou animals (p. 150), because he thinks the "two large wings . . . are subdivided by lines of gold into six appendages" (p. 148). There are such lines (but not of gold; the eyes are

outlined in gold, but the striations are dark blue or black) on the bull's wings, but they do not seem to depict separate wings; striations in the wings of the other three figures are less regular and in none of them seem to define separate "appendages."

24. The motif of the four rivers, usually flowing from a hill on or above which Christ's throne sits, is widespread. One of the best known examples is in the apse mosaic of San Vitale in Ravenna; one of the earliest (fourth century), the apse mosaic of Old St. Peter's in Rome, known now from a fresco copied from it before its destruction. Also from the fourth century, the motif occurs in one of the small apse mosaics of Santa Costanza: see Walter Oakeshott, *The Mosaics of Rome: From the Third to the Fourteenth Centuries* (Greenwich: New York Graphic Society, 1967), 64; 67–69, and figs. 29, 40, 41.

25. David Halperin points out that *Genesis Rabbah* 21:9 uses Ezek 10:20 to interpret Gen 3:24, for Chebar = *kebar*, "already, long ago," = *miqeddem*. "Certain rabbis may have equated the two words, and assumed that Ezekiel saw his visions by 'the river of Long-ago.' They may have gone on to equate this river with the 'river flowing from Eden' of Gen 2:10; or, perhaps, with the primordial waters in general" (Halperin, *Faces of the Chariot*, 229). It is unlikely, but not impossible, that a Christian interpreter might be acquainted with this ingenious midrash.

26. Spieser, *Thessalonique et ses monuments*, 158, my translation. Contrast Grabar, "Icone byzantine," 291, who says, "Il s'agit sûrement du Jourdain, le fleuve 'évangélique' qui s'ajoute aux quatre fleuves du Paradis de la Bible: ces quatre sources dominées par le Jourdain sont le pendant allégorique à l'image au-dessus, où le Christ apparaît entouré des quatre symboles des évangelistes." In one of the Apa Apollo frescoes of Bawit, often compared with the Latomou mosaic, there may have been some such demon figure beneath the wheels of the divine chariot, though the shape is indeterminable in the watercolor copy in the publication. Jean Clédat writes, "Sous les roues du char, il semble qu'il ya it une figure humaine couchée," and he speculates that it could be the vanquished Satan, as in Rev 20:7–10. But there is no river motif here. (Clédat, *Le monastère et la nécropole de Baouît*, 12:137 and n. 3.)

27. Ihm, *Programme*, 46.

28. Neuss, *Das Buch Ezechiel*, 86: "the Jordan, into which the seed of baptism has fallen," quoting a fragment published by A. Mai from catenae, *Scriptorum veterum nova collectio* IX (Rome 1837), 740. Cf. the comments by Theodoret of Cyrus, *Interpretatio in Ezechielem*, in *PG* 81, 1240–47.

29. The pioneering work of Gershom Scholem brought this tradition into the light of modern scholarship: see Gershom G. Scholem, *Major Trends in Jewish Mysticism* (3rd ed.; New York: Schocken, 1961); idem, *Jewish Gnosticism, Merkabah Mysticism, and Talmudic Tradition* (New York: Jewish Theological Seminary of America, 1954). Since Scholem's death, several scholars have both extended and revised his insights, among them Ithamar Gruenwald, *Apocalyptic and Merkavah Mysticism* (AGJU 14; Leiden: Brill, 1980); Peter Schäfer, ed., *Synopse zur Hekhalot-Literatur* (TSAJ 2; Tübingen: J. C. Mohr [Paul Siebeck], 1987); idem, *Hekhalot-Studien* (TSAJ 19;

Tübingen: J.C.B. Mohr [Paul Siebeck], 1988); idem, *The Hidden and Manifest God: Some Major Themes in Early Jewish Mysticism* (SUNY Series in Judaica; Albany: State University of New York Press, 1992). David Halperin especially has emphasized the exegetical core and popular connections of the tradition: *Faces of the Chariot,* cited above, and his earlier revised dissertation, *The Merkabah in Rabbinic Literature* (New Haven: American Oriental Society, 1980).

30. Philo, *Cher.* 27–28; *Fug.* 101; cf. *Mos.* 2.97; *Her.* 166. Neuss, *Das Buch Ezechiel,* 29–31, to the contrary notwithstanding, there is little if any evidence of influence from the Ezekiel vision on Philo's exegesis. Though he does speak of the Archangel as the "chariot driver" (ἅρματος ἡνίοχον, *Somn.* 1.157; Neuss, *Das Buch Ezechiel,* 30), there is no trace in this passage of any influence from Ezekiel. The Cherubim for Philo are always two in number.

31. Much of the evidence is gathered conveniently in Christopher Rowland, *The Open Heaven: A Study of Apocalyptic in Judaism and Early Christianity* (New York: Crossroad, 1982), 94–113 ("The Development of an Exalted Angel in Apocalyptic Literature"), with abundant secondary literature up until the time of writing.

32. See Jonathan Z. Smith, "The Prayer of Joseph," in *Religions in Antiquity: Essays in Memory of Erwin Ramsdell Goodenough* (ed. Jacob Neusner; SHR 14; Leiden: Brill, 1968), 253–94, and his introduction and notes to his translation in *The Old Testament Pseudepigrapha* (ed. James H. Charlesworth; Garden City, N.Y.: Doubleday, 1985), 2:699–712.

33. Alan F. Segal, *Two Powers in Heaven: Early Rabbinic Reports about Christianity and Gnosticism* (SJLA 25; Leiden: Brill, 1977).

34. I translate the Nestle-Aland[27] text, from P66, ℵ*, B, C*, L, Irenaeus, Origen, Didymus, et al., in the way that v. 1 seems to require. Later copyists simplified the statement by inserting the word "son."

35. See Jeffrey Earl Peterson, "The Image of the Man from Heaven: Christo-logical Exegesis in 1 Corinthians 15:45–49," Ph.D. diss., Yale University, 1997.

36. My teacher and colleague Nils Dahl saw this process more clearly than anyone else I know and has described elements of it in many essays, published and unpub-lished. Some of the most important are gathered in *Jesus the Christ: The Historical Origins of Christological Doctrine* (ed. Donald Juel; Minneapolis: Fortress, 1991).

37. E.g., Justin, *Dial.,* 59–62. Justin does not make use of Ezekiel's vision re-ports, however.

38. The survey in Part I of Neuss, *Das Buch Ezechiel,* remains authoritative, though there are many details that must be updated.

39. Neuss, *Das Buch Ezechiel,* 34–42; Halperin, *Faces of the Chariot,* 327–37. In the GCS edition of *Origenes Werke,* the fragments are collected in vol. 8 (GCS vol. 33, 1925).

40. *Hom. Ezek.* 1.6, GCS 33 (1925) 331: "'secus flumen' istud gravissimum sae-culi." Cited by Neuss, *Das Buch Ezechiel,* 37.

41. Halperin, *Faces of the Chariot,* 262–358.

42. Reuven Kimmelman has shown that comments on the Song of Songs by Origen and R. Yohanan of Tiberias form, as it were, two sides of a polemical conversation: Ronald Reuven Kimelman, "Rabbi Yohanan of Tiberias: Aspects of the Social and Religious History of Third Century Palestine," Ph.D. diss., Yale University, 1977. See also Halperin, *Faces of the Chariot*, 322–26, on "Origen and the Jews," with further references.

43. On the importance of the chariot in the liturgy, see Neuss, *Das Buch Ezechiel*, 63–65 and 82–84. He especially emphasizes the *cherubikon*, the solemn hymn that accompanies the introduction of the prosphora for its transformation (p. 83), and notes that in the Armenian liturgy, Christ arrives on the "chariot of the cherubim" (p. 84).

44. From *Catenae Graecorum Patrum in Novum Testamentum* (ed. J. A. Cramer; Hildesheim: Georg Olms, 1967), 2:189, on John 1:18. I owe the reference to Jaime Clark-Soles, and I have used her translation, slightly modified.

45. Neuss, *Das Buch Ezechiel*, 54, citing *PG* 48, 725–26. Gregory Nazianzus also takes the vision to demonstrate the ineffable nature of God, for even the prophet's depiction of the cherubim is impossible to grasp (Neuss, *Das Buch Ezechiel*, 42–44).

46. Irenaeus, *AH* 4.20.9–11; quotations from 20.10 (SC 100: 657) and 20.11 (SC 100: 272–73), my translations.

47. Mathews, *Clash of Gods*, 141.

48. Mathews, *Clash of Gods*, 119–41.

49. One cannot, I think, appeal, as Mathews implicitly does on pp. 118–19, to the legend included in Ignatius's "Edifying Narrative," that the mosaic miraculously and overnight replaced an image of the Mother of God commissioned by Princess Theodora, for the astonishment of the artist is that his composition has been replaced by "a likeness of the Lord Jesus Christ in manly form" (ἐν εἴδει ἀνδρικῷ). But of course that tells us only how it was conceived in the twelfth century, and in any case this point is not a material part of Mathews's argument.

50. *Clash of Gods*, chapters 1 and 2 and passim.

51. Spieser, *Thessalonique et ses monuments*, 160. I cannot agree with Spieser, however, in seeing the two as companions of Christ, as in other apse programs (he rightly rejects Grabar's proposal, based on such parallels, that they are Peter and Paul). Though it is true that the right-hand figure is not in fact looking at the vision, I do not see how the left-hand figure can be read in any other way than as reacting to the christophany. And, as Spieser says, there is "hardly any parallel" to the iconography of the two (p. 159).

52. Cf. Gerke, "Il mosaico," 185, "un antico filosofo in pura contemplazione."

Locating Interpreters

Gender Refusers in the Early Christian Mission

Gal 3:28 as an Interpretation of Gen 1:27b

MARY ROSE D'ANGELO

"I don't know what you mean by 'glory,'" Alice said.

Humpty Dumpty smiled contemptuously. "Of course you don't—till I tell you. I meant 'there's a nice knock-down argument for you!'"

"But 'glory' doesn't mean 'a nice knock-down argument,'" Alice objected.

"When *I* use a word," Humpty Dumpty said in a rather scornful tone, "it means just what I choose it to mean—neither more nor less."

—*Lewis Carroll*[1]

Among the most abiding lessons that I learned from Rowan Greer is the recognition that no interpretation is the progeny of two parents only. Indeed, interpretations resemble offspring less than the figures of an elaborate dance in which text and interpreter bob and weave in exchange with a cloud of partners, seen and unseen, to melodies whose changes they do not themselves perceive. Over the last thirty years, the highly dogmatic espousal of "historical objectivity" that condemned "eisegesis" in the allegorical and typological readings of ancient Christianity has largely been replaced with a more nuanced comprehension of the ways that every reading, including that of the contemporary historian, is deeply implicated in its own world, subject to and of its theologies, politics, and social and historical exigencies. This is due in part to the endeavors of scholars of the history of interpretation, like

Greer and Judah Goldin. But hermeneutical discussions, especially feminist hermeneutical discussions, have also contributed heavily.

By insisting that readings are constructed from specific locations of gender, race, and class, feminist interpretation has been instrumental in awakening contemporary interpreters to their own debts, particularly to interests less easily transcended than denominational differences, and so has helped to make the investments of ancient interpreters less distant, closer kin to recent ones. By the same insistence, it has added new dimensions to the questions about the sources and functions of ancient exegesis. And, I would suggest, its rather short history has become an illustration of the variability and multiplicity of interactions between texts and interpreters, even interpreters who profess the same allegiances.

One text that illustrates this particularly well is Gal 3:28. Except for a complaint concerning Paul's inconsistency in Lucinda B. Chandler's comments on 1 Timothy, this text received no attention in the *Women's Bible*.[2] But the mid-twentieth-century revival of Christian feminism largely hailed it as an "emancipation proclamation" for women. Krister Stendahl's *The Bible and the Role of Women*[3] gave this text a central role in his influential biblical arguments for women's ordination and equality in Christianity. Stendahl suggested that in Gal 3:26–28 Paul exploited a baptismal tradition. Noting the anomalous use of the neuter adjectives (male, female) connected by "and" in place of the expected "neither man nor woman," he suggested that "there is no male and female" (οὐκ ἔνι ἄρσεν καὶ θῆλυ) was actually a radical interpretation of Gen 1:27b: "male and female (ἄρσεν καὶ θῆλυ) [God] created them." This interpretation rejected the boundaries between male and female and pointed toward the human being as the image of God (Gen 1:27a). Elisabeth Schüssler Fiorenza built upon Stendahl's reading in her reconstruction of the movement Paul joined and propagated, which she called the early Christian mission. In her view the baptismal tradition proclaimed and enacted the early Christian mission's abolition of patriarchal marriage.[4]

While this proposal has been widely accepted, its implications are by no means unproblematic. Already in 1969, Madeline Boucher pointed to rabbinic traditions whose proclamations were at least as radical but which seemed to have no effect on the conduct of Jewish life.[5] She thus exposed two abiding issues in feminist treatment of the passage: the representation of Judaism as a negative contrast to Christian origins and the relation of the proclamation to practice.[6] The debate over whether Paul is to be read as "feminist" is well represented by the early exchange between Robin Scroggs and

Elaine Pagels.[7] Many interpreters, both feminist and more traditional, have seen the Jewish tradition of exegesis of Genesis 1–3 as responsible for Paul's strictures on women in 1 Cor 11:2–16 and the stipulations of 1 Tim 2:8–15 and even for the household codes and the prohibitions of 1 Cor 14:34–35.[8]

The picture is further complicated by another stream of interpretation of this text which, while acknowledging that the text had implications for social practice, was primarily interested in locating it in the history of religions.[9] Wayne A. Meeks's influential article on the text explored the phrase as one manifestation of the spiritual ambitions antiquity expressed through the "image of the androgyne." Reading Gal 3:28 with Col 3:9–11, Meeks argued that they testified to a "performative utterance" that announced and effected the restoration of the baptized to the originally androgynous image of God. He traced ancient social contexts and texts from Paul's letters that portrayed areas in the proclamation which might have justified wider roles for women in the Pauline communities.[10] Hans Dieter Betz, while allowing social repercussions of the transformation that bestowed androgyny, argued that it primarily envisaged a *transcendence* of biological distinction.[11] Dennis Ronald Mac-Donald argued that Gal 3:28 was Paul's revision of a "dominical saying" attested in a number of second-century contexts that grounded a spiritual tenet central to some gnostic groups.[12]

A recent feminist study by Lone Fatum has adopted this reading of "no male and female," identifying it as a proclamation of baptism into a divine image that was perfect maleness. She explains it as the result of an understanding of gender reflected also in Philo's categories of maleness and femaleness, which she sees as deriving from the Jewish culture Paul and Philo share.[13] She thus repudiates earlier feminist readings that argue for some liberating or egalitarian function.

The goal of this essay is by no means to choose among these contestants, but both to complicate the picture and to attempt to explain its complexity by suggesting that there is no reason to assume a single, universally agreed-upon meaning for the phrase, either for the communities who used the baptismal formula or for Paul. Elsewhere I have argued that the "image of the androgyne" in antiquity is by no means one image. Rather it is possible to distinguish at least four different images among the texts that have inspired the label of androgyny: the true hermaphrodite (almost always negative), the double-bodied creature of Plato's *Symposium* and the rabbinic tradition (a warrant for sexual union), the syzygies, or divine pairs of the gnostic cosmogony, and "making the two one" (the spiritual ambition of wholeness). These distinguishable "images" perform differing, though not necessarily mutually exclusive, functions in the religious world and the art of the first five centuries of the common era.[14]

Similarly, this essay proposes that as a "performative utterance" the baptismal proclamation "no male and female" invited and required its hearers to apply it and to specify its application by their enactment. That is, when they used the phrase it meant exactly what they wanted it to mean—or how they acted it to mean. But no what or how could be final or exclusive. Depending on their social location and communal experience, the folk of the early Christian mission could and did hear and appropriate it differently. The inconsistency later readers detect in Paul's dicta on women reflects the ways that this tradition was applied and reapplied in Paul's interactions with the communities to which he writes.[15] Materials from the context of Paul and the early Christian mission attest at least three functions of the phrase "male and female" that illuminate its several applications in the conversations between Paul and the communities to which he wrote.

First and most simply, "male and female" can function as a merismus indicating "all human beings, both male and female." Secondly, "male and female" can characterize a relationship of disadvantage. Third, "male and female" can refer to sexual intercourse or marriage. These functions are by no means mutually exclusive, but neither need they all be invoked by every use of the phrase. Thus the communities of the early Christian mission need not have agreed among themselves on what performance this utterance initiated and entailed, nor need they have agreed with Paul on what should be performed.

In what follows I shall delineate contexts for each of these functions, and suggest enactments of the proclamation that are reflected in Paul's letters. In many cases I shall be resuming earlier research, but I cannot claim to be comprehensive. Two factors dominate the material I have collected: the specific wording of Gen 1:27b and the similar statement in Gen 5:2b (i.e., "male and female" or rather "man or woman"), and the negative which renders the verse so startlingly radical as an interpretation.

"Male and Female" As Merismus: All Are Included

First, then, Gen 1:27b is a merismus; it designates the whole of a reality by naming its opposite poles: "male and female" means "all human beings."[16] This use is widespread in antiquity, not only for this pair, but also for "Jew and Greek, slave and free." In the case of "Jew and Greek" (or "Greek and barbarian") it usually expresses the universalistic (or more negatively, totalizing and imperialist) vision of Hellenism or of the empire.[17] Philo and Josephus both use all three pairs.[18] Although the merismus "man and woman" is far more frequent,[19] they also use the pair "male and female."[20] Philo's use of "male/female" as a merismus is somewhat specialized; for him this polarity designates one of the Platonic sections (τμήματα) that categorize all reality.[21] He understands this division to originate in Gen 1:27b, which created the species (εἴδη) of humanity potentially in the idea or genus (γένος).[22]

If these words in Gal 3:28 are regarded as a merismus, then "no male and female" in some way, like "male and female," means "all are included" in Christ through baptism. An excellent example of a text in which merismus provides an emphasis on the all-inclusiveness of humanity is Philo's injunction to name the particular parts of humanity when praying for the whole:

> And if you give thanks for human beings, do not do so only for the whole race (γένος), but also for its kinds (εἴδη) and most necessary divisions (τμήματα): men, women, Greeks, barbarians, those on the mainlands and those whose lot is cast on the islands.[23]

Two texts which have frequently been discussed as "parallels" to Gal 3:28 deserve special mention as examples of merismus. Neither of these texts involves a citation of Gen 1:27b; rather, the parallel in both cases is to the relation of "male and female" to one or both of the other two pairs in Gal 3:28. Neither directly influenced either the early Christian baptismal formula or Paul; rather, each provides an analogy to Gal 3:28.

One is the inscription of a private shrine in Lydian Philadelphia.[24] The inscription dates from the first century BCE and proffers entrance to the shrine to "men and women, free and slaves" (ἀνδράσι καὶ γυναῖξιν ἐλευθέροις καὶ οἰκέταις),[25] excluding those who have been polluted in some way, be they man or woman, slave or free. The other is a set of midrashic texts of very uncertain date (although substantially later than Paul). Three passages from *Seder Eliyyahu Rabbah* use a formula very close to the three pairs found in Gal 3:28: "Gentile and Israelite, man and woman, bondsman and bondswoman."[26] With their parallels[27] the texts from *Seder Eliyyahu Rabbah* are usually read to mean that all are equal in the sight of God.[28]

When the pair "male and female" is taken as a merismus, then it means "all human beings." Thus in some way the meaning of Gal 3:28 is: "all are included in Christ by baptism." Applied in this way the phrase need not claim any change of women's status through baptism. It has been argued that the proclamation had no practical application, that such texts as Gal 3:28 and *Seder Eliyyahu Rabbah* applied only *"coram deo"* (before God) or in the eschatological future and not in the social order.[29] And it is clear that Philo's counsel on prayer implies no challenge to the social distinctions it names. He speaks of "most necessary divisions"[30] and in his view these polarities are not only the basis of the eros that makes the world go round,[31] but also demand different social treatment:

> For who would talk in the same way to parents and children, being slave of the former by nature and master of the latter in virtue of the same cause? Who would speak in the same way to brothers, cousins, near relatives generally, and to those only distantly connected with him? to those associated with him, and to those with whom he has nothing to do; to fellow citizens and foreigners; to people differing in no slight nor ordinary degree in nature or age? For we have to talk in one way to an old man, in another to a young one, and again in one way to a man of importance and in another to an insignificant person, and so with rich and poor, official and non-official, servant and master, woman and man, skilled and unskilled.[32]

The Context in Paul's Letters

That Paul could understand Gal 3:28 as a proclamation of inclusion in Christ is clear; both the context in the baptismal tradition and the argument of Galatians require at least this meaning. Further, he uses an alternate form of the tradition in 1 Cor 12:13: "for in one spirit we have all been baptized into one body, whether Jew or Greek, whether slave or free." The author of Colossians uses a similar formula to express the inclusiveness of the community; in the new creation (by putting on the new humanity) all are included in God's image (Col 3:10–11). In Colossians, the status of the slave is in no way changed by the affirmation of inclusion; indeed, as in Philo, the appropriate distinctions are affirmed and sacralized by this author's household code, in which the slave is required to obey their fleshly "lords" (κύριοι), fearing the "Lord" (κύριος). But both 1 Cor 12:13 and Col 3:10–11 differ notably from Gal 3:28. 1 Cor 12:13 is expressed in the affirmative rather than the negative form. In Colossians, the form of the merismus has been dissipated by the addition of other distinctions, which are not expressed by pairs and are not mutually exclusive. Further, neither includes the pair "male and female." Thus it is nearly certain that for both the early community and Paul, Gal 3:28 was at least a proclamation of inclusion in Christ. But this reading must be regarded as minimal, for it necessitates neither the negative (as 1 Cor 12:12 shows) nor the reference to Gen 1:27b.

"Male and Female" As a Relation of Disadvantage: Gal 3:28 As Proclamation of Equality

The celebration of this verse as an "emancipation proclamation" comes from the conviction that "male and female" expresses a relation of disadvantage; thus, "no male and female" is understood as meaning "no more disadvantage between men and women." While this interpretation was long overshadowed by Pauline and post-Pauline texts prescribing the subordination of women, and has been disputed both by feminists and those who question feminist claims, the evidence is strong not only that the phrase instantiated an unequal relationship, and that its baptismal performance realized a sort of equalization, but also that Paul's argument in Galatians requires that the three pairs proclaim the end of disadvantage.

Women were certainly disadvantaged, even disabled, in religious and civil life in both the imperial and Jewish contexts.[33] A wide variety of ancient texts attest to the relation of disadvantage between men and women in the ancient world. Among the most widely discussed are prayers attributed to Plato and to Thales which give thanks for being born a human being and not an animal, a man and not a woman, a Greek and not a barbarian.[34] Rabbinic texts provide a Jewish revision which gives thanks for not having been created a Gentile, a woman, or a boor.[35] The sentiment eventually found its way into the liturgy as a thanksgiving for not having been born a Gentile, a woman, or a slave.[36] These prayers and other texts like them testify that women (like slaves, foreigners, and the ignorant) were perceived to be at a disadvantage.[37] But few of the texts recording this disadvantage use the words "male and female."

Here again, Philo provides an example of discourse which uses the words in this fashion. As was mentioned above, Philo treats "male" and "female" as philosophical categories, as species defining human and animal reality and created at Gen 1:27. These categories are moral and metaphysical as well as physical; the category "female" denotes all that is passive, weak, and distant from God.[38] Femaleness "clings to all that is born and perishes . . .";[39] it "is irrational and akin to bestial passions, fear, sorrow, pleasure and desire, from which ensue incurable weaknesses and indescribable diseases."[40]

Further, the categories male and female are embodied in a striking way in Philo's allegorical interpretation of the creation of humanity. The allegory is a moral or psychological one. The text of Genesis 1–3 provides a base on which the character of the soul is explained. For Philo, Adam/man symbolizes mind, while Eve/woman represents sense perception.[41] Sense perception is not always treated as negative by Philo, but the hierarchy is clear:

> He built it to be a woman (Gen 2:22) proving by this that the most proper and exact name of sense perception is "woman." For just as the man shows himself in activity and the woman in passivity, so the province of the mind is activity and that of the perceptive sense passivity, as in woman.[42]

Commenting on Gen 2:24, Philo is even more explicit:

> Observe that it is not the woman that cleaves to the man, but conversely the man to the woman, mind to sense-perception. For when that which is superior, namely mind, becomes one with that which is inferior, it resolves itself into the order of flesh which is inferior.[43]

While Philo's moral and metaphysical use of these categories might seem too specialized or too elevated to be relevant to Gal 3:28, this is not really the case. It derives from ancient constructions of gender identifying the male as active (penetrative) and the female as passive.[44] While these gender contructions have been translated into the categories of Philo's middle Platonism, they represent a confluence of traditions of philosophical interpretation of the Bible[45] with standard medical views, conventional wisdom, and popular misogyny.[46] But they are not primarily a feature of a "conservative Jewish" heritage; rather, they are produced by the desire to display the mores of the Greek-speaking imperial intellectual world.

The Baptismal Context

"Male and female" as instantiating a relationship of disadvantage is the function most strongly confirmed by the immediate context, both by the baptismal formula that originates in the early community and by Paul's argument in Galatians. First, the pairs "Jew and Greek, slave and free" also imply a relation of advantage/disadvantage.[47] In the first case the relationship of disadvantage is mutual: the Greek is disadvantaged religiously, the Jew is disadvantaged culturally.[48] In the case of slave and free, male and female, the disadvantage is one-sided in the social and legal realms. Thus it seems that the overcoming of the relationship of disadvantage is what is proclaimed in the formula. Indeed, two of the texts cited above as examples of merismus also attest to both the relationship of disadvantage and its annulment or suspension in religious contexts. The sanctuary inscription explicitly includes women and slaves, because they were not necessarily included in cult.[49] So too, the contrast "social order/*coram deo*" is an inappropriate measure of the praxis behind the texts in *Seder Eliyyahu Rabbah*. In each case that the formula is used in that text, it asserts that the usual or perceived disadvantage to women, slaves, and Gentiles does not stand. In the context of a discussion of who was permitted to bring a burnt offering, *Seder Eliyyahu Rabbah* proclaims that the recitation of Lev 1:11 substitutes for the daily offering, whether it is done by Gentile or Israelite, man or woman, bondsman or bondswoman.[50] According to their works the holy spirit rests upon all, Gentile or Israelite, man or woman, bondsman or bondswoman; so Deborah was able to prophesy, even though there was in her time a male, free Israelite prophet.[51] In responding to Moses' complaint after his punishment, God defends the impartiality by which all (Gentile or Israelite, man or woman, bondsman or bondswoman) are not only punished for sin but rewarded immediately for every commandment they fulfill.[52] This last text opposes the opinion that only those who are obliged to the commandments merit from them.[53] Thus these texts in *Seder Eliyyahu Rabbah,* and particularly the text on Deborah, make a claim not merely "before God" but also in light of community life and practice. This is also the case with Gal 3:28.

The suggestion that the proclamation originated in baptism invites the reconstruction of a ritual context for its use. Direct evidence about baptismal ceremonies at such an early period is lacking. But evidence from later rituals provides a plausible ritual location for Gal 3:27–28. In general, candidates appear to have been stripped, baptized nude, then clothed and welcomed into the congregation.[54] Later rituals and homilies rarely elaborate or interpret the garment of reclothing,[55] but Gal 3:27–28 might be seen as preserving a greeting to the newly baptized which commented upon their new and uniform clothing: "All you who have been baptized into Christ have put on (ἐνεδύσασθε) Christ. There is among you neither Jew nor Greek, neither slave nor free, no 'male and female.'"[56] Clothing, unclothing, and clothing over serve as metaphors for transformation in variety of texts from the first two centuries of Christianity.[57] In *Trimorphic Protennoia*[58] the baptismal context is explicit, and Col 3:9, 10, 12 uses the metaphor for the assumption of a new humanity according to the image of the creator, in which the distinctions of ethnicity and status are to be overcome by the practice of virtue.

Despite Seneca's frequently cited claim that the senate refused to prescribe special clothing for slaves lest they discern their own numbers,[59] clothing was a central and highly effective means of distinguishing social rank and a means that had been much strengthened during the Augustan "restoration."[60] The outer garments (toga, humation, stola), headgear (a pilleus, or liberty cap for freedperson, veils or fillets, civic crowns, etc.), and ornaments (rings, other jewelery, special shoes) were the main media of sexual and social distinctions.[61] The basic indoor garment, the tunic or χιτών, was much the same in form for men and women, citizen and non-citizen, slave and free, varying primarily in length, quality, and in trendier circles, in color. Adult women wore a floor-length version, while men's were usually shorter. But in ritual settings, free men also wore full-length tunics. Thus the early baptismal ritual might well have clothed the newly baptized in identical, highly traditional white full-length tunics of linen or wool. The mark of circumcision would of course be covered, while other distinctions of status were omitted. Some marks of distinction, for instance, slave collars or brands, could not be removed or hidden. But the baptismal context and proclamation would be a powerful sign against them.[62]

The Context in Galatians

If this picture of the baptismal context strongly affirms the meaning "no disadvantage," Paul's argument in Galatians also relies on this sense of the formula. His purpose in Gal 3:1–4:31 is to assure the Galatian communities that the Gentile is at no disadvantage in Christ, that there is no advantage to the Gentile in circumcision and the law, that in fact the believer is already "seed of Abraham, heir according to the promise." Calling upon their experience of baptism as a proof, he interprets both it and the deed of Christ as a kind of passage to majority (3:23–25; 4:1–7) through which believers attain "sonship" (3:26, 4:5)—the status of the adult heir, the full legal personhood which is not available to women, slaves, or foreigners under the law.[63] It is noteworthy that although in Galatians Paul has no particular interest in either slaves or women, the analogy that he uses has real relevance to both.

Performing the Utterance in the Early Christian Mission

The letters of Paul give some evidence of other members of the early Christian mission who are likely to have believed themselves to be enacting the baptismal tradition as an end to the disadvantage suffered by women—as well as by slaves and Gentiles. A number of them appear in Romans 16, where Paul greets a long list of missionaries in the Roman community by name. He has never been there, so it is probable that these are figures he encountered elsewhere who can vouch for Paul in the Roman community. They are by no means necessarily his converts or students; Junia and Andronicus, for instance, are said to have "been in Christ before" him. The greeting includes the names of a number of women leaders of the Roman community, coupling them with the same descriptors as are given to men.[64] The NRSV and NAB have acknowledged that the person hailed with Andronicus as "famous among the apostles" in Rom 16:7 should be a woman, Junia, not a man (Junias).[65] Phoebe (16:1–2, probably the letter carrier) should be described as "minister," not "deaconess" or even "deacon" (NRSV).[66] Some of these women, like Prisca (Rom 16:3–4), Junia (Rom. 16:7), Julia, and the "sister" of Nereas (Rom 16:15) seem to have worked as the partners of men, presumably their husbands. But others traveled alone, like Phoebe (Rom 16:1–2), Mary (Rom 16:6), and Persis (Rom 16:12), or appeared to have worked with another woman as a missionary partner, like Tryphaena and Tryphosa (Rom 16:12, see perhaps also Evodia and Syntyche in Phil 4:2).[67]

The point is not that roles that women take in Romans 16 lacked examples among religious communities in the ancient world. Yet Averil Cameron contended that the numbers of women mentioned in these positions reflects their status in their class, rather than their rarity.[68] Her observation is borne out by Ross Kraemer's study of women in Greek and Roman religions in the imperial world.[69] Bernadette Brooten has shown that women were leaders in the parallel Jewish communities, the Greek-speaking synagogue.[70] Even Juvenal gives some backhanded evidence that Jewish women were reputed to be prophets and interpreters of the Law.[71] Rather, the proclamation of Gal 3:28 found some realization in the community in which it was promulgated. It applied neither in the larger social order nor merely *coram deo,* but "in Christ" (ἐν Χριστῷ), in the community life where it validated practice that was not unexampled in the imperial world, but might otherwise have been suspect as destructive of the social order.[72] In later years, women leaders did become suspect within the community; the strictures of the Pastorals represent one early attempt to exclude women from communal authority

(1 Tim 2:9–15, 2 Tim 3:6–7). And later external critics of the movement painted Christians as dupes of deranged and disorderly women leaders.[73]

The traces of another practice based upon the baptismal context of the saying may appear in Paul's suspicions of disorderly conduct on the part of the women prophets of Corinth (1 Cor 11:2–16). In refusing the veil (or fillets, or hairdressing) when they prayed or prophesied in the assembly, these women may have been repeating the "unveiling" of baptism. The *Apostolic Tradition* specifically requires that women loosen their hair and remove jewelry before being baptized, and Aseneth is told that her head is as that of a young man on the day of her initiation.[74] They would have been displaying in the assembly the status they had acquired through and experienced in the new creation described by the pronouncement "no male and female" (Gal 3:28). Paul's confused and confusing attack on their practice produces interpretations of Genesis 1–3 that both reassert a gendered hierarchy (Gen 3:7–10) and either contradict or relativize it (Gen 3:11–12).[75]

"Male and Female" As Sex and Marriage: "No Sex and Marriage"

A third function of Gen 1:27, namely, that "male and female" means "sex and marriage," is the meaning for Gen 1:27 that is easiest to trace to the first century.[76] The negative of Gal 3:28 has a clear meaning in light of this interpretation and the rejection of sex and marriage is a posture (among others) in the early community that is attested by Paul's letters.

This reading of Gen 1:27 appears in the decision about divorce presented in the debate in Mark 10:2–12. The passage treats Gen 1:27 as prescriptive, as "what Moses commanded" (Mark 10:3): "From the beginning of creation, male and female [God] created them; . . . on account of this shall a man leave his father and mother and the two will become one flesh. So they are no longer two but one flesh. What therefore God has yoked together (συνέζευξεν), let not a human being separate" (Mark 10:6–8).[77]

In Matt 19:1–9, the exchange has been reorganized according to the author's understanding of the form of rabbinic debate, with special attention to the citation. Matthew completed Gen 2:24 (although not according to the LXX as we know it), treating Gen 2:24 as the commandment and Gen 1:27 as its explanation: "The one who created in the beginning made them male and female and said, 'For this cause shall a man leave his father and mother and cleave to his wife and the two will become one flesh.'" This revision may be partially motivated by the difficulty of seeing Gen 1:27b as a command.

Besides these two versions of the debate, the only use of the terms "male" and "female" together in the NT is Paul's condemnation of "unnatural" intercourse in Rom 1:26–27.[78] I do not wish to suggest that Romans cites Gen 1:27 here, but rather I wish to stress the association of the words with sexual practice.

From Qumran, the *Damascus Document* uses Gen 1:27b as a proof for lifelong monogamous marriage:

> The builders of the wall . . . are caught twice in fornication: by taking two wives in their lives, even though the principle of creation is, "male and female created he them" (Gen 1:27). And the ones who went into the ark "went in two by two to the ark" (Gen 7:9).[79]

As in the case of Mark, this text views Gen 1:27 as prescriptive.[80] This document sees no need to supply a clearer command, but the verse is backed up with a reference to the "male and female" animal pairs in Gen 6–7.

This combination draws attention to an omission in my discussion of the words "male and female." I have been treating them as if they could only reflect Gen 1:27b. But in fact they occur also in Gen 5:2; 6:19, 20; 7:2, 3, 9, 15, and 16. Gen 5:1–2 is clearly an alternate version, perhaps a restatement of Gen 1:27: "in the day when God created Adam, in the image of God [God] created him; male and female [God] created them . . ." (Gen 5:2 LXX). The other verses use the pair of words to describe the animals who are to enter the ark with Noah. It is clear that the purpose of these pairs is sex and procreation: "to bring up seed upon the earth" (Gen 7:3). This was recognized in the first century; Philo's comments upon these pairs assert that they provide a new creation.[81]

Philo's other uses of the words make clear that he too generally associates them with sex and procreation. He describes the purpose of the sections or species of Gen 1:27b as procreation.[82] He also uses "male" and "female" when he speaks of sexual intercourse.[83] Philo's pejorative definition of the category "female" is grounded in his perception of the female role in sex and procreation as "passive." His interpretation of Gen 1:27 is particularly striking. He distinguishes 1:27a from 1:27b so that 1:27a describes the creation of the pattern of humanity, the idea (γένος), while 1:27b describes the species (εἴδη). His distinction explicitly denies sexuality to the idea: "The one according to the image is an idea or type or seal, intelligible, incorporeal, neither male nor female (οὔτε ἄρρεν οὔτε θῆλυ), incorruptible by nature." Possession of maleness and femaleness is a requirement of bodiliness, reproduction, and corruption; what does not degenerate has no need of generation.[84]

Josephus' interpretation of "male and female" shows that for him also it means sexuality and reproduction. In *Antiquities* 1.32, "male and female" is transferred to Gen 1:25, the creation of the animals: like the birds and fish they are paired for generation.[85] *Antiquities* then goes on to explain that Eve was created because Adam was without a female sleeping partner and was gaping at all the animals with theirs.[86] Although Josephus' interpretation of Genesis undoubtedly serves his own purposes, this explanation (like many other details of his interpretive work) derives from a tradition that both precedes and survives him. It is usually attached to Gen 2:18, 20 as it is in *Jubilees* 3.3: "And during these five days,[87] Adam was observing all of these, male and female, according to every kind which was on the earth, but he was alone, and there was none whom he found for himself, who was like himself, who would help him."[88]

Among later texts ʾAbot de Rabbi Nathan B 8 and *Genesis Rabbah* 17.4 elaborate the story, relating that when Adam saw and named all the animals with their female pairs, he wanted to know why they all had a mate or yoke-fellow (*zwg*)[89] and he had none.[90] This interpretation identifies a "help like himself" (Gen 2:18, 20) as *zwg*, "mate" or "partner," a term that includes both companionship and sex.[91] The *Fragment Targums* translate "female" (*nqbh*) in Gen 1:27 and Gen 5:2 with *zwg*; the word meaning "help" in Gen 2:18 and 20 is then translated with *br zwg*.[92] *Neofiti I* uses *zwg* at Gen 1:27, 2:18, and 2:20, and the margin gives this reading at 5:2.[93] The word *zwg* is a loanword from Greek (ζυγόν, yoke).[94] It appears in the compound verb in the interpretation that Mark gives the combined citation of Gen 1:27 and 2:24: "What God has yoked together (συνέζευξεν). . . ." A more explicit (and probably later) version of the story that Adam was inspired to ask for Eve by seeing the animals with their mates claims that Adam tried out all the animals before God finally created Eve for him.[95]

Other rabbinic materials also interpret "male and female" to mean sex, procreation, and marriage in ways that echo the first-century interpretations. According to *Yebamot* 6.6, Beth Hillel ruled that a man must engage in sex ("increasing and multplying") until he has a boy and a girl child, in conformity with Gen 5:2.[96] This decision treats Gen 5:2 as prescriptive, as a commandment, much as Mark and the *Damascus Document* treat Gen 1:27b.[97] But for the most part, in the rabbinic traditions Gen 1:27b is the basis for speculation about the character of humanity (as it is at a highly sophisticated level for Philo) or for edification.

The compiler of *Genesis Rabbah* appears to see "male and female" in Gen 1:27 as describing procreation ("increasing and multiplying"), one of four characteristics human beings share with animals (as opposed to the four they share with the angels).[98] It may be that this interpretation takes the conjunction of "image of God" and "male and female" in Gen 1:27 as describing the human being's double nature (angelic and bestial). A similar viewpoint emerges when Josephus introduces "male and female" into the creation of the animals. Philo comments that the "true image" is "neither male nor female."[99]

In the vein of pious exhortation, *b. Yebamot* 63a interprets Gen 5:2 as a warrant for marriage: "R. Eleazar said: 'Any man who has no wife is no proper man; for it is said, male and female created He them and called their name Adam.'"[100] *Qoheleth Rabbah* 9.1 uses the second part of the verse similarly:

> R. Hiyya b. Gamda said: He is also an incomplete man, as it is stated, and blessed (i. e., married) them and called their name Adam (Gen 5:2), i.e. when they were both as one, [as the effect of marriage] they were called Adam, but when they are not both as one they are not called Adam.[101]

Thus in the tradition "male and female" functions as "sex and marriage" in a variety of ways. For Mark, the *Damascus Document* and the memories of Beth Shammai and Beth Hillel, it provides a commandment. Later traditions use it for exhortation. A tradition that emerges in *Jubilees* and Josephus, and perhaps also Mark, and continues through the rabbinic material identifies "female" as "sexual partner." Josephus, Philo, and *Genesis Rabbah* seem to see "male and female" as sexuality, one of the characteristics that human beings share with the animals.

The Context in Paul's Letters

The question then arises whether there is support for this function in the context of Galatians or of Paul's mission. It is difficult to find a direct role for Gen 1:27b as a description or prescription about sex and marriage in Galatians.[102] But it appears that "no male and female" played a role in Paul's correspondence with the Corinthians and that both Paul and the Corinthians understood this slogan to mean "no sex and marriage." The Corinthians espoused an ascetic stance that Paul cites and at least partially affirms in 1 Cor 7:1: "It is good for a man not to touch a woman."

That this stance is connected with the proclamation of Gal 3:28 is manifested by the way Paul argues for his counsel to stay in the state in which one was called. In 1 Cor 7:17–24 he commands that circumcised and uncircumcised, slave and free, stay as they are, in order to enforce his view that married and unmarried should do the same (7:8–16, 26–27), except when the death of a spouse or manumission by a master offer the opportunity of freedom. Thus for Paul, Jew and Greek, slave and free, married and unmarried, are parallel pairs. I suspect that Paul asserts that married and unmarried are *adiaphora*, against the Corinthians who believe that "no male and female" means that sex and marriage are among the ἀρχαῖα (original things) that have passed away in the new creation (2 Cor 5:17–18). They "live like the angels" (Mark 12:26) as they speak in "angelic tongues" (1 Cor 13:1). It is not necessarily the case that the baptismal pronouncement pledged its participants to celibacy; the Corinthians may have been the first to interpret baptism as a pledge or transformation to sexual asceticism. But, as has frequently been noted, they were certainly not the last. The author of Colossians warns against the counsellors of sexual asceticism (Col 2:20–23).[103] In the second century, the *Acts of [Paul and] Thecla* provides an example in which sexual asceticism is the content of Christian (or at least Pauline) preaching, while 1 Timothy inveighs against the rejection of marriage (1 Tim 4:3). Clement of Alexandria directs the major portion of the third book of *Stromateis* against groups that understand Christianity and abstinence as coterminal. Much later Augustine provides an orthodox example of a view that understands baptism as a pledge to a very high degree of continence, if not celibacy.[104]

Thus the third function of Gen 1:27b in antiquity has a real claim as an explanation of Gal 3:28. "Male and female" as "sex and marriage" is well attested in the first century as an interpretation of Gen 1:27, and helps to explain the choice of the words "male and female" rather than "man and woman." Further, it gives the negative in Gal 3:28 a clear meaning. Finally, 1 Corinthians provides evidence of a position based on just such a meaning.

Performance and Identity: A Nice Knock-Down Argument

Each of these three functions of "male and female" could ground the "no" Gal 3:28 offers to the primeval gendering of human beings; "no" to excluding the "weaker vessel"; "no" to the relation of disadvantage between the pairs; "no" to the desire of the flesh, or the bonds of marriage. These are by no means mutually exclusive readings; they are easily combined with each other, and with one or more of the images of "the androgyne"—of humanity as both two and one.

Elisabeth Schüssler Fiorenza's claim that Gal 3:28 proclaims the end of patriarchal marriage in the community, which was explicitly based on the function of Gen 1:27b as a warrant for sex and marriage, also implies a rejection of disadvantage.[105] Schüssler Fiorenza seems to envision an early community that had revised their sexual arrangements; although they continued to make monogamous sexual commitments, these unions were no longer established through and for the protection of the patriarchal family. Her suggestion has the advantage of explaining why the context in Galatians understands the text as a warrant for the end of disadvantage in the community, while the Corinthians appear to read it as an end to sex and marriage.

It is certainly the case that the disadvantages under which women labored in antiquity were created or arose as the safeguards of patriarchal marriage. Social disadvantages to women still serve this purpose. And there is plenty of evidence from antiquity. Both *tutela* and liberation from *tutela* functioned in the interest of the patriarchal family; both Philo and Paul envision marriage as a relationship of slavery for the woman.[106] The author of 1 Timothy not only seeks to exclude women from teaching roles, but also seeks to bind them to marriage and child-rearing (2:8–15; 5:3–16). And it is clear that many of the women who attached themselves to Christianity were converted specifically to Christian sexual asceticism.

But the differences between 1 Corinthians and Galatians suggest a less harmonious and indeed less organized picture than differing applications of a consensus on the end of patriarchal marriage. The disputes in Corinth militate against the view that the baptismal formula issued from or resulted in a community consensus.[107] Some members of some the communities may have understood their practice in this way. Notably those women missionaries of Romans 16 who worked with a male partner may have seen themselves as forming an alternative partnership, rejecting the structures of marriage with or without abstaining from sex. Even more, women who worked alone or with another woman chose an alternative to the patriarchal family. For some of these, the "double-bodied creature" who explains sexuality for Plato and the Rabbis may have offered an image of egalitarian partnership.[108]

But others may have understood the formula as a rejection of sex and marriage, with little or no effect on the proprieties of gender. It is noteworthy that in Rom 16:14, Paul addresses a single greeting to five male names and "the brothers" with them. The NRSV translation "brothers and sisters" may in fact obscure a very early grouping of male celibates. Such a group might well have been inspired by the ambition of spiritual unity expressed by the goal of "making the two one," subsuming all that is female into perfect manhood.

Despite Antoinette Wire's fascinating attempt to depict the conflict behind 1 Corinthians as a contest between two coherent theologies, that of the Corinthian women prophets and their supporters on the one side, with Paul and his Corinthian partisans on the other, and despite Thecla's joint sponsorship of teaching roles and celibacy for women, it is not necessarily the case that the sponsors of celibacy who believed "it is good for a person not to touch a woman" spoke in unison with the women prophets who led the congregation with their heads uncovered or their hair unbound.[109] And the man who "kept his virgin" might well have been able at the same time to keep his authority over her.

Ross Kraemer's study of women in the religions of antiquity remarked with some surprise that it was only in early Christianity that disputes over women's leadership played a significant role.[110] It cannot be shown that Gal 3:28 inspired any more agreement among those who sought to perform this utterance than it does among those who lay claim to its performance today. But it did leave to its successors that true glory of human gender, a nice knock-down argument.

Notes

1. *Through the Looking Glass, and What Alice Found There* (Boston: Books Inc., n.d.), 196.

2. Elizabeth Cady Stanton and the Revising Committee, *The Women's Bible* (1898; repr., Seattle: Coalition on Women and Religion, 1974), 163.

3. Krister Stendahl, *The Bible and the Role of Women: A Case Study in Hermeneutics* (trans. E. Sander; Philadelphia: Fortress, 1966).

4. Elisabeth Schüssler Fiorenza, *In Memory of Her: A Feminist Theological Reconstruction of Christian Origins* (New York: Crossroad, 1983).

5. Madeline Boucher, "Some Unexplored Parallels to 1 Cor 11:11–12 and Gal 3:28: The New Testament on the Role of Women," *CBQ* 31 (1969): 53–55.

6. Stendahl, *Bible*, faced the question of practice directly, arguing that the failure of early Christianity to implement the new creation in regard to slaves and women does not absolve later generations from undertaking that task (35–37). He

did, however, lay down the picture of Judaism as the patriarchal background of the proclamation and of early Christianity that has so frequently been accepted and elaborated (25–28).

7. R. Scroggs, "Paul and the Eschatological Woman," *JAAR* 40 (1972): 283–303; Elaine Pagels, "Paul and Women: A Response to a Recent Discussion," *JAAR* 42 (1974): 538–49.

8. See most recently, Lone Fatum, "Image of God and Glory of Man: Women in the Pauline Congregations," in *The Image of God: Gender Models in Judaeo-Christian Tradition* (ed. Kari Elisabeth Borresen; Minneapolis: Fortress, 1995), 50–133.

9. The popular appeal of this material has been enhanced by explorations of androgyny in Jungian spirituality; see e.g. Elémire Zolla, *The Androgyne: Reconciliation of Male and Female* (New York: Crossroad, 1981).

10. Wayne A. Meeks, "The Image of the Androgyne: Some Uses of a Symbol in Earliest Christianity," *HR* 13 (1974): 165–208.

11. Hans Dieter Betz, *Galatians: A Commentary on Paul's Letter to the Churches of Galatia* (Hermeneia; Phildelphia: Fortress, 1979), 195–96.

12. *Gos. Thom.* 22; *2 Clem.* 12.2; *Gos. Eg.* (Clement of Alexandria, *Strom.* 3.92.2–3.93.1). See Dennis Ronald MacDonald,*"There Is No Male and Female": The Fate of a Dominical Saying in Paul and Gnosticism* (Philadelphia: Fortress, 1987).

13. See note 8 above.

14. Mary Rose D'Angelo, "Trans-scribing Sexual Politics: Images of the Androgyne in Discourses of Antique Religion," in *Descrizioni e Iscrizioni: Politiche del Discorso* (ed. Carla Locatelli and Giovanna Covi; Labirinti 32, Collana del Dipartimento di Scienze Filologiche e Storiche; Trento: Editrice Università degli Studi di Trento, 1998), 1–32.

15. Fatum, "Image of God," 50–57, rejects the idea that there is any inconsistency in Paul's position on women.

16. For a discussion of Gal 3:28 as merismus, under the designation "espressione polare," see Francesco Sarracino, "Forma e funzione di una formula Paolina: Gal, 3.28," *RivB* 28 (1980): 385–406. He argues that the formula is Paul's own expansion of Gal 3:16, not a pre-Pauline tradition. His ground is Paul's use of merismus elsewhere. The nearly universal occurrence of merismus in antiquity makes his argument less than convincing.

17. On "Jew and Greek" see Betz, *Galatians*, 191–92, nn. 79–89.

18. See *Spec.* 1.211, 2.44, 165; Josephus *B.J.* 5.17; *Ant.* 15.136; *C. Ap.* 1.201; on "free/slave," *Abr.* 109; *Post.* 109; Josephus *Ant.* 14.313; 15.136.

19. See, e.g., *Legat.* 208; *Post.* 109; *Mos.* 2.247; *Decal.* 32; *Spec.* 1.138, 144, 211; 2.43, 146; 3.45, 48; 4.142, 203; *Prob.* 140; *Virt.* 220; *Abr.* 109; *Her.* 164; Josephus *Ant.* 4.209.

20. Both Philo and Josephus speak of "male and female gods" (Josephus *C. Ap.* 2.244; Philo *Spec.* 1.331, 2.164; *Decal.* 54); one cannot but suspect that the very mention of sexuality in regard to the gods is pejorative for Philo and Josephus. Josephus also uses "male" and "female" when listing the descendants of the heroic ancestors

(*Ant.* 9.158; 14.300; 17.12); elsewhere he uses the formula "so many males, the rest daughters" (*Ant.* 5.271; 6.129; 7.190, 243; 18.132; 20.92). M. de Mérode contends that "male and female" are synonyms for "man and woman" in Plato and Musonius Rufus: "Une théologie primitive de la femme?" *RTL* 9 (1978): 184–85.

21. *Abr.* 139; *Her.* 139; *Spec.* 1.211.

22. *Opif.* 76; *Her.* 139, 164; *Opif.* 134; *Leg.* 2.13 is less clear; it seems to treat male and female as *genera*.

23. *Spec.* 1.211 (translation mine).

24. W. Dittenberger, *SIG* n. 985. Trans. F. C. Grant, *Hellenistic Religions* (Indianapolis: Bobbs Merrill, 1953), 28–30.

25. Dittenberger, *SIG* 3.15; in line 53 the inscription uses δούλοις for "slaves."

26. *S. Eli. Rab.* (6) 7; (9) 10; and (13) 14. For English translation, see G. W. Braude and S. Kapstein, *Tanna debe Eliyyahu: The Lore of the School of Elijah* (Philadelphia: Jewish Publication Society, 5741/1981), 124, 151–52, and 188. In fact, there are two more sections in the midrash that use the pairs. See Boucher, "Some Unexplored Parallels," 53–55. On the date of the text—anywhere from the third to the tenth century—see Braude and Kapstein, *Tanna debe Eliyyahu*, 3–12.

27. *Yalkut* on Genesis 22 and Judges 4 seems to have been taken over from *S. Eli. Rab.* 6 (7) and 9 (10) as does *Lev. Rab.* 2.11; *Exod. Rab.* 21.4 is similar in thought to *S. Eli. Rab.* (13) 14.

28. See also Boucher, "Unexplored Parallels," 53–55.

29. Boucher, "Unexplored Parallels," 50–58.

30. *Spec.* 1.211, cited above.

31. *Cher.* 111.

32. *Post.* 109 (Colson and Whitaker, LCL).

33. The disadvantage to women and attempts to counter it are treated by Meeks, "Androgyne," 167–80. Schüssler Fiorenza, *Memory*, 42–95, 99–104, discusses the problems of describing the situation of women in antiquity. See also Bernadette Brooten, "Early Christian Women and Their Cultural Context: Issues of Method in Historical Reconstruction," in *Feminist Perspectives in Biblical Scholarship* (ed. Adela Yarbro Collins; Chico, Calif.: Scholars Press, 1983), 65–91.

34. Thales in Diogenes Laertius, *Lives* 1.33; Plato in Lactanctius, *Inst.* 3.19. Plutarch likewise attributes the other pairs to Plato but omits "a man and not a woman" (*Marius* 46.1).

35. *t. Ber.* 7.18,; *y. Ber.* 9.1; *b. Men.* 43b.

36. In *Birkot ha shahar* from the Morning Service of the synagogue liturgy. *B. Men* 43b testifies to the antiquity of this version.

37. For discussions of these texts, see Meeks, "Androgyne," 167–68; Schüssler Fiorenza, *Memory*, 217 and nn. 38 and 39. Dennis MacDonald, *Fate*, 123–24, views only the pair "male and female" as traditional. He suggests that the blessing may have influenced Paul to introduce the other two pairs. Boucher also suggests that the blessing may have influenced Paul's formulation of Gal 3:28. But the variations in the for-

mula and the difficulty of dating its entry into Judaism make it difficult to sustain the view that it influenced Paul.

38. For a full discussion of these categories, see Richard A. Baer, *Philo's Use of the Categories Male and Female* (Leiden: E.J. Brill, 1970).

39. *Spec.* 3.178 (Colson, LCL).

40. *QG.* 4.15 (Marcus, LCL); cf. *Leg.* 2.97; *Abr.* 102; *Sacr.* 103; *Cher.* 8, 50; *Det.* 28; *Somn.* 2.185 ; *Mos.* 68.

41. See especially *Leg.* 2.

42. *Leg.* 2.38.

43. *Leg.* 2.50.

44. *Abr.* 101; cf. *Aet.* 69; *QG.* 3.18; 4.15; *Sacr.* 103; *Leg.* 3.178.

45. On traditions of philosophical interpretation before Philo, see Thomas H. Tobin, S.J., *The Creation of Man: Philo and the History of Interpretation* (Washington, D.C.: Catholic Biblical Association, 1983).

46. The reasons Philo gives for the Essenes' celibacy approach in tone and content Juvenal's *Sat.* 6.

47. MacDonald, *Fate*, argues against the original unity of the formula.

48. Cf. Rom 1:14–16 "to Greeks and barbarians"; "to Jew first and then to Greek."

49. Schüssler Fiorenza, *Memory*, 213–14, sees this text's inclusion of women and slaves as representative of the mystery cults other than Mithraism; cf. Meeks, "Androgyne," 169.

50. *S. Eli. Rab.* (6) 7. The point is not the liberation of slaves, women, or Gentiles, but to inculcate the view that despite the fall of the temple, God supplies atonement for Israel.

51. *S. Eli. Rab.* (9) 10. Here the point is to defend the prophecy of Deborah against objections to the idea that women can prophesy. *Eliyyahu Rabbah* believed that there had been seven Gentile as well as seven women prophets: (28) 29.

52. *S. Eli. Rab.* (13) 14.

53. *Y. Ber.* 9.1 explains the reason a man should give thanks for not having been born a woman: a woman is not given the commandments. *Y. Ber.* 9.1 does not include the blessing for not having been born a slave. Presumably the reason is the same, as slaves are also exempted from the commandments. *B. Men.* 43b includes a protest that the case of the slave and the woman are the same. The blessing for not having been born a Gentile is because the Gentiles are "nothing beside him" (Isa 40:17).

54. Hippolytus *Trad. Ap.* 21 specifies that the baptizands be stripped, reclothed after baptism, and then brought into the assembly. See the reconstruction of Bernard Botte, *La Tradition apostolique de Saint Hippolyte: Essai de reconstitution* (LQF 39; Munster: Aschendorffsche Buchverhandlung, 1963); also *Hippolyte de Rome: La Tradition apostolique d'après les anciennes versions* (SC 11; Paris: Editions du Cerf, 1984). By the late fourth century the practice is clearly established. Egeria relates that in Jerusalem the candidates are baptized nude, then clothed and led into the Anastasis

with the bishop and from there to the Basilica of the Cross, where the congregation was assembled (*Itinerarium* 38.1–2). For a more extensive discussion, see Mary R. D'Angelo, "Veils, Virgins and the Tongues of Men and Angels: Women's Heads as Sexual Members in Ancient Christianity," in *Off with Her Head! The Denial of Women's Identity in Myth, Religion, and Culture* (ed. Howard Eilberg-Schwarz and Wendy Doniger; Berkeley: University of California Press, 1995), 131–64, esp. 136–37 and nn. 23–28.

55. Of particular interest is Theodore's reference to a practice of placing a linen stole over the head before baptism to proclaim the freeing of the candidate (Theodore of Mopsuestia, *Instructions* part 2 sermon 3).

56. See also Meeks, "Androgyne," 183–84 and n. 82; Wayne Meeks, *The First Urban Christians* (New Haven: Yale University Press, 1983), 151, esp. n. 49; 155, n. 68.

57. Rom 13:12, 14; 1 Cor 15:53–54; 2 Cor 5:3; 1 Thess 5:8; Eph 4:24, 6:11, 14; Col 3:10, 12; *Gos. Thom.* 22.

58. NHL 13, 1, 45.17–21.

59. *Clem.* 1.24.

60. Paul Zanker, *The Power of Images in the Age of Augustus* (Jerome Lectures 16; trans. Alan Shapiro; Ann Arbor: University of Michigan Press, 1988), 162–66.

61. See D'Angelo, "Veils," 137 and n. 25. The toga, as the badge of citizenship in the empire, was an object of particular concern in the Augustan reform; see Zanker, *Power*, 162.

62. See also D'Angelo, "Veils," 136–38. It should be noted, however, that Gregory of Nazianzus complains that the baptismal garment had become the occasion of ostentation (*Sermon on Holy Baptism* 23–24).

63. Betz, *Galatians*, 131, identifies the baptismal tradition as the centerpoint of the *probatio* section of the letter.

64. See Margaret MacDonald, "Reading Real Women through the Undisputed Letters of Paul," *Women and Christian Origins* (ed. Ross Shepard Kraemer and Mary Rose D'Angelo; New York: Oxford University Press, 1999), 199–220.

65. Bernadette Brooten, "Junia, . . . Outstanding among the Apostles," in *Women Priests: A Catholic Commentary on the Vatican Declaration* (ed. Leonard and Arlene Swidler; New York: Paulist, 1977), 141–45.

66. See Schüssler Fiorenza, *Memory* 170; Josephine Massengbyrde Ford, "Women Leaders in the New Testament," in *Women Priests*, 132.

67. Mary Rose D'Angelo, "Women Partners in the New Testament," *JFSR* 6 (1990): 65–86.

68. Averil Cameron, "Neither Male Nor Female," *Greece and Rome* 27 (1980): 65; see also the careful treatment of Roman women in Judith Hallett, "Women's Lives in the Ancient Mediterranean," in *Women and Christian Origins*, 13–34.

69. See Ross Shepherd Kraemer, *Her Share of the Blessings: Women's Religions among Pagans, Jews, and Christians in the Greco-Roman World* (New York: Oxford University Press, 1992); Lynn LiDonnici, "Women's Religious Lives in the Greco-

Roman City," in *Women and Christian Origins*, 80–102; for inscriptional evidence see Ross Shepherd Kraemer, *Maenads, Martyrs, Matrons, Monastics: A Sourcebook on Women's Religions in the Greco-Roman World* (Philadelphia: Fortress, 1988).

70. Bernadette Brooten, *Women Leaders in the Ancient Synagogue* (Chico, Calif.: Scholars Press, 1982).

71. *Sat.* 6.541–548; see Mary Rose D'Angelo, "Women in Luke-Acts: A Redactional View," *JBL* 109 (1990): 441–61; also Mary Rose D'Angelo in *Women and Christian Origins*, 194; see also Ross Shepherd Kraemer's remarks on the rabbinic materials in *Women and Christian Origins*, 71–72.

72. See M. de Mérode, "Théologie," 178; so also Stendahl, *Bible*, 32–35.

73. For references and discussion, see Margaret Y. MacDonald, *Early Christian Women and Pagan Opinion: The Power of the Hysterical Woman* (Cambridge: Cambridge University Press, 1996).

74. Botte, *La Tradition*, 21.

75. See Mary Rose D'Angelo, "The Garden Once and Not Again: 1 Cor 11:11–12 as an Interpretation of Gen 1:26," in *Intrigue in the Garden: Studies in the History of Exegesis of Genesis 1–3* (ed. Gregory Robbins; New York: Edwin Mellen, 1988), 1–42.

76. Phyllis Bird has suggested that this is the meaning of Gen 1:27b in the priestly narrative: "'Male and Female He Created Them': Genesis 1:27b in the Priestly Account of Creation," *HTR* 74 (1981):129–59; reprinted in Phyllis Bird, *Missing Persons and Mistaken Identities: Women and Gender in Ancient Israel* (Minneapolis: Fortress, 1997), 123–54.

77. Schüssler Fiorenza, *Memory*, 211, n. 22.

78. Cf. M. de Mérode, "Théologie," 178, n. 11.

79. CD 4.19–5.1; Florentino García Martínez, trans., *The Dead Sea Scrolls Translated: The Qumran Texts in English* (2nd ed.; Leiden: Brill; Grand Rapids: Eerdmans, 1996), 35–36. See also Chaim Rabin, *The Zadokite Documents* (Oxford: Oxford University Press, 1954), 17–19. Cf. Rabin's translation (16–18); also see Rabin, n. 1 on line 21, p. 17. See also Paul Winter, "Sadoqite Fragments IV, 20, 21 and the Exegesis of Genesis 1:27 in late Judaism," *ZAW* 68 (1956): 71–84.

80. On this see the discussion of the word translated "principle" in Lawrence H. Schiffman, *The Halakah at Qumran* (SJLA 16; Leiden: Brill, 1975), 49–54. For a different view, see Ginzburg, cited in Rabin, *Zadokite Documents*, n. 3 on 4.20, p. 16.

81. *Mos.* 2.60–61; *Praem.* 22.

82. *Her.* 164.

83. *Cher.* 43; *Opif.* 161.

84. *Opif.* 134; my translation (cf. Colson and Whitaker, LCL).

85. On Josephus' conviction that he renders the intention of scripture in changes of order, see H. W. Basser, "Josephus as Exegete," *JAOS* 107 (1987): 21–30, esp. 22–24. Basser makes an excellent case for Josephus' intentional revision of the creation of Eve, but neglects to consider the tradition that precedes Josephus.

86. *Ant.* 1.35.

87. Of the second week of creation (3.1). The chronology of *Jubilees'* creation account is somewhat confusing; the naming of the animals concludes with this observation, and is followed by the creation of Eve. But 3.8 claims that both Adam and "the rib, his wife" were created in the first week and she was shown to him in the second week.

88. Trans. O. S. Wintermute, in James H. Charlesworth, ed., *The Old Testament Pseudepigrapha* (2nd ed.; Garden City, N.Y.: Doubleday, 1985), 58. J. M. Evans, *Paradise Lost and the Genesis Tradition* (Oxford: Clarendon, 1968), 30–31, claims that *Jubilees'* revision of Gen 2:18–20 is intended to exclude the idea that a companion for Adam was sought among the animals. The inclusion of "male and female" here seems to me to do exactly the opposite.

89. *Gen. Rab.* 17.4, *bn zwg*.

90. *ʾAbot R. Nat.* 8. See the edition of Solomon Schechter, ed., *Aboth de Rabbi Nathan* (New York: Philipp Feldheim, 1967), 23. This opinion is introduced to resolve a problem about the view that Eve and Adam were created back-to-back, i.e., as the androgyne, or rather as a double-bodied creature. See also Anthony J. Saldarini, trans., *The Fathers according to Rabbi Nathan (Abot de Rabbi Nathan) Version B* (SJLA 11; Leiden: Brill, 1975), 77–79, nn. 16–23. But they seem to have originated independently. *ʾAbot R. Nat.* harmonizes them to answer the question why Eve was not given to Adam if she had been created with him. *Jub.* 3.8 also describes Adam and Eve as having been created at the same time and only shown to each other later. As far as I can tell from the translations of the Ethiopic, *Jubilees'* account precludes the idea that Adam was a double-bodied creature: "and he took one bone from the midst of his bones for the woman" (3.5; trans. Wintermute, *Pseudepigrapha*, 59).

91. See Samuel Krauss, *Griechische und Lateinische Lehnwörter in Talmud, Midrash, und Targum*, vol. 2 (1899; Hildesheim: Georg Olms, 1964), s.v. *zwg*, 1 (p. 240). Krauss also cites the nouns *zwwg* or *zywwg*, which were constructed from the same stem and mean marriage (243). See also Marcus Jastrow, *A Dictionary of the Targumim, Talmud Babli, Yerushalmi, and Midrashic Literature* (New York: Judaica Press, 1971), s.v. *zwg* and *zwwg*, 383.

92. These readings appear at Gen 1:27, 2:18, and 5:2 in the Paris ms., and at Gen 1:27, 2:18, and 2:20 in the Vatican ms., as well as the Leipzig and Nürnberg mss. See Michael A. Klein, *The Fragment-Targums of the Pentateuch according to their Extant Sources*, vol. 1 (AnBib 76; Rome: Biblical Institute, 1980), 44, 45, 48, 126, 129.

93. Alejandro Diez-Macho, *Neophyti I Genesis* (Madrid-Barcelona: Consejo Superior de Investigaciones Cientificos, 1968), 7, 11, 27.

94. Krauss, *Lehnwörter*, s.v. *zwg*, 1 p. 240.

95. *b. Yebam.* 63a; this seems to be an attempt to explain the beginning of Gen 2:23: "This time (*zoth hapaʿam*) flesh of my flesh. . . ."

96. Cf. *t. Yebam.* 8.4; *y. Yebam.* 6.6; *b. Yebam.* 61b–62a. An alternate version of Beth Hillel's opinion claims that they required a male *or* a female; this view does not

use Gen 5:2. The *Tosephta* attributes it to R. Jonathan, the *Babylonian Talmud* to R. Nathan. *Y. Yebam.* 6.6 attributes a rationale for this alternative to R. Abun.

97. Ben Witherington, "Rites and Rights for Women," *NTS* 27 (1981): 593–604, has claimed that the Rabbis interpreted Gen 1:27–28 together, and that "male and female" in Gal 3:28 expresses the command "increase and multiply." There are problems with the text on which he bases it: *b. Yebam.* 63b appears to envisage Gen 9:6 and 7, in which "male and female" does not appear.

98. *Gen. Rab.* 8.1, cf. 14.2.

99. *Opif.* 134.

100. *Qoheleth Rabbah* (London: Soncino, n.d.), 419. The text actually appears to say "any Jew." This text may assume that Adam was created as an androgyne. But the explicit reference is to marriage.

101. A. Cohen, trans., *Midrash Rabbah Ecclesiates* (London: Soncino, n.d.), 238–39. The material in brackets is the addition of the translator, who appears to see the reference to being as one (*kʾhd*) as a use of Gen 2:24. I have added the parentheses. The blessing in Gen 1:28 is frequently interpreted as a marriage blessing; see, e.g., *Gen. Rab.* 8.12, 13.

102. Witherington, "Rites," argues that Paul formulated Gal 3:28 to stand against the position of the Judaizers in Galatia who had been demanding not only circumcision but also obedience to the command to "increase and multiply" (Gen 1:28). Galatians shows no evidence of such a position on the part of Paul's opponents.

103. Mary Rose D'Angelo, "Colossians," in *Searching the Scriptures: A Feminist-Ecumenical Commentary* (ed. Elisabeth Schüssler Fiorenza; New York: Crossroad, 1994), 313–24.

104. See also Meeks, "Androgyne," 189–97.

105. Schüssler Fiorenza, *Memory*, 211.

106. *Hypoth.* 7.3 claims that the law requires a woman to serve her husband (δουλεύειν); Paul speaks of the death of a husband as the end of bondage (δέδεται) or slavery, in praxis in 1 Cor 7:39, and as an analogy in Rom 7:1–6. It should be noted that Paul sees this imagery as appropriate for either woman or man (1 Cor 7:15 δεούλεται, 7:26 δέδεται).

107. Schüssler Fiorenza, *Memory*, 143, has an answer to this. She argues that the Jesus movement had already abolished patriarchal marriage. Part of her basis for this view is a complex exegesis of Mark 10:2–9. I find her argument problematic, not least because Mark 10:2–9 appears to use Gen 1:27 as a proof of marriage.

108. D'Angelo, ""Trans-scribing Sexual Politics."

109. See Antoinette Wire, *Corinthian Women Prophets: A Reconstruction through Paul's Rhetoric* (Philadelphia: Fortress, 1990).

110. Kraemer, *Her Share*, 174.

Prolegomena to a Ritual/Liturgical Reading of the Gospel of Mark

CHARLES A. BOBERTZ

*A*nyone who would begin a new study of the Gospel of Mark which takes as a beginning premise the importance of ritual location, both for the creation of the text and its subsequent reception by Christian communities, must face a dizzying array of "prior questions." Two of the most important of these questions have to do with the history, place, and value of ritual studies in the current state of scholarship and one's operative understanding of "ritual location" applied to an interpretation of the text itself.

My work with ritual location and the interpretation of Mark is the distillation of a larger, more ambitious undertaking. This is to take seriously the "postmodern" location of much current scholarship—a location which appears to challenge any overreaching claim for an "objective" scientific interpretation of scripture and instead places more emphasis on the location of the reader as determinative of "meaning"—and to ask whether the liturgical gathering, historical and modern, might well be a location from which meaning (those gathered might say "the meaning") emerges.[1]

I should say outright that I have not as yet undergone a postmodern baptism. In my work I offer "historical" judgments about the nature and purpose of Mark's gospel. These judgments sound very much like the give-and-take of the historical-critical exegetical claims so often made within the modern academy. Yet insofar as I am aware, such judgments emerge from certain basic assumptions of mine about the ritual location of the text and, at times, of its readers. To change these assumptions would alter the interpretation—an admission that often pulls my reading away from more traditional historical-critical claims for objectivity.

In 1994 the journal *Semeia* came out with an issue devoted to the inter-section of new studies of ritual theory and practice and more traditional approaches to biblical texts. Both the avant-garde purpose of the journal and the fledgling nature of the articles signaled that scholars were breaking rela-tively new ground in the application of the study of ritual to biblical inter-pretation. Indeed, a cogently argued essay in this issue by Frank Gorman out-lines just why this is so.[2] Gorman posits three separate movements within the emergence of modernity that have served to blind us to the importance of ritual and, more important for my purposes here, have tended to inhibit scholarship from taking ritual seriously as a location for interpretation: nega-tive attitudes toward cult and ritual emerging from the Protestant Refor-mation; the Enlightenment's assumption that cult and ritual were not "rea-sonable" and therefore belong in the category of religious "superstition"; and the emergence of comparative religious studies as part of the historical-critical method.[3]

As is well known, within many Reformation movements there was a renewed emphasis on the superior value of inner experience in relation to, or even divorced from, outer or exterior acts such as ritual practice. Standing over and against any Catholic claim for the reality and efficacy of the sacra-ments was the central Reformation premise of salvation by faith alone. Both Luther and Calvin, for example, agreed that being a Christian was definitively related to the *inner* working of the Holy Spirit. It was by "hearing the word" that one encountered genuine Christian experience.[4] The exterior forms and ritual practices of Catholicism were now discounted as so much hierarchy and legalism. Such emphases within the Reformation also engendered a dis-tinctive pattern of biblical interpretation, namely, a Christocentric rather than an ecclesiocentric interpretation of the Bible (perhaps the ancestor to the modern quest for the historical Jesus). Such interpretations read the priestly and ritualistic passages of the Old Testament as merely prepara-tion for, and anticipation of, the superior teaching of Christ and Christianity. Christ was the "end of the Law" (Rom 10:4), not in terms of goal or fulfill-ment, but in terms of supersession over legal and cultic practices.[5]

Reformation supersessionism paved the way for the seventeenth-century Enlightenment's emphasis on the separation of the rational and reasonable elements of religion from ritual and cultic superstition,[6] a separation which in time gave birth to nineteenth-century theories on "progress" in religion—

the latter subject now increasingly studied within the Protestant academies of Europe. The history of religion was described as moving through stages from primitive—caught up in utilitarian and superstitious ritual—to reasonable and rational religion: one based on interiority, ethics, and morality. It was a remarkably modern and Protestant ideal.[7]

Mary Douglas, in *Purity and Danger*,[8] tells this story with particular poignancy, describing first the work of Edward Tylor on primitive cultures and then, of course, Robertson Smith's *Lectures on the Religion of the Semites.* The moral loftiness of Israel's religious concepts, her ethical idealism, in comparison to the religious and ethical concepts of her more "pagan" neighbors (those caught up in superstition and ritual), was beyond dispute. These "ethical" concepts gave rise in the course of history to the ethical ideals of Christianity. These in turn had "progressed" through their Catholic to their final, Protestant, form:

> The Catholic Church had almost from the first deserted the Apostolic tradition and set up a conception of Christianity as a mere series of formulae containing abstract and immutable principles, intellectual assent to which was sufficient to mold the lives of men who have no experience of a personal relation with Christ.[9]

Catholicism, ancient and modern, was tainted by "formulae" (rituals) and was clearly inferior to the higher forms of personal, revealed religion now available with modern Protestantism. As Douglas relates, this notion of religious progress, emanating from the halls of the academy, culminated in James George Frazer's *Golden Bough*,[10] which enshrined the "evolution" from magic (i.e., purely utilitarian ritual), to religion (a combination of irrational rites and rituals with ethical precepts), and finally to purely reasonable science. Thus the study of comparative religion in the latter part of the nineteenth and early twentieth century inherited and gave academic legitimacy to the Reformation and Enlightenment disparagement of the place of formal ritual in religious practice and experience.

To the extent that the modern historical-critical method of biblical studies was engendered by the Enlightenment's insistence on the hegemony of rational reason and caught up in the larger project of the comparative study of religion, so obvious in *Lectures on the Religion of the Semites*, we can begin now to assess how its interpretive practices and attitudes, its *tradition,* has carried within it a particularly negative assessment of ritual. The emergence and application of an almost fundamental principle of "scientific" objectivity in the comparative study of religion had its biblical studies counterpart in the application of Leopold von Ranke's famous description of the objective of historical studies as *wie es eigentlich gewesen* (how it actually happened). Both comparative religion and biblical studies were caught up in a false evolutionary schema which posited religious ritual either as unreasonable superstition or as part of an arrested stage of development toward the true religion of rational interiority.

Biblical scholarship in the twentieth century, to a large degree, accepted and expanded upon the anti-ritual tradition begun in the previous century. Rudolph Bultmann, by many accounts the most influential exegete of the twentieth century, claimed that at the heart of the New Testament, that is, after scraping off all the accretions (e.g., the sacramentalism in the Gospel of John), is the individual's existential awareness before God.[11] Clearly, this was the triumph of interiority over external form! Ernst Käsemann, an influential student of Bultmann, produced a thorough-going interpretation of Pauline theology based in the split between "law" (often taken to refer to "external" religious requirements and practices) and "gospel" (personal faith in Christ), an interpretation which is still widely influential among exegetes.[12]

With respect to the Hebrew Bible, Jon Levensen's recent work on the secular and modern traditions informing historical criticism has shown the extent to which the pioneers in the "scientific" criticism of the Hebrew Bible contrasted the ethical religion of the prophets with the "dead" religion of post-exilic Judaism. The latter was often characterized as the religion of ritual and harsh observances. This was the dead religion that Christ revived by breathing ethical interiority back into the corpse.[13]

My argument, therefore, is that integral to the history of biblical studies scholarship, as part of the history of modernity, is a built-in bias either against taking ritual seriously as constitutive of religious identity in the ancient world (dead religion) or toward seeing it as part of Jewish legalism trumped by Christianity.[14] The legacy of the devaluation brings with it the danger, at worst, of paying no attention to texts obviously marked by ritual (e.g., most of Leviticus),[15] and at best, of interpreting them merely as curious sidebars to those texts, such as the Gospels, which just might, because of their literal narrative form, grant some access to "what actually happened." Hardly ever is the idea entertained that the literal narrative form of the Gospels may be not so much history mythologized as mythology, built upon the symbolic structure of ritual, historicized.[16]

This of course brings me to the point of asking how scholarship informed by a liturgical and ritual religious tradition should distinguish itself in relation to the distrust of ritual within the modern history of the academic discipline. Put differently, is there at least the possibility that scholars standing *within* a tradition that by and large rejects the conclusions of the Reformation/Enlightenment concerning a conceptual dualism between mind/spirit and embodiment/ritual, would read and interpret the biblical texts differently than those not sharing this particular tradition? If postmodernism has brought us to the point of realizing our imbeddedness in and indebtedness to particular locations of discourse, *including that of the academy,* what difference does that make to the interpretation of texts?

In my own study of the Gospel of Mark I attempt to answer that question by the particular strategies and interpretive practices I adopt in reading the text, beginning with an affirmation of my location within a strong Catholic liturgical tradition. But on a basic theoretical level I should also like to address that question here. First, I would not claim that because of my stance within a liturgical community with its own tradition, only I, and others who stand with me in this location, will be able to read the text in this particular way. My project does not claim to be a "private interpretation" using private language. Rather, it uses recognized practices of scholarship, with attention to their discursive tradition, to offer a reading to others in my location. I also note that my work has been profoundly influenced by the academic study of cultural anthropology. I suspect that Mary Douglas's insights about the disparagement of ritual within the academy emerge, at least in part, from her location as an Irish Catholic in Britain. Yet I am not even aware of the religious tradition, if any, of the other cultural anthropologists whose work has shaped my own thinking, scholars such as Raymond Firth, Roy Rappaport, Nancy Jay, Clifford Geertz, and Victor Turner. What I am claiming is that their insights on the value of ritual—its ability to depict, communicate, and enact a symbolic world—have particular resonance to me as I read the gospel text self-consciously as a Catholic Christian. Hence, my interest in an interpretation that utilizes their insights *emerges* from my communal location as a Catholic, ritually joined with other Catholics in liturgy, and is meant specifically as a contribution to understanding the text from within this tradition. At the same time, I hope that others might find this interpretative approach interesting, perhaps even useful, as they read the text from their own traditions, whether that be purely the academy or particular churches or, like myself, some combination of "all of the above."

Second, and more important, I want to advance an argument that the description and communication of a symbolic world in ritual is an important aspect of the text of Mark that has been, with a few notable exceptions, practically ignored in modern scholarship on Mark. A greater self-awareness within the academy will make it less likely that interpretations embedded in prejudices often inimical to a sacramental tradition such as my own will carry the force of "objectivity" as they impact my tradition's understanding of itself. In this my own work has much the same venue as Jon Levensen's *The Hebrew Bible, the Old Testament, and Historical Criticism* has for the Jewish community.

I know I cannot offer a way out of the hermeneutical circle I have created here, nor do I want to.[17] My particular interest in the text as disclosive of ritual location ("then") is self-consciously derived from my location ("now"), not as a scholar presuming to find an objectivity which might well be false (and for that reason possibly all the more pernicious in its hegemonic claim) but as a believer gathered with other believers in liturgical ritual, a believer who desires to interpret truthfully, and therefore faithfully, the biblical text.[18]

Perhaps an anecdote is the best way to bring across my point here. In a class on the "quest for the historical Jesus" my students and I read John Howard Yoder's *The Politics of Jesus*.[19] Many would probably agree with me that the work, in its attempt to describe the "historical Jesus," reveals the hand of a person steeped in the Mennonite tradition of pacifism. There is a way in which the book is about and not about the historical Jesus. It is about Jesus in bringing home to us the radical nature of Jesus' call to peacefulness. Yet at the same time we are sure that Yoder has "seen" this aspect of Jesus' ministry more clearly because of his location within the pacificist Mennonite tradition. I submit that much more of our scholarship is like this than historical criticism, in its desire to be objective, would like to admit. And it is obvious that I do not think such attentiveness to location a bad thing. Yoder, *because* of his location within a tradition, revealed to me an aspect of Jesus that I—perhaps seeing through a Catholic lens tainted by Augustine—had not seen. My sense is that traditions reveal strong readings—the anti-ritual bias within the modern history of scholarship is but one example—and that readings ought to be in dialogue, perhaps temporarily even in dispute. For believers, the modern secular academy has a role to play in that dispute but cannot have the final say.

I have already hinted at my operative definition of ritual as a location in which a symbolic world is described and communicated to those gathered.[20] Ritual, therefore, has a role to play in social integration and maintenance, but that is not all it does. Ritual also has a dynamic quality. As Victor Turner describes it in *The Ritual Process,* the liminal unstructured state ("anti-structure") which is so often a part of ritual continually challenges as well as reinforces ordinary social structures found outside of the ritual process. It can act as a sort of dynamic social laboratory in which the necessity of social structure (roles and statuses) is mixed with liminal anti-structure in moments of encounter that can profoundly affect the evolution of social structures.[21]

I would not hesitate to agree with Mary Douglas's claim that we in the modern West, raised within what she terms the elaborated speech code of modernity, are often deaf to the way ritual can and does communicate in other contexts. Attentiveness to ritual, Douglas argues, is dependent not upon a level of social evolution (Pygmies enjoy the same deafness to ritual as moderns), but upon family/kinship structure. Where the positional family/kinship structure is highly positional, where roles and statuses are "given" and strictly enforced within a society, there often exists a ritual system that both communicates and reinforces, in dense symbolic speech, the many status requirements of the social system. Conversely, within a family/kinship system in which roles and statuses are not clearly defined and inculcated—a social system wherein a child never internalizes as "real" a pattern of social statuses and never experiences authoritative social control, which exalts the self-evident capacity of the social system to command obedience—in such situations the developed capacity to "understand" the particular aesthetic communication of ritual may be lacking.[22]

With appropriate modification, Mary Douglas's analysis of the relationship between ritual as a restricted speech code and positional social structure has heuristic value when considering the text of Mark or other early Christian literature. In the first place, there is no question that ancient society as a whole, from which early Christian groups emerged, was marked by highly positional social structure.[23] In addition to the capacity actually to "hear" ritual communication, such communication would have been necessary in relation to the boundedness or sectarian quality of a group, such as the early Christians, within the larger social system.[24] The symbolic world of a subgroup, its sense of a different reality, must be maintained against enormous social pressure to conform to the "ordinary" symbolic social reality of the larger society. Ritual would have been perhaps the most important means of ensuring the survival of such a group.

If this is so, then it stands to reason that a primary task of a *text* such as the Gospel of Mark would be the inculcation of a new symbolic reality by offering, in present threatening circumstances, a new way to understand and incorporate the ritual communication within the group. The text itself, I argue, emerged from continuing symbolic communication of ritual and offered back to the community a new way of "hearing" that same ritual.[25]

One good example of this manner of reading the gospel comes in a consideration of the story recorded in Mark 7:1–23: the confrontation of Jesus with the Pharisees over eating with common hands (κοιναῖς). This pericope has most often been interpreted within modern critical study as involving an early Christian attack on the complex ritual system of ancient Judaism for determining *kashrut*, in favor of some sort of internalized faithfulness or more "ethical" position espoused by the Markan Jesus.[26]

One prominent example of this sort of reading of the passage is a 1986 article by Jerome Neyrey.[27] In an essay that clearly shows how hidden anti-ritual ideological convictions can be present within a "social scientific" interpretation of early Christian texts, Neyrey contrasts the criterion of membership in the Markan Christian community as "concern [with] the interior and the heart"[28] with the Jewish community's maintenance of a particularistic purity system manifest, one is led to suppose, in exterior ritual forms. He argues, for example, that in the perspective of the Gospel of Mark, the Jewish "core value" was holiness, while Jesus' "core value" was mercy. The Jews are shown to possess a strong purity system marked by "particularity," and this is to be contrasted with a weaker Christian purity system that was more "inclusive."[29]

Yet if we consider even briefly the wider narrative context of Jesus' demonstrations of mercy in this Gospel, for example, the healing of the paralytic in Mark 2:1–12, it becomes obvious that what is at stake in almost all such narrative portrayals of Jesus is the Christian community's claim to possess the eschatological prerogative to forgive sins: "'But that you may know that the Son of man has authority on earth to forgive sins'—he said to the paralytic—'I say to you, rise, take up your pallet and go home'" (Mark 2:10–11 RSV; cf. Mark 1:4). The heart of the Christian claim in the narrative is actually to *be*—in the context of the ritual gathering—the eschatological community of physical and moral perfection.[30] The claim, against other groups no doubt, is that the ritual gathering (which one enters through baptism) is a space without sin and *therefore* a space of physical perfection (healing and resurrection). The capacity of the group to declare the forgiveness of sins is the sine qua non of the truthfulness of such a claim.

The contrast in the story of Mark 7:1–23, therefore, is not "inclusive mercy" versus "exclusive holiness," as if the ancient Christian community enjoyed or claimed some moral and ethical superiority to the Pharisees. Rather, it is a Christian claim for absolute "holiness" (physical and moral perfection) which is here being advanced against an (implied) Pharisaic claim for holiness. It is a struggle between ancient religious communities moving toward exclusive self-definition vis-à-vis each other.

In contrast to the notion that the Markan community in its narrative portrayal of Jesus is somehow breaking down exclusive and exclusionary boundaries of purity (for example, in Jesus being touched by the menstruating woman of Mark 5:25–34 or the declaration that all foods are "clean" in Mark 7:18–19), one instead might infer from such texts the dramatic and exclusive eschatological claim of the early Christian community: the greater holiness (wholeness) which marks the integration of previous physical and social distinctions is the hallmark of the new, *ritually pure*, eschatological community. The woman with the hemorrhage is no longer ritually *impure; all* foods are now *kosher*. If anything, however, the boundaries of purity, that which marks the common from the sacred, are even higher in the Markan community. A very stringent sexual ethic is pronounced (Mark 10:11–12; cf. 1 Cor 7:10–13); ordinary social life is disrupted (e.g., Mark 3:31–35; 10:21); what is more, the potential price of ritual participation in baptism and Eucharist is martyrdom (Mark 10:35–40).[31] In the story of Mark 7:1–23 we do not see the early Christian community "progressing" from ritual communication bound up with positional statuses—the Pharisaic demarcation of the "holy" from the symbolic world of the larger society—to an ethical interiority (a religion of the heart), but rather a movement from one form of ritual communication marking the boundaries of one group (Jews) to another form of ritual communication marking the boundaries of another group (the early Christian community represented in Mark's narrative). This is not a move to an elaborated speech code in which ritual communication is only so much noise, but rather a dramatic claim for a new eschatological authority established and sustained by the *new* ritual communication (baptism and Eucharist) within the Christian community. The story in Mark 7:1–23 is a prelude to the new and specific demands for ritual Eucharist incorporating the Gentiles in the story of Mark 8:1–9 (cf. 8:19–21).[32]

My concern here not to offer a point by point refutation of one article among the vast outpouring of scholarship on Mark in recent years, but rather to make clear by example a glaring tendency of scholarship in the historical-critical period, namely, to interpret the Gospels as if they were not produced by early Christians who were shaped by and practiced external, particular, and highly exclusive rituals. All too often Jesus becomes like one of us moderns: brandishing interior ethical morality over against the ritual "legalism" of the opposition Jews.

I conclude this brief essay with two main observations: (1) given our knowledge of the highly positional social structure of ancient society, we should presume that the ancients were expertly attuned to the dense restricted speech of ritual communication; where we don't notice this, it is probably because we are not looking; (2) we should also presume that early Christians, constituting a new and highly intentional social group, bounded and in great tension with the larger society, effectively communicated and enacted their new symbolic world in the form of particular and exclusive rituals. That such presumptions make a great difference in reading the text of Mark is something I have begun to hint at here.

NOTES

1. Following Foucault, Catherine Bell, *Ritual Theory, Ritual Practice* (Oxford: Oxford University Press, 1992), 13, suggests that "the nature of objectivity itself rests on historical paradigms and strategies of human inquiry effective within a specific milieu." In turn, Jon D. Levensen, *The Hebrew Bible, the Old Testament, and Historical Criticism* (Philadelphia: Westminster/John Knox Press, 1993), 30, argues that historical-critical inquiry must recognize itself as a tradition, a community of interpreters, rather than the Archimedean point from which all other traditions are judged. Moreover, historical-critical interpreters often assert a secular analogy to religious revelation: definitive insight, not empirically proved, into the meaning of things not directly experienced, things which might be differently interpreted by those who had the experience.

2. Frank H. Gorman, "Ritual Studies and Biblical Studies: Assessment of the Past, Prospects for the Future," *Semeia* 67 (1994): 13–36.

3. Mary Douglas, *Natural Symbols: Explorations in Cosmology* (New York: Pantheon, 1970), 7, characterizes the move toward anti-ritualism in three phases: first, the contempt for external ritual forms, second, the private internalizing of religious experience, and third, the move toward humanist philanthropy. She characterizes the development of anti-ritualism in the modern academy as the "central problem of religious history" (p. 8).

4. Gorman, "Ritual," 3. As a young Catholic biblical studies graduate student at Yale, I still remember the profound interest in the *kerygma* (the proclamation of the "word") as perhaps "the" operative category of interpretation in my biblical studies classes. Perhaps it was the dissonance of that experience which first fostered my interest in the importance of location in the act of interpretation.

5. See Mark McVann, "Introduction," *Semeia* 67 (1994): 7–8. A good discussion of this perception of the split between law (ritual) and gospel in the history of scholarship can be found in Howard Eilberg-Schwartz, *The Savage in Judaism: An Anthropology of Israelite Religion in Ancient Judaism* (Bloomington: Indiana University Press, 1990), 46.

6. Contrasted with the Enlightenment emphasis on human freedom and autonomy, ritual had to be evaluated negatively: "Ritual, consisting of prescribed and mindless rules, did not allow for the free choice of the individual" (Gorman, "Ritual," 17). Indeed, any religious practice not consonant with the Enlightenment's own definition of "reason" was impugned with the label "superstitious" (Eilberg-Schwartz, *Savage*, 46). Moreover, such a rational approach to religion ultimately reduced religion to an inner cognitive structure (as in Hegel): the practice of religion was the expression of ideas, beliefs, and thoughts. Hence what one might term an interpretive dualism developed, distinguishing between mind and body, thought and action, and religious "experience" (important to romanticism) and particular practices. The work of several prominent ritual theorists, e.g., Catherine Bell, Ronald Grimes, and Roy A. Rappaport, is largely devoted to overcoming this dichotomy.

7. One is reminded here of Kant's opinion concerning Judaism, that it did not qualify as a religion because it demanded only outward observances and possessed no requirements for a moral disposition. See the discussion of Kant in Eilberg-Schwartz, *Savage*, 58.

8. Mary Douglas, *Purity and Danger* (London: Routledge, Kegan and Paul, 1966), 7–28. See also *Transition and Reversal in Myth and Ritual* (ed. H.S. Versnel; Studies in Greek and Roman Religion 6; Leiden: Brill, 1993), 21–22.

9. Douglas, *Purity*, 18, quoting Robertson Smith.

10. New York: Collier Books, 1922.

11. Rudolph Bultmann, *The Gospel of John: A Commentary* (Philadelphia: Westminster, 1971), 218–37; cf. Raymond E. Brown, *The Gospel according to John* (New York: Doubleday, 1966), cvii.

12. Ernst Käsemann, *Perspectives on Paul* (Philadelphia: Fortress Press, 1971), 138–66. Käsemann is worth quoting here: "In view of the frankness with which ecclesiology in its various variations is made on all sides the decisive criterion of theology, it is worth giving critical attention to the question of whether superstition has not contributed more to the continuity of church history, theology and Christian institutions than faith. . . . Demythologizing is one of the tasks of historical criticism, and it is true that a very much better understanding of the Christian message can be achieved with its help" (p. 153). One might well judge the history of Pauline scholarship in the twentieth century as revolving around the axis of "law versus gospel." See, e.g., Vincent Smiles, *The Gospel and the Law in Galatia: Paul's Response to Jewish-Christian Separatism and the Threat of Galatian Apostasy* (Collegeville, Minn.: Liturgical Press, 1998).

13. Levensen, *Hebrew Bible*, 10–32.

14. See the discussion in Douglas, *Purity*, 1–36.

15. Philip J. Budd, *Leviticus* (Grand Rapids: Eerdmans, 1996), 25–38.

16. Work has begun in this direction, however. In particular see the studies of Mark McVann, "The Passion in Mark: Transformation Ritual," *BTB* (1988): 96–101; "Reading Mark Ritually: Honor, Shame and the Ritual of Baptism" *Semeia* 67 (1994):

179–98; Brenda Dean Schildgen, *Crisis and Continuity: Time in the Gospel of Mark* (Sheffield: Sheffield Academic Press, 1998).

17. Nancy Jay, *Throughout Your Generations Forever: Sacrifice, Religion, and Paternity* (Chicago: University of Chicago Press, 1992), 8, has a cogent discussion of this dilemma: our imbeddedness in a particular tradition enables us to interpret and also prevents us from interpreting perfectly.

18. This is also, I should say, the way I currently situate myself in the postmodern dilemma, a dilemma which appears to offer only an indeterminacy of meaning and asks us, on the basis of no other criteria, to trust such a claim. Hence, insofar as the postmodern location has made us more aware of the elusive nature of objectivity, it has helped us avoid idiolatry through falsely ascribing truth. It has not vitiated the necessity of faith (a postmodern's faith is in indeterminacy), faith which I judge to be constituted within the gathered assembly.

19. Grand Rapids: Eerdmans, 1972.

20. My debt to Durkheim via Douglas, *Purity*, and Clifford Geertz, *The Interpretation of Cultures* (New York: Basic Books, 1973), is perhaps more than apparent here. Durkheim asserted that ritual was the means by which collective beliefs and ideals were simultaneously generated, experienced, and affirmed as real. See Bell, *Ritual*, 20; McVann, "Introduction," 7; Jay, *Generations*, 134. Mary Douglas defines "ritualism" as the heightened appreciation for symbolic action (Douglas, *Symbols*, 8). I have also been influenced by Bobby Alexander's definition (following Victor Turner) of ritual as a symbolic, self-reflective performance that makes a transition to time and space out of the ordinary. See Bobby C. Alexander, *Victor Turner Revisited* (Atlanta: Scholars Press, 1991), 23. Less influential in my work has been Rene Girard's understanding of ritual sacrifice as an activity that controls mimetic desire (which leads to violence) by directing all violence against a single victim—the victim thus becoming the "other" that makes social cohesion possible. See the discussion in James G. Williams, "Sacrifice and the Beginning of Kingship," *Semeia* (1994): 78–79; Jay, *Generations*, 131.

21. I would hasten to add here that it appears, on this analysis, that the activity that had the *most* to do with the dramatic social changes in antiquity wrought by the emergence of the Christian churches was ritual. It was not—to refute one widely popular line of interpretation stemming from Max Weber and popularized through Hans Von Campenhausen's *Kirchliches Amt und geistliche Vollmacht* (Tübingen: J.C.B. Mohr/Siebeck, 1953; ET *Ecclesiastical Authority and Spiritual Power;* Stanford: Stanford University Press, 1969)—the routinization of some free-willing charisma which resulted in a stolid hierarchical church. Rather, the "charisma" was part of the ritual structure of the church from the beginning. See the discussion in James Burtchaell, *From Synagogue to Church* (Cambridge: Cambridge University Press, 1992), 344–52.

22. See the extensive discussion of this part of Mary Douglas's work in Lyndon Farwell, "Betwixt and Between: Anthropological Contributions of Victor Turner

and Mary Douglas toward a Renewal of Roman Catholic Ritual" (Ph.D. diss., The Claremont Graduate School, 1976), 52–100.

23. In particular the Gospels presume, by the very tenor of particular sayings and depictions of Jesus, that the underlying social structure of ancient society would have provided a population attuned to ritual communication. Such scenes as the story of Jesus with his family in Mark 3:31–34 (cf. 6:1–6), as well as the seemingly independent saying recorded in 3:35, would hardly have the jarring effect apparently intended if social status and position within family were of little concern. The same holds true for the familial Q sayings in Luke 14:26 (Matt 10:37)— "If any one comes to me and does not hate his own father and mother and wife and children and brothers and sisters, yes, and even his own life, he cannot be my disciple"—and Luke 9:59–60 (Matt 8:21–22)—"To another he said, 'Follow me.' But he said, 'Lord, let me first go and bury my father.' But he said to him, 'Leave the dead to bury their own dead.'" The provocation of such sayings depends on fully positional family social structure. It should also be noted that, in addition to the fact that the ancient Mediterranean social world was markedly positional with respect to family and overall social structure, it was also a world, for example within Jewish communal life, in which such expectations were communicated and reinforced by a continuous and involved ritual system.

24. When a social group grips its members in tight communal bonds, the religion is ritualist; when this grip is relaxed, ritualism declines, hence the most important determinant of ritualism is the experience of closed social groups. See Douglas, *Symbols*, 13–14.

25. It seems to me that those who place the origins of the text of Mark within the exigencies of persecution would be amenable to aspects of the analysis offered here. See, e.g., Bas M.F. Van Iersel, "Failed Followers in Mark: Mark 13:12 as a Key for the Identification of the Intended Readers," *CBQ* 58 (1996): 244–63. The necessity of maintaining a plausible symbolic universe in the midst of concerted opposition and persecution would heighten the necessity of ritual communication.

26. See, e.g., C.E.B. Cranfield, *The Gospel according to St. Mark* (Cambridge: Cambridge University Press, 1963), 244; James A. Brooks, *Mark* (Nashville: Broadman Press, 1991), 119. For secondary references pertaining to this passage, see Robert H. Gundry, *Mark: A Commentary on His Apology for the Cross* (Grand Rapids: Eerdmans, 1993), *ad loc.*

27. Jerome Neyrey, "The Idea of Purity in Mark's Gospel," *Semeia* 35 (1986): 91–128.

28. Neyrey, "Idea of Purity," 113.

29. I shall only mention what is surely another noteworthy irony in this description of the two communities, namely, that Neyrey's study pays almost no attention to the *Christian* "external" ritual system of baptism and Eucharist and the prominent role this plays in the narrative of Mark. Such an omission serves to highlight an issue which is surely of great importance to post-Holocaust Christian theology: a lack

of sensitivity to the importance of ritual forms can perpetuate false dichotomies (Jews are "legalistic," Christians are "inclusive") between Christians and Jews in the narrative.

30. One notes a similiar understanding in 1 Cor 11:17–34. There Paul warns that Christians who profane the ritual act will suffer *physical* maladies (v. 30). The converse must also be true: the "true" ritual space is a place of physical wholeness.

31. Neyrey also argues that Jews found scriptural legitimation in the Pentateuch (is the ritual system implied here?), while Jesus found his legitimation in the election of Abraham and the prophets (interiority?). Such an interpretation seems to miss Jesus' appeal to Genesis to establish a new standard of sexual purity in Mark 10:6–8, or the bold pronouncement that his claim to messianic status is rooted in the symbolic world of the pentateuchal ritual sabbath (Mark 2:27–28), or his claim to possess the sacrificial system's capacity to atone for sin (Mark 2:5).

32. *Mutatis mutandis,* the same holds true as a reading of Mark 3:31–35. The repositioning and restructuring of the family (Mark 3:35) into a bounded and intentional group at odds with their former social structure is both made possible by and reinforced through ritual communication—a communication that is even written into the narrative plot itself as these new disciples apparently, by the sixth chapter, gather for the Eucharist in the wilderness.

The Transfiguration of Christ
The Transformation of the Church

FREDERICK W. NORRIS

Students of Rowan Greer learned to know him as priest and scholar. In everyday life his critical eye is always informed by his deep sense of mystery, worship, and pastoral care. One published indication of that synthesis is his *Broken Lights and Mended Lives*.[1] Thus to look at the Transfiguration of Christ in connection with the transformation of the Church reflects his influence, my concerns, and the interests of the texts, both biblical and patristic.

Western Christian tradition has a place within its worship for the Transfiguration, but not one as strong as that of Eastern Orthodoxy. Roman Catholic liturgy celebrates it, as do Anglican services and many of the more liturgical Protestant traditions that pay attention to the church year. In Eastern Orthodoxy, however, the Feast of the Transfiguration is one of the twelve high festivals. We know from early Christian art that it was recognized as an important theme in some church buildings throughout the empire. The apse mosaics in the Church of St. Catherine at Mt. Sinai and the Church of Sant' Apollinare in Classe near Ravenna show how significant the event was, not only to a monastic community and to a common congregation, but also to the emperor who financed the building programs. Other depictions of the Transfiguration also occur both in architectural art and manuscript illustration.[2] It was meaningful for Christian worshippers who could not read as well as for those who could.

In my own heritage within Christian Churches/Churches of Christ, the Transfiguration is seldom celebrated. Correcting that deficiency is itself a clear indication of how the reclaiming of liturgical traditions, particularly

Orthodox ones, can support the claim of an apparently Protestant heritage to pay close attention to Scripture. The Gospel of John does not include the Transfiguration of Christ, but each synoptic Gospel does (Matt 17:1–3; Mark 9:2–13; Luke 9:28–36). In them the event is placed between one of Jesus' predictions of his death and the healing of a boy with a troubling or evil spirit. The outline of the story is quite similar in each Gospel.

Mark's account opens with Jesus taking Peter, James, and John up a mountain after an interval of six days from the last event. There Jesus is transfigured; his clothing begins to shine a brilliantly bleached white. Both Moses and Elijah appear and talk with him. Peter and the other two are so frightened that Peter does not understand what he is saying when he suggests building three tabernacles to honor Moses, Elijah, and Jesus. A cloud overshadows them and a voice from the cloud declares that Jesus is the beloved Son who should be heard. Moses and Elijah disappear and Jesus stands alone (Mark 9:2–8).

Luke's version says that after eight days the four go up the mountain to pray. While Jesus is in prayer, the semblance of his face changes as well as his clothes. Moses and Elijah appear with Jesus in glory and speak to him about his departure. The three disciples observe this glory in the midst of fighting sleep. After Moses and Elijah disappear, Peter suggests three tabernacles be built, but he does not know what he is saying. While he is speaking the cloud covers them, they are afraid, and the voice speaks of the chosen Son. Jesus then stands alone. The disciples tell no one of what happened (Luke 9:28–36).

Matthew develops a story outline somewhat similar to that of the other two synoptic writers, but details vary. His account agrees with Mark against Luke that the interval is six days, but with Luke against Mark that both Jesus' face and clothes shine. Yet Matthew fails to mention Peter not knowing what he says, something that both Mark and Luke declare. The voice from the cloud announces that this is the beloved and well-pleasing Son. The three are so terrified by the voice that they fall on their faces and must be touched by Jesus; when they look up, Jesus is alone. On the way down the mountain, Jesus tells the three to keep quiet about the event until after the Son of Man is raised from the dead. They ask Jesus why teachers of the law said that Elijah must precede the Son of Man; Jesus responds that Elijah has already appeared. The disciples understand that the Elijah who has come is John the Baptist (Matt 17:1–13).

Post-biblical theological comments on the Transfiguration are widespread. John McGuckin, in his wise and balanced book *The Transfiguration of Christ in Scripture and Tradition*, makes no claim to have ferreted out all the references.

Yet he both studies and translates passages from various pieces on the Transfiguration: twenty-one Greek theologians from Irenaeus to Gregory Palamas, and ten Latin theologians from Tertullian to Ambrose Autpertus. His conclusion is clear and justified:

> The Fathers evidently pursue three concerns: the wonder of the event as a theophany, the power of the event as a salvific act of God, and the promise of the event as a paradigm of the Resurrection of Christ's saints. Within the whole tenor of the Patristic analyses two great themes emerge and they are firstly the vision of Christ's radiance as a manifestation of his own essential deity, a glory that did not come on him from without but rather proceeded out to his disciples from within; and secondly that the power which shone out from Jesus on the nucleus of his church should be interpreted as his promise of Easter transfiguration for that church universally.[3]

McGuckin sees the continuing life of the Church, particularly his Eastern Orthodox tradition, wrapped up in the Transfiguration that develops within the context of the mystery called deification.[4] The gospel accounts emphasize brilliant glory in the midst of humiliation, resurrection promised in the midst of death. Within the Church the Transfiguration acts as "an ascetical symbol" calling for "a sensitivity and strength of soul similar to that possessed by Christ himself."[5]

I have no quarrel with McGuckin's conclusions; indeed I have suggested in meditations before the celebration of the Lord's Supper within my home congregation that the Transfiguration be remembered because of its connection with the consensual and cogent doctrine of deification.[6] But within the comments of early Christian exegetes—another clear interest of Greer's[7]—here viewed primarily from Origen's *Commentary on Matthew* and Chrysostom's *Homilies on Matthew,* the Transfiguration receives a central place in describing both the full revelation of God and the transformation of the Church. I would like both to deepen and broaden the picture McGuckin provides by making three observations.[8]

First, in reference to modern NT studies both as an academic discipline and a need of the Church, Origen and Chrysostom are caught by the details of the texts and their relationships to other biblical passages. They give evidence of critical intellect engaged with Scripture. At the same time they always treat the details and relationships of those texts theologically from a group of assumptions held by the communities in which they worship, ones that brightly color their interpretations. When Luke states that the event happened about eight days after Jesus' prediction of his death and both Mark and Matthew say six, the apparent discrepancy must be handled. John Chrysostom tries to combine the two dates by indicating that the number "eight" represents "the very day on which He spoke, and the one on which He led them up." The "six" stand only for "the days between them."[9]

Even the tiniest difference should be explained if at all possible, but this does not depend upon a wooden understanding of inerrancy. The fathers' sense of the trustworthy character of Scripture can have them speak about its lack of errors, but they never protect the Bible with the doctrine of inerrancy that was developed in seventeenth-century Protestantism. Origen insisted that Scripture was divine; it always had a spiritual meaning, but it did not always have a bodily meaning. At times literal absurdities were intentionally woven into the text in order to alert the reader that deeper truths were underneath the surface text problems. Here divine verses had to include literal errors if they were to lead toward eternal truths.[10] Many seventeenth-century Protestants identified the inerrant text as the literal one. They put forward an infallible Bible to counter what they saw as a fallible tradition. Patristic divines were not, however, caught up in such a restrictive sense of truth that any difference in the texts would sink the ship. These earlier theologians were never so deeply absorbed with intra-Christian debate that they forgot their pagan audience. They fought "heretics" but they lived within religiously pluralistic times. Defending a totally consistent scriptural text, the same in every account, would be derided by their pagan opponents as proof of dreadful complicity. For them both unity in faith and diversity in detail are important. Although his views may be contested at points, Chrysostom says it well.

> Why, when there were many disciples, did only two apostles and two of their followers write? (Paul's disciple, the other Peter's, along with Matthew and John wrote the gospels.) Because they did nothing pridefully but everything to assist [others]. Wasn't one gospel writer enough to tell the whole [story]? Yes, but if four write, neither at the same times, nor in the same places, neither having met each other nor having talked about it, and then they speak as if they were one mouth, [their agreement] serves as a great proof of the truth.
>
> Of course someone will say, "But they clearly disagree in a number of places." Yet [such disagreement] is itself evidence for their truthfulness. If they did agree about everything exactly according to time, place and even specific words, not one of our adversaries would believe that

they hadn't met together and cooked it up on the basis of some human scheme. That kind of full agreement never arises from simplicity, [more from complicity]. Even the disagreement in small things frees them from suspicion and shows their character.

And if [a detail] about times or places is different, it does not wound the truth which they express. As we go through [Matthew], as far as God empowers us, we will point out such things. What you need to recognize, along with other things we have mentioned, is that among these main leaders, those who have formed our life and have woven our teaching together, there is no disagreement on even little points [of significance].

What do they then agree on? That God became man, that He worked miracles, that He was crucified, that He was buried, that He rose again, that He has commanded what we need for salvation, that He has given a law that does not contradict the Old Testament, that He is a Son, that He is only-begotten, that He is true Son, that He is of the same nature as the Father, and many things like these. In such matters they always fully agree.

If they have not all mentioned every miracle, one these and another those, don't get upset. If one [of the gospel writers] had told [every story of a miracle], the accounts of the others would have been superfluous, but if each one had given only an account of new deeds, each different from the other, there would be no evidence of their agreement. Therefore they have told many common [stories] while each has told something distinctive. That way each is not superfluous, thrown aside because his [gospel] serves no purpose, and each offers a perfect test that their statements are truthful.[11]

Chrysostom also pays attention to what is not said. He notices that Matthew describes an incident from which he was excluded because he was not preferred. Telling the story indicates the apostle's own humility. He also spares the feelings of the other disciples not chosen to go up the mount by not mentioning their names. That would emphasize their exclusion. Comments about the virtue of the apostles come easily to his mind even from the silences.[12]

For both Origen and Chrysostom the persons of Moses and Elijah on either side of Jesus Christ show that the Law and the Prophets are unified in Him.[13] But Origen expresses it best because he deals with the point in the context of those who know Scripture and teach the Gospels to the Church.

[W]hen you see anyone who not only has a thorough grasp of the theology about Jesus, but also clearly explains every passage of the gospels, be sure to tell him that the garments of Jesus have certainly become as light to him. For when the Son of God in His transfiguration is so known and seen that His face is as the sun and His garments as white as light, Moses— the law—and Elijah—the prophets, one standing for all—both talking with Jesus will appear before the person who sees Jesus in this form . . . Indeed if anyone sees the glory of Moses, having recognized the spiritual law as conversation in harmony with Jesus, and the prophets' wisdom which is hidden in mystery (1 Cor 2:7), he sees Moses and Elijah in glory when he sees them with Jesus.[14]

Both commentators treat the Transfiguration passage in its immediate context within the Gospel of Matthew. They work through the text pericope by pericope. But each also uses verses from Matthew, both further back and further on, to word his own comments on these verses, a kind of argumentation that is similar to modern redaction criticism.[15]

Origen shows how much he reads the Gospels harmonically. He imports into his comments on Matthew, indeed as an important key to the interpretation of that Gospel, the statement from Mark that Peter did not know what he was saying when he suggested that three tabernacles be built (*Comm. Matt.* 12.40). Chrysostom does something similar; both employ a group of texts from the Gospel of John to make sense of the context.[16] For the modern reader, they tend to think of the Gospels in the sense of a synopsis more like that of Aland than that of Huck.[17] Thus there are features of patristic exegesis which resemble quite closely some of the central concerns of modern historical-critical studies.

As a second observation that broadens McGuckin's view, there is a deep tradition of ethical admonition that complements, in fact completes, the great story of Transfiguration and promised resurrection. Perhaps the richest interweaving of theology and ethics is found in Origen. For him the detail "after six days" represents the created world. This is allegory, to be sure, but it is expressed in terms rather moving for members of the Christian community.

If therefore any one of us wishes to be taken by Jesus, and led up by Him into the high mountain—having been chosen to view His transfiguration—we must go beyond the six days. We can no longer hold onto the things that are seen, neither love the world, nor the things of the world. [We should avoid] feeding any worldly lust, the desire for bodies and for the riches of the body, the glory which is fleshly. [We must not concentrate] on those things which naturally distract and drag the soul away from better and more divine things, those that bring it down and anchor it in the deceit of this age, in wealth and glory, and the rest of the lusts which are the enemies of truth. (*Comm. Matt.* 12.36)

It is, of course, proper that the greatest sense of the Transfiguration is focused on Jesus Christ himself. As Origen says: "He appeared to [the disciples] in the form of God in which He formerly was, so that to those below He had the form of a servant, but to those who had followed Him after the six days to the lofty mountain, He did not have that form, but the form of God" (*Comm. Matt.* 12.37). Christ was not transfigured before all, but He can be transfigured before people other than the apostles:

[I]f you wish to see the Jesus transfigured before those who ascended the lofty mountain along with Him, look with me at the Jesus of the Gospels, as more simply apprehended, and as one might say known "according to the flesh," by those who did not go up that mountain. [Look at Him] through the works and words which lift us up to the lofty mountain of wisdom. He is rather known no longer after the flesh, but known in His divinity by means of all the Gospels, and seen in the form of God according to their knowledge; for to them is Jesus transfigured, and not to any of those below. When He is thus transfigured, His face also shines as the sun in order that He may be seen by the children of light. [They] have put off the works of darkness, and put on the armor of light, and are no longer the children of darkness, but have become the sons of day, and walk honestly as in the day. When Jesus is seen that way, He will shine on them not simply as the sun, but as the one shown to be the sun of righteousness. (*Comm. Matt.* 12.37)

The more seriously one takes the Transfiguration and understands all that the Gospels say about Christ, the more one is transformed from works of darkness to works of light, from dishonesty to honesty, from unrighteousness to righteousness. Theology and ethics are not separate disciplines; they are combined realities. The ideal is ascetic, but it may also apply to daily activity outside a monastery.

Chrysostom deepens this sense of life alight by talking about specific everyday matters. He urges his hearers along with him to lay aside our filthy garments, . . . put on the armor of light and the glory of God will enfold us. . . . [The three disciples saw Christ brightly transfigured], but if we will see Him . . . not as they did on the mount, but in far greater brilliance . . . , later He shall come in the very glory of the Father, not only with Moses and Elijah, but also with the vast number of angels. . . . And to some He will say, "Come, blessed of my Father; for I was hungry, and you gave me meat; . . . "Then shall the righteous shine forth as the sun." . . . Nobody there will appear rich or poor, mighty or weak, wise or unwise, slave or free; those masks will be smashed. The judgment will concern only their deeds. (*Hom. Matt.* 56)

Some will be condemned, thrown into darkness and the furnace. The reasons are rather simple but deadly:

[A] dreadful disease, beloved, terrible and crying out for attention, has arisen in the church. Some who have left unheeded the warning not to accumulate earthly wealth by honest work but to open their homes to the needy, make a profit from other men's poverty. Some have devised a shrewd theft, a plausible greed. . . . Don't tell me about outer laws. We will all be punished unless we refrain from oppressing the poor and from using their need and necessity as an occasion for shameless money-making. You have wealth to relieve poverty, not to compound your gain through it. Your public show of relief makes the calamity worse. You sell benevolence for cash. I don't forbid selling, but only [sell what you have] for a heavenly kingdom. Your interest rate of one percent per month will not earn you immortal life

. . . Don't you recognize that even in the old law this is prohibited. But someone says to me "When I am paid the interest, I give it to the poor." Better not to help the poor than to offer them [funds] from that source . . . , such an evil increase is like forcing a beautiful womb to give birth to scorpions. Why should I talk about God's law? Even you call this [interest] "dirty." . . . And if you ask Gentile lawmakers, they will reply that they also see this as a demonstration of absolute shamelessness. People who hold high honored office in the senate by their law are forbidden from dishonoring themselves by charging such interest. (*Hom. Matt.* 56)

Thus theology and practical economics are viewed together, the Transfiguration of Christ and the transformation of the Church. Some of the interests of modern liberation theologies can be found in these interpretations of Scripture.

As a third observation on McGuckin's conclusion, we need to understand ourselves, writing near the beginning of the twenty-first century, as somehow related to the context of postmodernism. While rejecting the extreme sense that words mean either nothing much or nearly everything, we can seize the day and plump for a Christian reading of the fathers. We cannot insist that reading them within the Church is the only possible interpretation, but it is certainly a legitimate and strong one. The *Wirkungsgeschichte* of any biblical text is remarkably significant for the Church. We have conceded too much to contemporary biblical specialists who do philological and historical work within a paradigm they generally describe as distanced, objective investigation. How distanced? How objective? NT studies is a subdiscipline that too often depends on rather narrow views of reality, parts of which were learned from the age of Western Enlightenment rationalism, which have now been discredited by contemporary physics, biology, and chemistry, as well as historical and literary investigations.[18] Such outlooks occasionally struggle with the accounts of the Transfiguration of Christ or the calls for a spiritually transformed Church. The miraculous is frequently defined poorly and treated as suspect.[19]

Origen and Chrysostom show us that patristic commentators are rather savvy and humble deconstructionists. On the one hand, they do not propose the sense of truth and a "literal" reading of the Bible that appeared in the seventeenth century and desperately needed many of the correctives proposed by modern historical-critical exegesis. On the other, they are only pre-critical in a significant sense if "pre-critical" means being unlike most nineteenth- and twentieth-century specialist exegetes. Obviously we cannot adopt their work as if we could move back into their times and ignore issues of our own era which did not concern them. They recognized a much deeper religious pluralism than is sometimes granted, but none of them knew the full extent of our globe or our universe. Science and its technologies have put us in a far different place. We will be much the poorer, however, if we do not study their exegesis carefully and draw from it insights and methods that can serve us well. They wrestle with textual details; they expect a text to offer some resistance to their interpretations. And they read from deep within a worshipping Christian community that finds events such as the Transfiguration not merely enlightening, but lightening-like, frightening yet comforting, lighting the trail toward the poor and firing the soul for life eternal. How ancient that reading is. But also how postmodern.

Notes

1. Rowan A. Greer, *Broken Lights and Mended Lives: Theology and Common Life in the Early Church* (University Park: Pennsylvania State University Press, 1986).

2. For a fascinating treatment of the Sinai apse mosaic see Jaš Elsner, *Art and the Roman Viewer: The Transformation of Art from the Pagan World to Christianity* (Cambridge Studies in New Art History and Criticism; Cambridge: Cambridge University Press, 1995), 111–18. Erich Dinkler (*Das Apsismosaik von S. Apollinare in Classe* [Wissenschaftliche Abhandlungen der Arbeitsgemeinschaft für Forschung des Landes Nordrhein-Westfalen 29; Köln: Westdeutscher Verlag, 1964], 25–50) refers to a written source for a depiction of the transfiguration in the bishop's church at Neapolis in the mid-sixth century (*Chronicon Episcoporum S. Neapolitanae Ecclesiae*, 22) and offers pictures of two extant mosaics in Rome, one in SS. Nereus et Achilleus dating about 800 and another in S. Prassede, the chapel of Zeno, dated to 820. He also pictures scenes from illustrated manuscripts: Florence, Bibl. Laur. Cod. Plut. I, 56, fol. 7r, the Gospel of Rabula, canon list 3; Paris, Bibl. Nationale, Cod. gr. 510, fol. 75; Athos, Iwiron, Cod. 1, fol. 303r; Rome, Bibl. Vat., Cod. gr. 1156, fol. 329v; Munich, Bayer. Staatsbibl. Cod. lat. 4453, the Gospel of Ottos III, fol. 113r; Utrecht, Bibl. der Rijksuniversiteit, Ms. 32, Utrecht-Psalter, fol. 83v; and Florence, Bibl. Laur., Cod. Plut. VI, 23, fol. 34v. Those are assembled for his argument; others could be viewed.

3. John McGuckin, *The Transfiguration of Christ in Scripture and Tradition* (Studies in the Bible and Early Christianity 9; Lewiston, N.Y.: Edwin Mellen, 1986), 125.

4. McGuckin, *Transfiguration*, 138–39.

5. McGuckin, *Transfiguration*, 141.

6. For a scholarly development of the theme see my "Deification: Consensual and Cogent," *SJT* 49 (1996): 411–23.

7. See Rowan A. Greer, *The Captain of Our Salvation: A Study of Patristic Exegesis of Hebrews* (BGBE 15; Tübingen: J.C.B. Mohr, 1973), and with James Kugel, *Early Biblical Interpretation* (LEC; Philadelphia: Westminster, 1986).

8. These come primarily from my research as a consultant for the Matthew volume in *The Church's Bible*, general editor Robert Wilken, to be published by Eerdmans.

9. John Chrysostom, *Hom. Matt.* 56. Throughout I have adapted the translation in NPNF[1] 9–10.

10. Origen, *Princ.* 4.1.1–4.3.5 (trans. G.W. Butterworth, *On First Principles* [New York: Harper Torchbook, 1966], 256–97). The argument sketched here survives in the Greek fragments and thus does not depend upon what one thinks about Rufinus' Latin translation.

11. John Chrysostom, *Hom. Matt.* 1.

12. John Chrysostom, *Hom. Matt.* 1.

13. John Chrysostom, *Hom. Matt.* 56; Origen, *Comm. Matt.* 12.38.

14. Origen, *Comm. Matt.* 12.38. Throughout I have adapted the translation in ANF 9.

15. John Chrysostom, *Hom. Matt.* 56–58, uses Matt 4:24; 5:20; 8:2, 26; 11:14; 13:43; 14:29; 16:4, 6–12, 14, 21–22; 20:20, 22; 22:13; 25:23; 26:34–35, 41. Origen, *Comm. Matt.* 12–13, shows knowledge of Matt 4:9, 16, 23; 8:5; 9:20; 13:31, 39; 15:22; 16:16, 20–23; 21:19–21, 22, 25; 24:35, 37; 25:35; 26:29–75.

16. Chrysostom uses Mark 9:6, 21–24, 32; Luke 9:31–33, 45, 54–55; 18:1–5; 23:24; and John 1:21; 4:25; 9:16; 10:33; 12:28–29, 47; 13:37. Origen employs John 1:2, 29; 4:46; 5:2; 8:31, 34, 44; 11:25; 13:27; 14:6, 30; 17:3; 18:36.

17. Albert Huck, *Synopse der drei ersten Evangelien: Mit Beigaben der Johannischen Parallelstelle* (13th ed.; Tübingen: J.C.B. Mohr, 1981), and *Synopsis quattuor evangeliorum: Locis parallelis evangeliorum apocryphorum et patrum adhibitis* (13th ed.; ed. Kurt Aland; Stuttgart: Deutschen Bibelgesellschaft, 1985).

18. See my "Black Marks on the Communities' Manuscripts," *JECS* 2 (1994): 443–46 (1994 North American Patristic Society Presidential Address).

19. For a nuanced historical study of such themes see Rowan A. Greer, *The Fear of Freedom: A Study of Miracles in the Roman Imperial Church* (University Park: Pennsylvania State University Press, 1989).

Enduring, or, How Rowan Greer Taught Me to Read

STANLEY HAUERWAS

Beginning with Friendship

I must begin with friendship. That Rowan claimed me as a friend has everything to do with how he taught me how to read. Such a claim seems odd today, but then it was Rowan who taught me the oddness of our now thinking it odd to think that friendship and reading are separate activities. In the ancient world it was assumed that reading and friendship were interrelated. Thus the importance of our friendship for how Rowan taught me to read and, in particular, to read the Scripture.

Some might think us unlikely friends. We are very different. Rowan is urbane, I am not. He went to Yale. I went to Southwestern University in Georgetown, Texas. He is a scholar's scholar. I am not. He actually knows what he is talking about. I am never sure I "know" anything, yet I must go on talking. I suppose that is the difference between historians and theologians in our time. But then one of the lessons Rowan taught me was to distrust the very distinction between history and theology. Nevertheless, in our time the distinction between historians and theologians is undeniable—thus the "oddness" of my contribution to this volume. I have to talk about "methodological" questions because I do not know, for example, Paulinus of Pella the way Rowan knows Paulinus of Pella. Indeed, I only know Paulinus because Rowan taught me to understand the importance of the life of Paulinus.

That Rowan has taught me the importance of lives such as that of Paulinus is inseparable from our friendship. I was never formally Rowan's student, but

I have always been his student. It was Rowan who taught me to be suspicious of the "historical critical" method as *the* way to get at the meaning of the biblical text. It was Rowan who taught me that there is something quite curious about the curricular division between New Testament and Patristics. And it was from Rowan that I began to understand that the study of Scripture only makes sense as a theological task of the church. I suspect that Rowan never knew he was my teacher, but like most good teachers Rowan never notices how he teaches those lessons that animate his life.

Friendship between a teacher and a student is not, of course, always possible. A teacher/student relationship is not a relationship between equals. Yet equality is a slippery notion. Thus Aristotle, with his usual insight about things human, notes that friendship does not so much require a strict equality between friends but rather creates equality through common judgments.[1] Such judgments require time, indeed, such judgments make time possible. Rowan and I have now been friends for over thirty years, which means the character of our friendship has changed, but what has not changed is that we remain friends bonded not only by the history of our friendship but by common loves.

Over the years, of course, we have discovered not only common judgments, but differences—he loves dogs, I love cats. I am angry about the church's accommodation to the world; he is bemused. I am at war with the current intellectual formations that produce and that reproduce the knowledges that legitimate liberal Protestantism; Rowan goes his own way willing to ignore them if they will ignore him. I am angry he is ignored. He would be aghast if the significance of his work were discovered. It never occurs to him to think of his work as "having significance." What a "silly" thought. All of which is to say that the very character of this essay, where I show the significance of his work, or at least the difference it has made for the way I "do" theology, would not be altogether welcomed by him. But as he would say, "There you have it."

In short, what I want to show is that Rowan Greer must bear at least some of the blame that I am labeled a "sectarian, fideistic, tribalist." The way he taught me to "read" the Bible through the Fathers forced me to challenge the very notion of "history" as a given. The notion that "history" is just "there," moreover, is part of the legitimating structure of modernity necessary for schooling us to believe the way things are is the way things have to be. By teaching me to read differently, Rowan taught me that being a Christian could not help but make one odd.

In truth, I suspect that such "oddness" is one of the "likenesses" that Rowan and I have always seen in one another. Indeed, some may think, not without cause, that our willingness to be "out of step" with the world around us is pathological. There are, of course, differences in the way we have gone about being odd. For Rowan it is a way of living. I have turned it into a career. Rowan is less likely to make the mistake of confusing our oddness with being Christian, but I should like to think our willingness to live against the stream might in some ways be of use to God.

"Broken Lights and Mended Lives": Helping Christians Live Historically

In the preface to *Broken Lights and Mended Lives,* Rowan observes that his approach in the book is peculiar for two reasons: (1) he attempts to enter the world of early Christianity on its own terms, and (2) he is sympathetic to the early Church, since he finds himself to be "a convinced Christian, at least as convinced as an Anglican can be."[2] Rowan notes that some may find these "peculiarities" to be an indication that he has abandoned any attempt at objectivity, which would be tantamount to repudiating the conventions of modern scholarship. He denies that such is the case, noting that we must aim for disinterested and impartial assessment of the historical while never forgetting that we will never be able to remove our prejudices altogether.

I confess I am not convinced that he can have it both ways. Of course, everything hangs on what you mean by "objectivity," "disinterestedness," and "impartial." I am not opposed to attempts to be objective, but I assume "objectivity" merely names one's willingness to locate his or her work in some context or other, so that others equally committed to similar endeavors can help us know the limits and possibilities of what we are trying to do. To be sure, the wonderful thing about Rowan is that he has never been preoccupied with devising a theory about history; rather he simply got on with it. For if anyone has exemplified what might be called theology in a historical mode, it has been Rowan.

Let me try to explain these last remarks by contrasting Rowan's way of doing history with recent proposals of George Marsden. The argument Marsden makes in *The Outrageous Idea of Christian Scholarship* might appear quite congenial to the way Rowan works as a Christian historian.[3] Marsden's defense of Christian scholarship certainly seems to support Rowan's attempt to provide sympathetic accounts of the Fathers. Yet I believe Rowan's way of working to be much more radical than Marsden's proposal allows.

For example, Marsden draws on William James in conceiving of the modern university as the embodiment of pragmatic liberal discourse. An apt metaphor for the university is a corridor in a hotel. In one room off the corridor, a man writes an atheistic volume; in another, a person prays for strength; and in yet another, a chemist investigates the properties of a substance. James concludes that these diverse scholars jointly own the corridor "and they must pass through it if they want a practicable way of getting into or out of their respective rooms."[4] Marsden notes that he finds this image quite congenial, because if it is the modus operandi of the contemporary university, then there is no justification for marginalizing all religious viewpoints.

Those that work as Christian historians are therefore identified by their subject matter more than by any peculiar method. Marsden concedes that Christians and non-Christians will likely use precisely the same methods for determining certain matters of historical fact, for example, the date on which Washington crossed the Delaware. Putting the matter more forcefully, Marsden claims that as a matter of fact "explicitly Christian convictions do not very often have substantial impact on the techniques used in academic detective work, which make up the bulk of the technical, scientific side of academic inquiry."[5] Marsden calls this "methodological secularization." According to this perspective, most historical work centers on a body of natural phenomena equally accessible to all. The Christian historian can accept this common ground, while not ignoring its "spiritual dimensions as created and ordered by God."[6]

There is no question that Marsden's heart is in the right place. But unfortunately his account of history nicely confirms Nietzsche's suggestion that such an understanding of history can only be an attempt by the living to bury the past. As Nietzsche puts it:

A historical phenomenon clearly and completely understood and reduced to an intellectual phenomenon, is for him who has understood it dead: for in it he has understood the mania, the injustice, the blind passion, and in general the whole earthly darkened horizon of that phenomenon, and just in this he has understood its historical power. So far as he is a knower this power has now become powerless for him: not yet perhaps so fast as he is a living being. History, conceived as pure science and become sovereign, would constitute a kind of final closing out of the accounts of life for mankind. Historical education is wholesome and promising for the future only in the service of a powerful new life-giving influence, of a rising culture for example; that is, only when it is ruled and guided by a higher power and does not itself rule and guide.[7]

It may seem quite unfair to attribute to Marsden Nietzsche's view that objective history is the way the living exact revenge on the dead. Marsden would surely object that he has no wish to make history a "pure science." But it is not a question of intention, but of execution. If Christian historians are to be Christians in their writing of history, it is not enough for them to differ only in what they choose to study. The truth is that Christians and non-Christians alike may use quite different methods and ways to date when Washington crossed the Delaware. Nothing is more controversial than the calendar. After all, few matters are more normative than dating, if you remember that 1776 is not a fact but a story. The expression "Washington crossed the Delaware" is not a brute fact, free-standing, intelligible in isolation from one narrative or another.[8]

The extraordinary thing about the way Rowan has done history—the way he has taught us to be readers of Irenaeus, Theodore, Origen, Gregory of Nyssa, Augustine, and so many more—is his learned innocence about the matters that exercise Marsden. Rowan never needed James's permission to do history from a Christian standpoint. He just did it, and in the doing he helped us understand not only Theodore but what Theodore's work was about— namely, God. Theology, to be sure, is a broken light; but if such a light does not make a difference for how the historian works, then the very way history is done, the way we are taught to read "the past," cannot help but reproduce a world in which God does not matter. Accordingly, Rowan has not written in an attempt to make the story he tells "intelligible to anyone," whoever that may be, but rather his history has been done at the service of those who desire to live lives appropriate to the view that God matters.[9]

Rowan, without calling attention to how he works, makes no hard and fast distinction between history and theology. He does not because he could not, given the texts he was helping us read. He therefore takes as his task in *Broken Lights and Mended Lives* to help us see the relationship between theological developments and Christian behavior. As he puts it,

the broken lights are meant to mend lives; vision ought to be translated into virtue. How may the Christian destiny, the vision of Christ's victory, be related to the Christian life? To what degree does that life participate in the destiny, and to what degree does it merely anticipate it? Moreover, is the translation meant to include all people and capable of doing so? These issues could be addressed in a number of ways. For example, we might examine what were supposed Christian virtues with a view to discovering their relation to theological themes. But what seems remarkable to me about the Christian vision of Christ's victory is the consensus of the Fathers that this victory is mediated to us through the common life of the Church. (17–18)

Broken Lights and Mended Lives is written to help us understand that Christian theology is not just more thought. For the church Fathers, knowing the good and doing the good could not be separated. "The Christian life was for them a growth toward perfection, and as the Christian's knowledge grew, so did his virtue. Similarly, progress in virtue meant progress in knowledge; and the dialectic pressed the Christian forward toward his destiny" (75). Thus questions of the humanity of Christ took the form of metaphysical issues of substance, but—like all important theological and metaphysical questions— could not and cannot be abstracted from inquiry about how we are to live.[10] Consider, for example, this illuminating paragraph from *Broken Lights and Mended Lives:*

The place we have seen given to the individual in Cappadocian monasticism correlates with Nyssa's understanding of the individual. By thinking of individuality in terms of relationship, Nyssa suggests that the more fully Christians are related to one another in Christ, the more they realize their true identity. As relations of the one human nature of Christ, which is the image of God, all human beings are meant to find their perfection in the completed and perfected image of God. This destiny is in some measure a present possibility when the members of the monastic community bring their gifts to the service of one another. The balance Basil attempts to strike between the cenobite and the hermit is one that is defined by the image theology we find in Nyssa's thought. If we ask how we are to imagine or to understand Nyssa's corporate understanding of human nature, we must think of the monastery where all hold everything in common, using and possessing one another's gifts. (171)

In short, *Broken Lights and Mended Lives* helps us see why "theology in the early Church was always directly and indirectly concerned with the common life of Christians. From one point of view, theologians attempted to put into words the corporate experience of the Church. The Christian story, continuously repeated in the reading of Scripture and in the liturgy, found its focus for the Fathers of the Church in the victorious Christ, the new humanity. And even more the technical aspects of early Christian theology were designed to explain this Christ and his significance" (vii). Rowan knew how to do "postmodern" historiography before there was a postmodern historiography. He did not need "theory" to help him know how to "do history." He had something much more important than theory—he had, and has, the confidence that comes only through many readings that the Fathers meant what they said about God.[11] Moreover, if what they said about God is to be presented "objectively," then what they said about God must make a difference for how, as well as to whom, we tell their stories.

Living between The Two Cities

That history is written to and for a specific community is but a reminder, as Marsden suggested above, that the historian's work both reflects as well as serves a politics. Some may object to the account I have given of how Rowan taught me to read as an attempt at self-justification, just to the extent that I read him in support of my peculiar theological politics. It is one thing to read Rowan's account in *Broken Lights and Mended Lives* as underwriting my contention that the very distinction between theology and ethics (and history) can distort the character of Christian speech, but it is quite another matter to suggest that his account of the church is congruent with my "sectarianism." He is, after all, an Episcopalian—which is not exactly like being a Mennonite.

But then I am not a Mennonite. I have always insisted that I am a *High-Church* Mennonite. That means I am a Methodist or, perhaps more candidly, I am trying to live and write and think according to what I think Methodism should be. Methodism, moreover, has at least some claim to be within the Episcopal tradition. By saying I am a High-Church Mennonite, I am trying to suggest the Mennonite understanding of the church's position toward the world is possible only if such a church is sustained by the kind of theology found in the church Fathers and, in particular, in that confession we call the Nicene Creed.[12]

Even if Will Willimon and I stole the title *Resident Aliens* from Rowan's depiction of "alien citizens" in *Broken Lights and Mended Lives,* the verbal similarities may hide deep differences.[13] Rowan, after all, does describe the Christian caught between church and world as "a marvelous paradox" (141). In order to explain the paradoxical character of Christian existence, Rowan provides wonderful accounts of Tertullian and Clement, noting how the latter saw Christian release from bondage to custom and idolatry as a freeing not only *from* the world but also *for* the world (149).

Rowan, moreover, provides a quite sympathetic account of Constantine's effect on Christian thinkers such as Chrysostom, Eusebius, and Lactantius. These theologians and churchmen, while no doubt wanting to put the church to the cause of *Romanitas,* never lost the tension between the transforming character of Christianity and the establishment of the church as the religion of Rome. Yet, Rowan observes, there is little evidence that the lives of ordinary citizens were transformed in any obvious or far-reaching way by Christianity, which may indicate that the ideal itself had become corrupted insofar as it lost touch with the paradox of alien citizenship. Which leads Rowan to observe that he is "tempted" to the view "that, however viable as an ideal, alien citizenship cannot be put into practice, at least on a social scale" (156–57).

By "social scale" I think Rowan means that the gospel cannot run an empire. The gospel, however, did create monasticism, which Rowan characterizes as "a protest against a Church gone public and an attempt to retain the spirit of the martyrs" (157). Indeed, in his wonderful chapter on monasticism in *Broken Lights and Mended Lives,* "The City on a Hill," Rowan observes that monasticism, even in its most radical forms as protest against the Church, remained tied to essential practices such as the celebration of the Eucharist (165–66). Thus Basil, like Chrysostom, thought monasticism to be "a light shining into the surrounding world, persuading people towards the ideal of the Christian life. The monastic ideal is meant to be a leaven in the Church and in all society" (170). Here we have no Troeltsch-like claims that monasticism is a forerunner of a sectarian withdrawal from the world. Instead, Rowan helps us see the complexity of the "alien" character of the Christian witness in a world falling apart.

Yet in truth I suspect Rowan does not think monasticism is *the* way, or at least the only way, that the alien character of our existence as Christians finds expression. In the last chapter of *Broken Lights and Mended Lives,* "The Collapse of the West," Rowan observes:

> As I have pointed out, the monasteries in the early Middle Ages served the double function of refuges and of foundations for the reordering of society. There is something to be said for the view that the Church began by providing deliverance from the disasters that attended the collapse of Roman rule in the West, but ended by becoming the basis for a new

order of society. A pattern that can be discerned in the first centuries of the Church's existence, leading to the new order of the Christian Empire, seems to repeat itself when we examine the end of late antiquity and the birth of the new order of the Middle Ages. Is this a way of looking at our own times? And are we living in the midst of the death of an old culture in which Christ brings us not so much an ordering of our society as a deliverance from it? (206)[14]

Broken Lights and Mended Lives can be read as a meditation on how we are to live as Christians assuming a positive answer to these questions.

Accordingly, Paulinus of Pella becomes for Rowan a central character for instructing us how to endure when we live in a world coming apart. For the story of Paulinus, the story of how a fairly worldly young man lost possessions and power in the changing empire, is, as Rowan tells, a story of endurance. Paulinus regards his life as God's gift; for, as he says, God has reasonably chastened him "with continual misfortunes, he (God) has clearly taught me that I ought neither to love too earnestly present prosperity which I knew I might lose, nor to be greatly dismayed by adversities wherein I had found that his mercies could succor me." To which Rowan adds the following observation: "His Christian faith did not empower Paulinus to take an active and constructive part in the events of his time, nor did it lead him to withdraw from society to the security of the monastery. But it did enable him to endure, and in that enduring there is testimony to the victory of Christ" (196).

Paulinus thus becomes for Rowan the exemplification of Augustine's account of the fall of Rome in *The City of God.* Augustine, according to Rowan, rightly refuses to interpret the fall of Rome as apocalyptic, since Augustine does not accept the theory that the Christian empire was sacred. Yet he also denies that the disaster can be anything less than tragic:

> The paradox of the Christian life is that the evils we suffer in our earthly pilgrimage must be taken with absolute seriousness, but so must the destiny that awaits us in the City of God. There are no victories or defeats in the present that really matter. All that counts is the final victory for the saints in the age to come. The practical implication of Augustine's view is that what matters is to endure. The Christian can be neither fully involved in society nor fully withdrawn from it. . . . I am persuaded by Faulkner's view that we cannot alter the tragic character of human life, but that we can endure and so prevail. (205–6)

I cannot deny, in contrast to Rowan, that the position I have been developing regarding the church's position vis-à-vis liberal social orders may seem to entail more active stances than that captured by the phrase "mere endurance." For one thing, I would never qualify endurance by "mere." Nor would Rowan, I think, if I have rightly understood his account of endurance. Indeed, Christian endurance may take quite aggressive stances (monasticism being one example) toward the world. I am, moreover, quite sympathetic with figures such as Paulinus just to the extent that they teach us how to go on in a world where we have no means of locating ourselves or even of determining if we might be lost.[15]

Yet finally—and I suppose many would take this to be the nub of the matter—it must surely be the case that Rowan remains at best indifferent to, if not supportive of, a Constantinian social strategy by the church. Or perhaps, put more accurately, Rowan simply assumes that the accusation of Constantinianism does not do justice to the complexity of lives like that of Paulinus.[16] Yet my attack on Constantinianism has never denied the importance of witnesses like Paulinus. Rather, the question has always been what kind of church disciplines, disciplines such as knowing how to read our Christian past in the way Rowan has taught us in *Broken Lights and Mended Lives*, are necessary to make lives like Paulinus possible even today.[17]

Ending with Friendship

Which brings me back to friendship. For if, as Rowan suggests, Christians are to live "both in this world and in light of the next," as well as "preserve both the holiness and the catholicity of the Church" (211), we will do so only to the extent God has made us his friends and, thus, friends with one another. Such friendship but names the possibility that God's victory in Christ is made possible. In an extraordinary "summing up" of Christian doctrine, Rowan observes:

> As Irenaeus says, it was necessary that the victory be human; and yet only God could win it, and only the union of God and humanity could make it effective. The development of the doctrine of the Trinity serves to enable the Church to define the Victor as God without compromising Christian commitment to the heritage of Jewish monotheism; the christological debates revolved around how to maintain that the divine Victor was also the human Victor and the human being given victory. Christ is

the Mediator. Both divine and human, he is the saved Savior and the sanctified Sanctifier. Thus, the Christian can see in him not only the power of God to save, but the ways in which that power works: It conquers death, whereby the Resurrection of Christ becomes the principle for the general resurrection in which all shall partake, and it conquers the sin and blindness that separate human beings from God. And so redemption carries with it the idea of God's triumph over sin and his self-disclosure as perfect Truth, Goodness, and Beauty. The physical, moral, and spiritual dimensions of Redemption are all rooted in the classical accounts of Christ as divine and human, as the Victor who also supplies the paradigm of what victory means. (208)

That Rowan taught me how to read, how to be friends with those who make up that great tradition called Catholic, by claiming me as friend is not simply a biographical point. Such is the way God has chosen to befriend us by becoming one of us. Another name of "the way" is called Church. I am forever grateful that Rowan helped me discover that "way."

NOTES

This essay is published by permission of the author, who retains copyright.

1. For an analysis of Aristotle's account of friendship, see Stanley Hauerwas and Charles Pinches, *Christians Among the Virtues: Theological Conversations with Ancient and Modern Ethics* (Notre Dame, Ind.: University of Notre Dame Press, 1997), 31–54.

2. Rowan Greer, *Broken Lights and Mended Lives: Theology and Common Life in the Early Church* (University Park: Pennsylvania State University Press, 1986), viii–ix. All paginations to this book will appear in the text.

3. George Marsden, *The Outrageous Idea of Christian Scholarship* (New York: Oxford University Press, 1997).

4. Marsden, *Outrageous Idea*, 45–46.

5. Marsden, *Outrageous Idea*, 47.

6. Marsden, *Outrageous Idea*, 91. For a similar view, see Grant Wacker, "Understanding the Past: Reflections on Two Approaches to History," in *Religious Advocacy and American History* (ed. Bruce Kuklick and D. G. Hart; Grand Rapids: Eerdmans, 1997), 159–78. One of the difficulties with the way Marsden and Wacker make their case is that they continue to state the "problem" in terms that assume the legitimacy of liberal practices. For example, Marsden says that anyone teaching religion should not "proselytize" (*Outrageous Idea*, 53), but it is hard to imagine any course about matters that matter in which the teacher does not want to change the lives of the

students. Or as Wacker puts the question: "Should historians impose value judgments on their narratives above and beyond the layers of evaluation that are already present in everything that they do?" ("Understanding the Past," 162). The problem is not with the answer Wacker gives to this question, but that any answer one gives is a mistake because the question is wrongly put. "Impose" implies the historian has some further judgment to make that is more determinative than how the story is told in the first place. What Marsden and Wacker fail to see is that the game is up as soon as you use the language of "values." The issue is what descriptions, which often may not appear "value laden," are determining how the story is told and for whom.

7 Friedrich Nietzsche, *On the Advantage and Disadvantage of History for Life* (trans. Peter Preus; Indianapolis: Hackett Publishing Co., 1980), 14.

8. Why, for example, do we teach courses in divinity schools called "American Church History," rather than "The Church's Story of America"? Often those who teach "American Church History"—which, of course, is increasingly under pressure to become "American Religious History"—do so appealing to Augustine's two cities as a justification for writing the "secular" history of the church in America. Yet such a view betrays Augustine, who, if he followed the same mode he used in the *City of God,* would write to help Christians see why that entity called America is a blip on God's radar screen.

It is, of course, quite a different matter for secular historians. For example, Joyce Appleby, Lynn Hunt, and Margaret Jacob in their book *Telling the Truth about History* (New York: W. W. Norton, 1994) note that historians influenced by postmodernist literary approaches have become more aware that their supposedly matter-of-fact choices of narrative techniques and analytical forms have social and political ramifications. These three authors try to go beyond "current negative or ironic judgments about history," however, by accepting the impossibility of total objectivity and completely satisfying causal explanations in order to have history serve a more intellectually alive democratic community. The latter they identify as the "kind of society in which *we* would like to live" (pp. 228–29). It simply does not occur to them that Christians might have a problem with that "we."

9. This does not mean that the Christian theologian cannot learn from or use the work of those who are not Christian. God, in Aquinas' phrase, works through secondary causes, inadequate as they are. Indeed, it may well be possible that some "secular" historians may provide better accounts of God's work through Israel and the Church than those who work explicitly as Christians. For example, see Michael Baxter's enlightening critique of accounts of the Catholic church in America by Catholic historians in "Writing History in a World without Ends: An Evangelical Catholic Critique of United States Catholic History," *Pro Ecclesia* 5 (1996): 440–69.

10. I am not suggesting that Rowan alone is working in this fashion. For example, George Huntston Williams wrote wonderfully illuminating articles helping us see how issues involved in the Arian controversy were inseparable from questions of

the status of the emperor in relation to the church. See his still classic article, "Christology and Church-State Relations in the Fourth Century," *CH* 20 (1951): 273–328. The work of Robert Wilken and Peter Brown has been invaluable for helping us to imagine our forebears' struggles to lead less broken lives. See in particular Robert Wilken, *Remembering the Christian Past* (Grand Rapids: Eerdmans, 1995). Wilken observes, "If love is no virtue and there is no love of wisdom, if religion can only be studied from afar and as though it had no future, if the passkey to religious studies is amnesia, if we can speak about our deepest convictions only in private, our entire enterprise is not only enfeebled, it loses credibility. For if those who are engaged in the study of religion do not care for religion, should others?" (p. 23).

There has been a rebirth of work dealing with the so-called Middle Ages that is enriching the Christian imagination in a similar fashion. I am thinking in particular of the work of Eamon Duffy, David Aers, Sarah Beckwith, Miri Rubin, John Bossy, and Frederick Bauerschmidt. I am not suggesting these authors are all in agreement, as they obviously have quite different views about their subjects, but what such work so helpfully does is aid us in recovering a sense of the embodied character of Christianity which we have largely lost today.

11. One of the delightful aspects of Rowan's work is his ability to avoid current theological divisions by simply forging ahead, confident that what he has learned through years of reading the Fathers makes sense. For example, many of us avoid the language of "experience" like the plague, assuming that any appeals to experience cannot help but reproduce the anthropological reductions of Protestant liberalism. George Lindbeck's strictures in *The Nature of Doctrine* (Philadelphia: Westminster, 1984) against the "experiential-expressive" model of religious language only increased our distaste for any appeals to experience. Yet in a few short paragraphs in *Broken Lights and Mended Lives*, Rowan provides an extraordinary account of experience by using Clement's account of Eunomos and the Pythic grasshopper in the latter's *Exhortation to the Heathen*. It seems that Eunomos was competing in a lyre contest at Delphi when one of his strings broke. A grasshopper flew to his lyre, supplying the missing note. The Greeks regarded this as a tribute to Eunomos' excellence as a musician, but Clement saw the grasshopper as the divine song that transforms and completes the human song. This latter song, according to Clement, is the Word of God, that "composed the universe into melodious order, and tuned the discord of the elements to harmonious arrangement, so that the whole world might become harmony." Rowan observes that Clement identifies this new song with God's agent in Creation and Redemption and that Clement appeals both to scriptural witness to the Redeemer and to Christian experience of Redemption as a vision of the new freedom and a transformed moral life (p. 9). I cannot imagine how theology can do without such an appeal to that kind of experience.

12. For a similar perspective, see Frederick Norris, *The Apostolic Faith: Protestants and Roman Catholics* (Collegeville, Minn.: Liturgical Press, 1992). It is no accident, of course, that Norris is also Rowan's student.

13. Actually the title *Resident Aliens* was suggested by my wife, Paula Gilbert. The title came to her while reading the manuscript by the recurring observation in the book about Christians as aliens. We had probably stolen that phrase from Rowan, but then Paula had also read *Broken Lights and Mended Lives* not long before reading Will's and my book. Thus the tangled path of "influence."

14. Rowan, like Peter Brown, possesses the extraordinary ability to find the particular exemplar for explicating complex historical developments—e.g., his use of Galla Placidia to help us understand that the "fall of the West" to the barbarians was not exactly a clear case of "us" against "them." I reread these pages in *Broken Lights and Mended Lives* (189–92) just after I had finished Brown's *The Rise of Western Christendom* (Oxford: Blackwell, 1996). Brown's account may in certain respects be more "complete," but I was struck again by how much I had learned about the story Brown tells from Rowan's account in *Broken Lights*.

15. For a more extended discussion of the theological implications of being so "placed," see my *Wilderness Wanderings: Probing Twentieth-Century Theology and Philosophy* (Boulder, Colo.: Westview, 1997). I suspect one of the reasons some have difficulty "pinning me down" (i.e., why won't he act like the "sectarian" he clearly must be) is because I find many of the vestiges of "Constantinianism" so useful for Christians in this time between times. Forms of Christian "rule" inherited from the past can become quite useful forms of resistance now that Christians no longer rule.

16. This kind of objection to the general characterization, "Constantinianism," has been developed by Nicholas Wolterstorff in a review of John Howard Yoder, *The Royal Priesthood: Essays Ecclesiological and Ecumenical* (ed. Michael Cartwright; Grand Rapids: Eerdmans, 1994), in *Studies in Christian Ethics* 10 (1997): 142–45. Wolterstorff challenges Yoder's alleged assumption that Constantinianism names the pattern of identifying the church with the world. Wolterstorff asks, "is it true that Constantine's revolution amounted to the church *identifying* itself with the (secular) power structure? It's true that the company of the baptized became pretty much coterminous with the subjects of the state in the Holy Roman Empire; and it's true that the emperors saw themselves as responsible for many aspects of church life which Yoder and I both think the state ought to keep out of. But did anybody really think of church and state as *identical*? As Yoder acknowledges, the history of late antiquity and the middle ages is full of instances of bishops standing up to princes. Wouldn't everybody at the time have regarded these conflicts as church-state conflicts, not as conflicts between two different bureaus of one organization?" (p. 144). Yoder is perfectly capable of answering such questions, but I think it worth observing in the context of this paper that Yoder's account of Constantinianism has never denied the point Wolterstorff is making. Yoder's concern is rather with recovering for the church practices that can make possible the kind of discriminating judgments about the church's relation to the social orders in which it finds itself, for which Wolterstorff seems to be calling. Constantinianism at the very least names the assumption that there is something called "the state" that requires theological legitimation, and as a result Christians are

made less able to make the discriminations necessary to maintain their tension with the world.

17. I have focused on Paulinus of Pella as the paradigm of how to respond to a collapsing empire because Rowan identifies Paulinus' response with his own. But one should not forget that Rowan also treats Sidonius and Cassiodorus as deserving our respect for their quite different responses to the collapse of the West. Christianity for Sidonius was simply part of the landscape, so being a bishop was not different than being a civil servant. Rowan notes that no matter how accommodated Sidonius' account of Christianity might have been, it is nonetheless the case that his commitment to the Church enabled him to take an active part in helping his people adapt to life under barbarian rule. Cassiodorus responded by forming a double (i.e., male and female) monastery committed to the study of Scripture, because for him "to study the Scriptures is to participate in the age to come, and in this way the monks have withdrawn from this age. On the other hand, Cassiodorus insists that the monastery has an obligation to be active in caring for the stranger and for the neighboring people. Baths have been built conducive to the healing of the sick, and the monastery exists in part to be sought by others. 'The peasants must be instructed in good morals,' and they may not be burdened 'with the weight of increased taxes.' The comment is interesting because it presupposes a dependence of the local people on the monastery" (p. 203). I am aware that the response of Cassiodorus looks more like the kind of ecclesiology for which I have argued and there is certainly truth to that. But I am equally aware that Sidonius and Paulinus also have to exist and, even more important, be remembered by us.

Works of Rowan A. Greer

Theodore of Mopsuestia: Exegete and Theologian. Westminster, U.K.: Faith Press, 1961.

"The Antiochene Exegesis of Hebrews." Ph.D. diss. Yale University, Department of Religious Studies, 1965.

"The Antiochene Christology of Diodore of Tarsus." *Journal of Theological Studies* 16 (1966): 327–41.

"The Image of God and the Prosopic Union in Nestorius' *Bazaar of Heraclides.*" In *Lux in Lumine: Essays to Honor W. Norman Pittenger,* edited by Richard Norris, 46–61. New York: Seabury Press, 1966.

"The Use of Scripture in the Nestorian Controversy." *Scottish Journal of Theology* 20 (1967): 413–22.

The Captain of Our Salvation: A Study in the Patristic Exegesis of Hebrews. Tübingen: Mohr (Siebeck), 1973.

"Hospitality in the First Five Centuries of the Church." *Monastic Studies* 10 (1974): 29–48.

As editor. *The Sermon on the Mount with an Introduction, Parallel Texts, Commentaries.* Oxford: Printed for the members of the Limited Editions Club, 1977.

Foreword and Introduction to *Origen: Selected Works,* translated by Rowan A. Greer, xv–xvi; 1–37. New York: Paulist Press, 1979.

"The Dog and the Mushrooms: Irenaeus's View of the Valentinians Assessed." In *The Rediscovery of Gnosticism,* vol. 1, edited by Bentley Layton, 146–75. Leiden: Brill, 1980.

"The Analogy of Grace in Theodore of Mopsuestia's Christology." *Journal of Theological Studies* 34 (1983): 82–98.

"Alien Citizens: A Marvelous Paradox." In *Civitas: Religious Interpretations of the City,* edited by Peter S. Hawkins, 39–56. Atlanta: Scholars Press, 1986.

Broken Lights and Mended Lives: Theology and Common Life in the Early Church. University Park: Pennsylvania State University Press, 1986.

"The Leaven and the Lamb: Christ and Gregory of Nyssa's Vision of Human Destiny." In *Jesus in History and Myth,* edited by R. Joseph Hoffmann and Gerald A. Larue, 169–80. Buffalo, N.Y.: Prometheus Books, 1986.

With James L. Kugel. *Early Biblical Interpretation.* Philadelphia: Westminster Press, 1986.

"Pieces of the Constantinian Puzzle: A Review of *Pagans and Christians* by Robin Lane Fox." *This World* 19 (1987): 127–31.

Review of *Earth and Altar: The Evolution of the Parish Communion in the Church of England to 1945,* by Donald Gray. *Anglican Theological Review,* 70 (1988): 112–13.

The Fear of Freedom: A Study of Miracles in the Roman Imperial Church. University Park: Pennsylvania State University Press, 1989.

Review of *Messianic Exegesis: Christological Interpretation of the Old Testament in Early Christianity,* by Donald Juel. *Journal of the American Academy of Religion* 57 (1989): 198–200.

Review of *Authority in the Anglican Communion: Essays Presented to Bishop John Howe,* edited by Stephen W. Sykes; *Quadrilateral at One Hundred: Essays on the Centennial of the Chicago Lambeth Quadrilateral 1886/88–1986/88,* edited by J. Robert Wright; *The Study of Anglicanism,* edited by Stephen W. Sykes and John Booty. *Anglican and Episcopal History* 58 (1989): 225–31.

"The Man from Heaven: Paul's Last Adam and Apollinaris' Christ." In *Paul and the Legacies of Paul,* edited by William S. Babcock, 165–82. Dallas: Southern Methodist University Press, 1990.

Introduction to *Homiletica from the Pierpont Morgan Library,* edited by Leo Depuydt, v–xxiii. Louvain: Peeters, 1991.

"Reckonings in the Study of the Ancient Church." *Anglican Theological Review* 73 (1991): 234–39.

"Reflections on Priestly Authority." *Saint Luke's Journal of Theology* 34 (1991): 103–13.

Review of *The Search for the Christian Doctrine of God: The Arian Controversy,* by R. P. C. Hanson. *Journal of the American Academy of Religion* 59 (1991): 835–39.

Review of *Theodore of Mopsuestia on the Bible: A Study of His Old Testament* Exegesis, by Dimitri Z. Zaharopoulos. *Anglican Theological Review* 73 (1991): 73–74.

"The Transition from Death to Life." *Interpretation* 46 (1992): 240–49.

"Who Seeks for a Spring in the Mud? Reflections on the Ordained Ministry in the Fourth Century." In *Theological Education and Moral Formation,* edited by Richard John Neuhaus, 22–55. Grand Rapids: W. B. Eerdmans, 1992.

Review of *Doctrine and Practice in the Early Church,* by Stuart G. Hall. *Anglican and Episcopal History* 62 (1993): 579–80.

Review of *Visible and Apostolic: The Constitution of the Church in High Church Anglican and Non-Juror Thought,* by Robert D. Cornwall. *Anglican Theological Review* 76 (1994): 379–81.

Review of *The Cruelty of Heresy: An Affirmation of Christian Orthodoxy,* by C. FitzSimons Allison. *Anglican and Episcopal History* 64 (1995): 233–34.

Review of *The Oxford Movement in Context: Anglican High Churchmanship,* by Peter B. Nockles. *Anglican Theological Review* 77 (1995): 247–48.

"Sinned We All in Adam's Fall." In *The Social World of the First Christians: Essays in Honor of Wayne A. Meeks,* edited by L. Michael White and Larry O. Yarbrough. Minneapolis: Fortress, 1995.

"Augustine's Transformation of the Free Will Defense." *Faith and Philosophy* 13 (1996): 471–86.

Review of *Ambrose of Milan and the End of the Arian-Nicene Conflict,* by Daniel H. Williams. *Anglican Theological Review* 78 (1996): 667–70.

Review of *Journeying into God: Seven Early Monastic Lives,* by Tim Vivian. *Coptic Church Review* 17 (1996): 103–4.

Review of *Remembering the Christian Past,* by Robert L. Wilken. *Modern Theology* 12 (1996): 377–78.

"Anglicanism as an On-going Argument." *Witness* 81 (1998): 23.

"Cicero's Sketch and Lactantius's Plan." In *The Early Church in Its Context: Essays in Honor of Everett Ferguson,* edited by Abraham J. Malherbe, Frederick W. Norris, James Thompson, Everett Ferguson, Rowan A. Greer, and Harold W. Attridge, 155–74. Leiden: Brill, 1998.

"The Good Shepherd: Canonical Interpretations in the Early Church?" In *Theological Exegesis: Essays in Honor of Brevard S. Childs,* edited by Christopher R. Seitz and Kathryn Greene-McCreight, 306–30. Grand Rapids: W. B. Eerdmans, 1998.

Christian Life and Christian Hope: Raids on the Inarticulate. New York: Crossroad Publishing, 2001.

Contributors

CHARLES A. BOBERTZ is associate professor of theology at St. John's University School of Theology and Seminary, Collegeville, Minnesota. He is the author of a work on Cyprian (University of Notre Dame Press, forthcoming) and articles on the history of ancient Christianity as well as a member of the Mark Group of the Society of Biblical Literature and the Mark Task Force of the Catholic Biblical Association.

DAVID BRAKKE is associate professor of religious studies at Indiana University. He is the author of *Athanasius and Asceticism* (1995; reprint, Johns Hopkins University Press, 1998) and articles on Athanasius, monasticism, and early Christianity in Egypt.

MARY ROSE D'ANGELO is professor of New Testament at the University of Notre Dame. She is the co-author of *Women and Christian Origins* (Oxford University Press, 1999) and has published widely on topics concerning gender in the New Testament and early Christianity.

STANLEY HAUERWAS is Gilbert T. Rowe Professor of Theological Ethics at Duke Divinity School. Among his many books is *Sanctify Them in the Truth: Holiness Exemplified* (Abingdon Press, 1999).

MARTHA F. MEEKS was trained in painting and art history. She was known for her New England landscapes in watercolor, acrylic, and pastel, and for wall hangings and liturgical banners.

WAYNE A. MEEKS is Woolsey Professor Emeritus of Biblical Studies at Yale University. He is the author of numerous works on the New Testament and early Christianity, most recently *In Search of the Early Christians: Selected Essays of Wayne A. Meeks* (Yale University Press, 2002).

FREDERICK W. NORRIS is Dean E. Walker Professor of Church History and professor of world mission/evangelism at the Emmanuel School of Religion. He is the author or editor of many works on the early church and world Christianity, including *Faith Gives Fullness to Reasoning: The Five Theological Orations of Gregory Nazianzen* (Brill, 1990). He is co-editor of volume 2 of the forthcoming *Cambridge History of Christianity.*

RICHARD A. NORRIS, JR., is professor emeritus of church history at Union Theological Seminary in the City of New York. He is the author of several works on the theology of the early church, including *Manhood and Christ: A Study in the Christology of Theodore of Mopsuestia* (Clarendon Press, 1963).

ALAN SCOTT is the author of *Origen and the Life of the Stars: A History of an Idea* (Clarendon Press, 1994). He serves as a pastor of the Flanders Baptist and Community Church in East Lyme, Connecticut.

ARTHUR BRADFORD SHIPPEE teaches at Queens College of the City University of New York. He is the co-author of *The Pastor: Readings from the Patristic Period* (Fortress Press, 1990) and has published articles on John Chrysostom's catechetical homilies.

MICHAEL B. SIMMONS is Bishop Ordinary of the Missionary Diocese of the Gulf Coast within the Province of St. Peter, Communion of Evangelical Episcopal Churches, and assistant professor of history at Auburn University, Montgomery, Alabama. He is the author of *Arnobius of Sicca: Religious Conflict and Competition in the Age of Diocletian* (Clarendon Press, 1995) as well as articles on Porphyry and ancient Christian and pagan soteriology.

FREDERICK W. WEIDMANN is associate professor of New Testament at Union Theological Seminary in the City of New York. He is the author of *Polycarp and John: The Harris Fragments and Their Challenge to the Literary Traditions* (University of Notre Dame Press, 1999) and articles on the New Testament and Apostolic Fathers.

Index

NEW TESTAMENT

RABBINIC TEXTS

PATRISTIC AND OTHER ANCIENT CHRISTIAN SOURCES

OTHER ANCIENT SOURCES